THE POISON TREE

THE
POISON
TREE

A True Story of
Family Terror

Alan Prendergast

AVON
PUBLISHERS OF BARD, CAMELOT, DISCUS AND FLARE BOOKS

AVON BOOKS
A division of
The Hearst Corporation
105 Madison Avenue
New York, New York 10016

Copyright © 1986 by Alan Prendergast
Published by arrangement with The Putnam Publishing Group
Library of Congress Catalog Card Number: 85-30080
ISBN: 0-380-70346-7

The Putnam edition contains the following Library of Congress Cataloging in Publication Data:

Prendergast, Alan.
  The poison tree.

  1. Jahnke, Richard. 2. Crime and criminals—Wyoming—Cheyenne—Biography.
3. Parricide—Wyoming—Cheyenne—Case studies. 4. Family violence—
Wyoming—Cheyenne—Case studies. I. Title.
HV6248.J243P74   1986   364.1′523′0924[B]   85-30080

First Avon Printing: July 1987

A POISON TREE

I was angry with my friend:
I told my wrath, my wrath did end.
I was angry with my foe:
I told it not, my wrath did grow.

And I waterd it in fears,
Night & morning with my tears:
And I sunned it with smiles,
And with soft deceitful wiles.

And it grew both day and night,
Till it bore an apple bright.
And my foe beheld it shine,
And he knew that it was mine.

And into my garden stole,
When the night had veild the pole;
In the morning glad I see,
My foe outstretchd beneath the tree.

—WILLIAM BLAKE,
    Songs of Experience

CONTENTS

PART ONE

THE HOUSE ON COWPOKE ROAD

As a little childe riding behind his father, sayde simply unto him, Father, when you are dead, I shal ride in the Saddle.

—STEFANO GUAZZO,
Civile Conversation

1

The city of Cheyenne stands on the high, windswept plains of southeastern Wyoming, at the junction of two interstate highways. Half an hour's drive from Nebraska and Colorado, it is a crossroads town, an outpost on the edge of vast and sparsely settled country—a web of railroad yards, motels, gas stations, fast-food franchises, state and federal offices, and military barracks.

Although it has been the state capital for almost a century, Cheyenne doesn't fit in with the popular image of Wyoming. The fabled land of Old Faithful, black bears, and Marlboro men working horseback beneath purple mountains' majesty—what locals still call "the *real* West"—lies hundreds of miles northwest. Cheyenne represents another side of Wyoming. The city was created out of the white man's need for a cheap stopover on the way to somewhere else, and that fact has colored much of its history. It is an encampment of fifty thousand people but home to very few. Many of its citizens are bureaucrats, blue-collar transients, upwardly mobile Midwesterners, or young families stationed at Warren Air Force Base, waiting for the next promotion, transfer, new job: a way out. Until something better comes along, they end each day in the shadow of the real West—along with the traveling salesmen, the truckers disengaged for the night, and the sons of the pioneers—all huddled together in a ring of bright lights against the encompassing darkness of the Great Plains.

In recent years, development in Cheyenne has marched north. Five miles north of downtown, outside the city limits but within the confines of Laramie County, several dozen houses are scattered along the rolling hills of sagebrush and prairie grass. The settlement is known as Cowboy Country. In the language of realtors, Cowboy Country is not a suburb but a "rural subdivision," a place for people who want to live out in the country but not too far from the comforts of town. The moderately expensive brick houses sit on two- to four-acre lots in splendid solitude. The more desirable properties hug the bare hillsides like upper-

2

class bunkers, sheltered from the hammering wind and out of sight of one another. The view is one of empty skies and endless prairie.

Looking out upon a treeless hump of sagebrush every day, it is easy to pretend that you are alone here, that your neighbors don't exist, that Cheyenne itself has disappeared. The illusion can be particularly strong at night, when the streets that wind through Cowboy Country—unpaved, unlit roads with names like Lariat Loop, Bronco Trail, and Cowpoke Road—vanish into the hollow blackness of the prairie. At night the great "out there" closes in on you, and it is possible to feel trapped in the so-called wide open spaces of the real West.

It is even possible to feel that you have been imprisoned at the very edge of the world.

Snow came early to Cheyenne in the fall of 1982. It was nothing like the ferocious blizzards that routinely sweep across southern Wyoming in late winter and early spring, closing I-80 and confounding the schedules of long-haul truckers. Still, the light dusting every few days muddied the streets and made the locals grateful for the sporadic sunshine. By the middle of November several inches of fresh snow covered the surrounding plains, and the persistent wind raised wisps of powder on the hilltops, like swirling jinn dancing on the bleached dunes of the Great American Desert.

The season encouraged early rising and quick action, for the days were getting shorter. November 16, a Tuesday, dawned brisk and clear, but morning sank quickly into afternoon, and the sun disappeared completely before five o'clock. Within minutes of its fall the temperature plunged below freezing, and a cold, crisp, moonless night gripped the prairie.

It was one of the blackest nights of the year. Cowboy Country was swathed in darkness—all except for one solitary strip of Cowpoke Road, where, shortly after sunset, one house was ablaze with lights from one end to the other.

The house was a spacious one-story of pale red brick, with white trim, white shutters, and a white four-poster facade, a vaguely neocolonial style popular in Cheyenne. There was one just like it, only bigger, up the road two hundred yards. A steep ridge behind the house hid the larger model and the rest of its neighbors from view. One of the last addresses to be erected on

Cowpoke, one of the last to be sold, the house cast its light forlornly on the deserted hills around it.

On the east side of the house was an attached, two-car garage and a concrete driveway that sloped downward thirty feet to a wash of gravel that led to the road. Like the house, the driveway was flooded with light. Only two areas of the house remained dark: the garage itself and a large room on the south side, adjacent to the front entrance.

Deborah Jahnke paced distractedly in the darkened front room, returning every few moments to the window to gaze out upon the empty road. When she stood still her fingers flew up to her temples and brushed her hair back over and over, until she felt the need to pace again.

She was seventeen years old but struck some people as much younger. This was partly because of her size—she was two inches over five feet tall, with spindly arms and small hands—and partly a matter of her fidgetiness, her thick, unruly shock of brown hair, and the girlish clothes she sometimes wore; all of which gave her the aspect of a street urchin in a Truffaut movie. To others, though, she seemed much older than seventeen. Her figure was petite but well defined; her large, somber green eyes roamed everywhere in conversation and seemed to miss nothing; and there was a strained quality to her incessant talk, a forced cheerfulness in her manner, that suggested she carried with her the half-submerged troubles and anxieties of a much older woman.

Tonight Deborah was having difficulty persuading herself to leave the living room. Living room! The name was a joke. No one "lived" there, really, just as no one did family-type things in the "family room," and no one ever came in through the front door of the house. No one even went into the living room. There was no reason to, nothing there. When they moved in they didn't have enough furniture to fill this huge, stark, homely place; so sorry, kids, no living room. The room was dark and empty, and maybe that was why she felt safe and didn't want to come out, even though Richard had told her to stay away from there.

A sharp ringing broke into her thoughts. She stopped pacing to listen. Telephone in the kitchen. *Don't answer the phone,* Richard had said. Well, she could answer it if she wanted to. But that would be a mistake. *Whatever can go wrong will go wrong.* Murphy's Law. Richard's Law. Her law, too.

Somewhere in the back of her mind she counted the rings.

Two. Three. Four. She wandered into the kitchen. Five. The ringing stopped. She walked past the phone into the family room and stood there, shifting uneasily from one foot to the other.

Don't worry, Deborah. I'll take care of him.

She didn't like wearing shoes; as a rule, she didn't wear them in the house. They were off—zoom!—flung to the far reaches of her room as soon as she walked in the door. But she had them on now because Richard had told her to get ready. She knew she should have fetched her coat, too, but she didn't want to do that, not until it was absolutely necessary. *Come on,* her brother had said, *first I'm going to get you out of here.* But what the hell was taking him so long? Whatever can go wrong will go wrong, whatever can go wrong—

"Deborah?"

"In here," she called.

"I can't find the goddam car keys."

Richard Jahnke stood just inside the kitchen, studying his sister intently. He was fifteen months younger than Deborah but seven inches taller. His pale blue eyes were strangely accented by the dark lines beneath them. The natural shadowing made his eyes seem huge; sometimes it gave him a sunken, haunted look, as if he hadn't slept for days. Tonight his face was flushed, and there was something hard and glittering in his eyes that Deborah had never seen before.

"You're kidding me," she said.

"I can't find them anywhere," Richard said, an edge rising in his voice. "He must have hid them."

"Oh God."

"You're going to have to stay here," he said.

"Sure. Sure," she murmured. "Okay, whatever . . ."

"You're going to stay, then?"

"Yeah. I guess," she said. She added quickly, "I mean— yeah. It's like you said: whatever can go wrong will go wrong. If I wasn't here, I guess that's when you'd need me."

"Okay." He started to leave, then stopped, still framed by the doorway. "Does that mean—you'll help me? Will you help me do it?"

She looked away from him.

"No. I can't, Richard. I can't. I'm sorry, but—"

"Okay. You wait here."

"—I'm not as strong as you are . . ."

He was gone again, moving quickly toward Dad's bedroom at the east end of the house. She sat down on the couch and waited, trying to think of something, anything, to get her mind off what was happening. She hated this house, with its white walls and white posts and white trim; she'd always hated it. Countless times she'd imagined what she would do with it if she were given the chance . . . what wonderful colors she'd give it . . . tear up the brown carpets, throw out the heavy Spanish furniture, redo the whole place in Art Deco maybe . . .

It was no use. She could hear Richard going wild in Dad's room, pulling rifles out of the gun cabinet and ammunition out of the big box by the bed.

She wondered if she should go talk to him, but she couldn't think of anything more to say. She had never seen him so upset before. He was trying so hard to take charge, he was being so . . . *active*. He had been like this ever since Mom and Dad left and she found him cleaning up the mess in the kitchen. Deborah told him how truly, utterly sick she was of all this crap, how she couldn't wait until she was out of here and off to college. Richard told her she was dreaming, it was time to do something. And he went on and on about Mom, and the things she told Dad he had said to her that he didn't even say; how the hell could she do that, he'd had enough of both of them. (Deborah had agreed with him. It was about time he saw that Mom was part of it, too. Besides, that *was* a pretty shitty thing for Mom to do; Deborah knew that her brother didn't say those things.) And then Richard took the peach carnations out of the vase, the ones Dad had brought home and Mom had gushed over as if they were some kind of rare orchid or something, and he threw them in the trash compactor. He muttered something like, *She's on his side now—* spat it out, really, his voice so strangled that Deborah could hardly understand him. He was breathing hard, his hands shaking with fear or pain or maybe simple rage. She asked him what he was going to do, and he told her, *Don't worry, Deborah, he's never going to touch you again . . .*

Richard reappeared in the doorway. He had a rifle in each hand and a revolver in a holster on his belt. He held out the rifles for her inspection.

"Which one do you want?" he asked.

Deborah looked from one weapon to the other. They were both big, black, ugly things, with long, evil snouts. One did seem smaller and more attractive than the other, but after a few moments she shrugged.

"The one that kicks the least," she said.

Tuesdays are busy at the Casa de Trujillo in Cheyenne. The business comes on Tuesday because the restaurant is closed on Sunday and Monday, casting patrons adrift in a town not known for its Mexican food. At 5:30 P.M. on Tuesday, the sixteenth of November, the Casa was almost full, and Richard and Maria Jahnke did not have a reservation. Fortunately, a table had just been cleared at the back.

That suited Maria just fine. She settled into her chair with a sigh of relief. It had been one hell of a day, buster, what with the house a mess and Richie smarting off and Big Richard losing that famous temper of his—on this of all days, mind you, the twentieth anniversary of the night she met him—and then that business at the light at Yellowstone and Prairie on the way over here; how did that old man get so old running red lights like that, she thought for sure they were gonna die this time. But no such luck, my friend. Richard spun the Volkswagen to a screaming halt in the middle of the intersection and honked at the other driver and unburdened himself of the torrent of bad words he kept ready for such occasions. Then they were on their way again, like bats out of hell. The last thing they needed now was a wait for a table, that would only get her husband started again, as waiting for anything always did. Better they should have this little corner to themselves.

They had hardly ordered, it seemed, when their food was brought to them. The service was amazing, Maria thought, considering the number of people in the place. She was glad that they hadn't been given a table closer to the other diners. That was another thing that set Richard off; if there were people nearby, sooner or later he would find one that offended him somehow. He would nudge her and urge her to take note of someone's table manners: *Look at that pig, isn't that disgusting? Look, Maria, take a look for yourself.* Or he would catch someone glancing their way and glare back at him, as if to say, *You looking at my wife? You looking for trouble, asshole?*

Can you believe it? As if anyone would be ogling the wife of Richard Chester Jahnke; as if anyone even noticed her. Several times when they went out together, Maria had tried to picture what she and Richard must look like to the rest of Cheyenne. It was a painful thought, but she had managed it: here's this dumpy little housewife in slacks, a real beauty queen, not even forty and already worn out; and this jowly, balding, fussy little man with the big belly, coming on like Mr. Macho Mustachio in his brown leather jacket, chewing on his cigar, trying to stare them all down with those huge, pale blue eyes. Who was going to care? He was lucky people didn't laugh in his face.

They said little after the food came. When they were almost finished, Richard asked her what was bothering her. He seemed to want some assurance that she was having a good time; after all, it was their anniversary. His mood was perilously difficult to read at times like this. Like all true romantics—and Maria herself was one, she knew all about it—he was so darned unpredictable. After the big fight with the kids at the house, and the near-accident on the way here, and all the cursing for the rest of the drive, Maria didn't want to get him started again. Yet she knew she had to say something.

"I can't help it," she said. "I'm going crazy in that house."

It was her usual opening gambit. When things got out of hand at home she threw up her hands and told them all to stop it, she was going crazy. Not that anyone seemed to hear. She slaved like a dog for all of them and yet no one paid any attention to her; for all they cared she could go bonkers or kill herself.

"Those little bastards," her husband said. "They make me sick."

"Please, Richard."

"I can't wait for them to get the hell out. You heard me, didn't you? I told him, 'You don't like it here? Then leave. Who's stopping you?' And if she wants to go with him, fine. Good riddance."

"Do you have that letter that came today?" she asked.

"Oh yeah, I was going to look at that," he said, pulling a piece of paper from his jacket.

"It's from the church."

"I can read."

"They're starting this counseling program for families," Maria began, choosing her words carefully. "I think it sounds interesting. Let's face it, Richie and Deborah need help. I need help"—the last thing she wanted to say was *you need help*—"we all need help."

"Little bastards. They screw everything up."

"Richard, I'm tired," she said, trying to head off another round of swearing. "I'm tired of living the way we do. All the fighting, all the yelling. We don't have a family life, we really don't, and I can't stand it anymore. I really do need some counseling."

"Well, maybe we should look into it," he said, in a tone so agreeable that she would always remember it with the greatest astonishment.

"You'll go with me?" she asked.

"Yeah," he said. "But I don't care what they say. It's not going to change a thing. Those little bastards make me sick."

"Please, Richard, can't we have a meal in peace?"

Deborah cradled the carbine in her arms and paced the length of the family room for the sixth or tenth or twentieth time, like a sleep-stunned mother up all night with her colicky child. After a few more turns she gave up and put the carbine back on the couch, knowing that any moment Richard would come in and tell her to pick it up again.

Another rifle, a mini something or other, stood against the wall next to the fireplace. Deborah didn't know much about it. Richard had talked about it and about the other guns he had put all over the house, but all she remembered was what he had said about the carbine: *This is thirty shots. All you have to do is point it and pull the trigger.* Sure, this is a loaded weapon here on the couch, and all I have to do is pull the trigger. Sure, Richard, no problem.

"Richard?"

He had disappeared again. She doubted he could hear her. He had turned on the radio in the kitchen and the stereo in her room, each tuned to a different station, and the resulting din made conversation from room to room difficult.

At first she had followed him around, until he finally told her to stay with the carbine. He had passed through the family room on his way from the garage to his room, from his room to the basement, from the basement to Mom's bedroom, from Mom's bedroom to the gun cabinet and the garage. Several times he had caught her straying from the gun or wandering off toward the inviting darkness of the living room, and he had scolded her: *Stay*

*with that rifle. Stay away from the garage. Keep out of the living
room. You're safer right here.*

But how did he know that? She had watched him take a rifle
into her room, then change his mind and come back out with it.
Stay out of your room, you could get pinned down there.
Together they had rounded up the dogs and cats—she had looked
all over for Leo, the tabby, but he was still missing—and put
them in the basement. But he had put guns down there, too, so
how safe was that? She had wanted to ask him about that, but
every time she started to say something he cut her off. "Bullshit,"
he snapped. "Bullshit."

And now she didn't even know where he was. There is no way
in hell this is going to work, she decided. Richard doesn't really
know what he's doing. He's going to screw up and get us both
killed.

She picked up the carbine once more, then put it back on the
couch and wandered through all the rooms she was supposed to
avoid. The way Richard acted, you'd think the whole house was
mined, ready to go up in flames. She touched nothing and found
no one. Finally, she knocked softly on the door leading to the
garage and opened it.

The garage was dark. As the light streamed in behind her she
could make out the Chevrolet station wagon and the Scout parked
side by side. White plastic blinds masked the glass panes in the
sliding overhead door in front of the cars, but the floodlights in
the driveway were strong enough to provide an eerie backlighting
from outside. Richard was sitting on the front bumper of the
station wagon, his face bathed in the pale light from the driveway.

"Oh, there you are," she said.

He turned around quickly. "What the hell are you doing
here?"

"I just wanted to know where you were."

"I told you to stay away from here."

He squeezed around the station wagon and came toward her.
He had changed into a darker shirt, a purple velour pullover. His
green plastic ROTC whistle dangled from a cord around his neck.
Far from being flushed, his face was now chalky white.

"Okay, I'm going," she said.

He followed her back inside, like a parent marching a troublesome child off to do her chores. She went obediently to the
family room, then turned to face him and burst into tears.

"I'm really scared," she said.

"It's okay," he said.

"I mean, is this necessary?"

"Nothing's going to change," he said. "I have to do this tonight."

She sat on the couch. At length she managed to stop crying and look up. Richard was still standing there.

"I have to go," he said. "Look, just stay here. It'll be okay."

"Well, if something radical happens, what do I know? What do I tell people?"

"Just tell them the truth, Deborah."

He was already in the kitchen, on his way back to the garage. She called to him once, but the radio was between them, and she didn't know if he heard her. She called again, louder, and he looked back expectantly. "What is it now?" he asked.

"Are you going to kill Mom, too?"

2

After dinner Maria asked her husband to take her to the Laramie County Library. A card had arrived today saying they were holding *Rage of Angels* for her. She read all of Sidney Sheldon's novels as fast as they came out. Richard understood how it was; he devoured James Michener and James Clavell in much the same way. When she came out of the library clutching her book, he asked her, what next? And she told him she was ready to go home.

"Are you sure? I'll take you anywhere you want to go," he said. "What about Pet City?"

Pet City, the pet store in the Frontier Mall, was one of his favorite places. There were always a few pups in the window so cute you couldn't help but laugh. They used to go there to visit Alfie, a black-and-white spotted mongrel with short legs and a long tail. Alfie was so ugly that no one would buy him, until the price finally dropped to seven dollars and Richard, in his usual unpredictable way, brought the puppy home and coolly deposited him in front of the children. He liked to brag about his seven-dollar dog, as if he'd made the deal of the century—but if you knew him the way Maria did, then you knew he felt sorry for Alfie and wanted to give him a good home. He loved dogs more than anything.

They went to Pet City every Friday night; they had been there last Friday and would be going again in three days. Maria was feeling heavy from dinner, and it had been one hell of a day, buster, so she told him no, not tonight, I just want to go home, we can play chess and read. Their big night on the town had lasted less than ninety minutes.

He drove fast. Along the way he started talking about the children again, how he wasn't going to put up with this shit anymore, and Maria realized she had misread him again. She thought the idea of a little chess game would relax him, but he was in a worse mood than ever. By the time they reached Yellowstone Road, Maria felt like opening her door at the next stop and climbing out, slamming the door in his face, the way Richie did sometimes. Well, not like Richie, exactly; Richie usually did that to *her* when she was trying to tell him something. Richie was acting so cruel toward her lately, telling her to shut up, no respect for his own mother. . . .

He roared onto Cowpoke and gave the Beetle a final burst of gas as he hit the gravel turnoff. Then he cut the engine and the lights and coasted to a stop at the right edge of the driveway, leaving a clear path for the two cars parked in the garage.

"Did you leave the lights on in your bedroom?" he asked her.

"I don't think so," she said.

"They're on now."

"It's probably Deborah," she said. "I bought some shampoo on sale. She must've gone in there to get some and forgot to turn the light off."

"Garage door's closed, too."

The garage door, which they always left open a few feet so Alfie and Rusty could get in and out, was completely down. "Now why would they do that?" Maria asked.

"Who knows?"

"Maybe the wind blew it down."

"The dogs can't be too happy about it."

"Oh, boy," she said. "I'll bet they can't wait to get out. They're gonna jump all over you and lick you to death."

He smiled as he opened his door.

> *I make my living off the evening news*
> *Just give me something, something I can use*
> *People love it when you lose*
> *They love dirty laundry . . .*

The radio in the kitchen was tuned to a Top Forty station in Cheyenne. The song of the moment was "Dirty Laundry" by Don Henley, a former member of the Eagles. It was all over the airwaves that month. Richard recognized it immediately, from the first twitchings of its ominous, driving beat. He followed it in his head as the synthesizer kicked in with its angry refrain. The tune was reminiscent of Otis Redding's "Tramp"—but less genial, as if someone had taken the chorus from that song and trained it to attack.

It's interesting when people die
Give us dirty laundry . . .

He fingered the whistle around his neck as he sat on the front bumper of the station wagon with a shotgun resting between his knees. The shotgun was a 12-gauge, pump-action Smith and Wesson with a shortened but still legal 18-inch barrel. A Dan Wesson .357 magnum revolver was strapped into a holster on his right hip. A sheathed hunting knife and two speed-loaders in a black case, for quick reloading of the revolver, hung from his belt on the opposite hip.

Dirty little secrets
Dirty little lies . . .

The familiar putt-putting of the Volkswagen coming up Cowpoke Road brought him to his feet. He put the whistle to his lips.

Maria shifted her book and her purse to one hand and struggled with the door handle with the other. Her husband walked around to her side to open her door for her, as he always did. She told him no, you go on ahead; she was so full from dinner, she wanted to take her time; go on, the dogs are probably dying to get out.

She had climbed out of the Volkswagen and was walking with her head down, stepping daintily from the gravel to the cement driveway, when the explosion came. She dropped her book and purse and froze like a startled sinner, stunned by the thunderous arrival of Judgment Day.

Richard Chester Jahnke stood at the opposite end of the driveway, a few feet from the handle of the garage door. He had spun around to face her with a strange smile or grimace on his lips. His right arm swept out in a horizontal arc, hacking at the air. Then a second explosion, louder than the first, burst from behind him, and he twisted and dropped to the pavement.

"Oh my God, oh my God," Maria shrieked.

She ran to him. He was lying on his back in the driveway, his feet at a diagonal to the garage. Glass and splinters from the garage door had sprayed all around him. His eyes were open and glassy, and a white foam bubbled from his mouth. She tried to feel his pulse at the neck, but her hands were shaking too much.

She put her head to his heart and saw a red stain spreading on the right side of his chest.

She stood up. Seemingly without effort—and surely without any awareness that she might be endangering her own life—she lifted the garage door and rushed into the house. She dialed 911 on the kitchen phone and wailed that her husband had been shot. The operator was terribly slow; Maria had to repeat the address, and then the stupid woman tried to keep her on the line. Maria hung up and headed toward the bedrooms at the west end of the house. As she passed through the family room, she saw a rifle lying on the couch.

The children's rooms were empty. In her own room a window was wide open, the screen removed.

She seized two embroidered cushions from the couch in the family room and returned to the driveway with them. Richard liked to sleep with two pillows. As she eased them under his head, she realized how cold he was and wondered why she hadn't thought of bringing a blanket. She crouched over him and hugged him fiercely, trying to give him the warmth from her own body.

"Please don't die," she cried. "You can't die."

Timothy Olsen was driving east on Riding Club Road when he heard the report of a shooting over the radio of his patrol car. Olsen, a deputy with the Laramie County Sheriff's Office, was working the four-to-midnight swing shift with his partner, Dennis Anderson. They were on their way to Anderson's house for dinner, a circumstance that placed them only a few blocks from Cowpoke Road. Olsen asked the dispatcher to repeat the address. Anderson noted the time: 6:28 P.M.

Two minutes later they turned off Riding Club onto Cowpoke. Olsen cut the car's outside lights as a precaution. The call was too fresh; a suspect might still be in the area. Olsen had been with the sheriff's office for only two years, and he planned to be around a lot longer.

They had no difficulty finding the house. As they came around the ridge that hid 8736 Cowpoke from its neighbors, they saw a short, auburn-haired white female kneeling over a white male in the harshly lit driveway. Olsen pulled up to within fifteen yards of the couple, turned on the flashing overhead light, and emerged behind the protection of his car door. He called to the woman to walk toward him. She refused.

"Where's the ambulance?" she cried.

With Anderson covering him, Olsen left the car to check on the victim. The man had a hole the size of a quarter above his right nipple. Olsen seized the man's right wrist and searched for a pulse. He couldn't find one.

He asked the woman what had happened. She told him that her husband had been shot on his way to the garage and that a rifle was lying on the couch inside.

The woman insisted on staying with her husband. Olsen returned to the patrol car to call for backups. Further questioning of the woman was interrupted by the arrival of an ambulance carrying three emergency medical technicians and an EMT student. Olsen urged them to be careful. They paused by the ambulance and looked around nervously.

"Do something!" the woman screamed. "He's not dead, he can't be dead!"

One of the paramedics asked her to step aside. He knelt down and began to cut the clothes off her husband.

Deputy Robert Bomar was the third officer on the scene. He arrived ten minutes after Olsen and Anderson and moments after the ambulance. When he first heard the report on the radio, Bomar thought the address sounded familiar; when he saw Maria Jahnke standing in the driveway, he knew why. Although he had never been to 8736 Cowpoke before, he knew something unpleasant about the people who lived there.

He leaned over the paramedics and took a hard look at the face of the victim. The man was a criminal investigator for the Internal Revenue Service. Bomar had met him and his wife six months ago, in the course of a routine inquiry concerning their son. The case had been turned over to the county social services agency the same day. The brief encounter hadn't left Bomar with an overly favorable impression of Richard Chester Jahnke. Still, no one deserved to go like this; the killer would have to be caught. And Bomar, a quiet, sandy-haired, poker-faced officer, already had a strong suspect in mind.

Bomar walked toward the garage. The sliding door was up, the way Maria had left it, and he could see another door on the far wall that led into the house. Deputy Olsen stopped him and explained that an official search had yet to be done—if the victim had surprised a burglar, which seemed likely, there was a strong possibility that the suspect or suspects were still inside. Bomar had his own ideas about that, but the two agreed to search the house together while Anderson secured the garage entrance behind them. With Bomar leading the way, the two officers entered the house with their pistols drawn.

"Richard!" Bomar called. "Come out with your hands up."

No one answered. They passed through the kitchen to the family room. Just inside the doorway, leaning against the wall by the fireplace, was a Ruger .223-caliber mini-14 rifle. Across the room, lying on top of a blue denim vest on the couch, was an M-1 .30-caliber carbine.

They checked a bathroom on the far side of the family room, then headed down a narrow hallway to the three bedrooms at the west end of the house.

In the master bedroom they found a Dan Wesson .357 magnum revolver in a brown leather holster. It was lying on the floor beside one of the twin beds in the room, along with a case containing two speed-loaders. They also found two loaded handguns in the closet.

They looked out the open window and saw its missing screen on the ground below. Lying next to it was a fat paperback book with a white cover. The title was *The Portable Jung.*

The bedroom to the right of the master bedroom contained a great number of books and dolls, several large stuffed animals, and a small ceramic Buddha head. It appeared to be a girl's room, and they found no weapons there.

The bedroom to the left of the master bedroom appeared to be a boy's bedroom, with model airplanes on shelves and a poster of a bosomy but clothed woman on one wall. They saw a backpack on the bed and a sheath knife on the floor beside the bed.

A quick check of the living room and dining room yielded nothing. At the east end of the house was another bedroom—or, more accurately, a small room with a washer and dryer and a bed crammed into it. Several shotgun shells were scattered on the bed and across the floor. At the foot of the bed was a large cardboard box overflowing with holsters and boxes of ammunition. A Remington .22-caliber rifle and a Winchester 12-gauge shotgun stood against the wall inside the door, next to a gun cabinet containing several shotguns, handguns, and single-shot and semi-automatic rifles.

A door adjacent to the east bedroom led downstairs to the basement. As Bomar opened it, a black cat that had been at the top of the stairs swept past him.

"Richard!" he called.

Two large dogs, a German shepherd and a black-and-white spotted mongrel, looked up at him from the bottom of the stairs. The basement was one enormous unfinished room with a bare concrete floor. A Smith and Wesson 12-gauge shotgun rested on a Ping-Pong table in the middle of the room. A Sako .30-06-caliber rifle lay on a couch behind it, next to a box of cartridges on a glass coffee table.

They returned to the garage and found another Smith and Wesson 12-gauge shotgun on the hood of the station wagon. Olsen tapped something with his foot and looked down to find several expended shotgun shell casings scattered between the two cars and beneath them. The sliding garage door was poised above their heads. There were two jagged holes in the white blinds above the door handle. Four more holes, only a few inches apart, stared back at them from a wooden panel below the door handle.

Olsen and Bomar studied the shotgun on the hood of the station wagon without touching it. More methodical searches of the house that night would turn up more rifles and a handgun under the beds in the master bedroom, as well as an air pistol and a cocked, loaded Colt .45 automatic under the bed in the boy's room: a total of fourteen rifles, twelve handguns, and seven shotguns, thirty-three guns in all. Many of them were loaded. But you didn't have to be Sherlock Holmes to figure out which one was the likely murder weapon.

Bomar returned to the driveway. Maria was pleading with the attendants to ride in the ambulance. Anderson was trying to persuade her to go with him. Bomar quietly took her aside.

"Mrs. Jahnke," he said, "where is your son?"

"I don't know," Maria replied. "Richie and Deborah were both here when we left, but Richie was supposed to go to an open house at school tonight."

"Did your husband and your son have a fight today?"

"They were arguing earlier, but then we left."

"Mrs. Jahnke, did your husband hit your son today?"

"No," she said. "Well—maybe." Her eyes darted away from him, back to the huddle of paramedics around her husband.

"Could your son have been involved in this?"

"I don't know. I suppose it's possible. I'm not trying to cover up for anyone, I just don't know," she said.

To Bomar it appeared that Maria was highly uncomfortable answering his questions. She was distracted, perhaps—yet he noted that she didn't seem to register any shock or surprise at the idea that her son might have shot her husband. In any case, he was unable to question her further. Anderson was waiting to take her to the hospital. Bomar knew someone else would pick up the questions from there.

Two more patrol cars pulled into the driveway. Bomar reported what he knew about the case to a sergeant from the sheriff's office. He was told to canvass the neighborhood for people who might have heard or seen something.

He discovered that five of the neighbors in the more immediate area had heard gunshots, and one had heard Maria screaming. Others were not at home at the time or had heard nothing. At one house Bomar used the phone to call the sheriff's office.

"Pull the child abuse report on Richard Jahnke, Senior," he said.

The emergency medical facility closest to Cowboy Country is Memorial Hospital in downtown Cheyenne. Deputy Anderson drove Maria there, not nearly fast enough to suit her. She didn't understand why the officers wouldn't let her ride in the ambulance with her husband, why a sheriff's deputy had been allowed to go in her place. What if Richard needed her? What good was a deputy going to do him?

At Memorial they asked her to wait in a break room next to the emergency receiving area. Deputy Anderson and a nurse waited with her. Maria found a phone and called her mother-in-law in Chicago; she told her that Richard was in critical condition and that she would call back as soon as she had any more news.

When she returned to the break room more nurses and police officers had arrived. They all looked at her.

Then a deputy she did not know told her what everyone else in the room must have already known or suspected; what had seemed likely to Tim Olsen when he first felt for the victim's pulse; what had been evident to the paramedics who attempted

cardiopulmonary resuscitation for twenty minutes; what had
become indisputably obvious to the emergency room team as they
worked on the patient for another twenty minutes, pumping him
full of drugs and fluids and giving him electric shocks, all of
which failed to produce a spontaneous heartbeat or any kind of
blood pressure, leaving them with a body that was turning blue
before their eyes, a body ravaged by four gunshot wounds: two in
the right side of the back, another in the left hip, and a fourth in
the right side of the chest.

The deputy told her that her husband was dead.

3

It was the longest night of Maria's life, a wandering, groping nightmare that led her in tears and confusion to unfamiliar places. Everywhere she went, people asked her questions, and the questions reminded her that Richard was gone, she was alone now. Alone! Was there anything more terrible?

Months later, when she could talk about the death of her husband with composure, memories of the night he died still haunted her. They pursued her like a pack of wild dogs; they invaded her dreams and shattered her sleep. It wasn't just the horror of that violent moment, or the numbness that came with the knowledge that he was dead, or even the anguish of learning who had killed him. All these stages of the ordeal had marked her, but there was something else, too. Something that gnawed at her—not just the way he died or even the why of it, but the timing of his death, the fatal coincidences that surrounded it.

That he should be taken from her on that particular night, twenty years after they first met, twenty years to the day . . . a day they had celebrated every year, just as they did every birthday, Valentine's Day, and the day of their wedding—but privately, so privately that up until that night their own children weren't aware that November 16 was a special day to them. It was like something out of a bad novel. Maria loved a magical coincidence as much as the next person, but this was more coincidence than she could stand.

Yet their life together had been ruled by coincidences. The story began with a chance meeting on a bus she had boarded by mistake, a bus that took her the wrong way and then broke down. However appropriate the bus trip might be as a paradigm of her marriage, it would be rejected by any scribbler of romances as too convenient, a shameless violation of all the taboos; real lovers don't meet that way. And then to have it end exactly twenty years later, on the secret anniversary of that magical moment in Santurce—but that was how it was. That was Maria's

21

story, the one she lived, and she was stuck with it. Some of the more painful scenes from the intervening years slipped away from her, but she never lost sight of the coincidences. And she could recall the first time she met Richard Chester Jahnke in astonishing detail, with the unsettling clarity of an ominous dream. In fact, she could recall the night she met her husband much better than she would ever be able to remember the night of his death.

It was November in Puerto Rico, her second fall on the island since she and her mother had come back from New York. She was nineteen years old and had her own apartment in Santurce, a small town lost among the suburbs of San Juan. It was a Friday night, and she was late for work.

She worked from ten-thirty in the evening until six-thirty in the morning at the telephone company as an overseas operator. She'd had the job almost two years and liked it very much, so much that she usually arrived an hour early. That gave her enough time to put on her makeup, chat with the other girls, and get ready for the long night ahead. But that Friday night she had dinner with her aunt and uncle, and the three of them started to talk, and the time flew by, and when she looked up at the clock she knew she was going to be late.

Her aunt insisted on making sandwiches for her and filling her thermos. Maria ran four blocks to the bus stop and boarded the bus as it was leaving. She couldn't find her dime, so she had to sit down and forage in her bag—among the makeup, the sandwiches, the thermos, the toothbrush and lotions and powder and perfume, all the things a girl needs to freshen up when she works the night shift—and pay the man and sit down again, quite flustered now.

To calm herself, she started reading the other people on the bus. This was a regular game of hers. She read faces, clothes, shoes, and jewelry, tried to imagine where each person was going on a Friday night in Santurce. Although it was late, she could tell from the number of lunch buckets that many of the people on the bus were headed for the night shifts at the factories.

She had noticed the American when she first boarded the bus. He was sitting at the front, in one of the side seats opposite the driver. He had huge blue eyes and a well-scrubbed, peachy complexion. He wore a freshly laundered pair of white cotton pants and a black short-sleeved shirt: a very clean-cut *yanqui*. His shiny black shoes and closely trimmed brown hair marked him as U.S. Army issue. There were two army bases in the San Juan area, Fort Brooke and Fort Buchanan, and Maria wondered what he was doing so far from either one of them.

From time to time his eyes roamed the bus and settled on her for a moment—not a leer, which would have made her avert her eyes, but a polite, studious glance, as if he played the same game she did. She appreciated neatness and good manners, and there was something about the American—so compact and muscular and trim, with that healthy glow in his cheeks—that pleased her.

She didn't have time to dwell on this. The bus made a turn it wasn't supposed to—at least, her bus never turned onto this street—and she realized she was on the wrong bus. She didn't know if she should get off now and walk back to her stop or wait and see where this one would take her. The right thing to do would be to ask the driver, but she'd already made a mess of things going back and forth with her dime, and it was terribly difficult for a shy girl to get up in front of everyone and ask directions—bus drivers could be so rude sometimes. The streets rolled by, and she felt herself starting to panic. She was going to be late for work and maybe get fired.

Then the bus lurched to a stop in the middle of a small, dark street. The driver swore; the bus shuddered but didn't move. The driver stood up, said something about engine trouble, and ordered everyone off the bus.

The other riders groaned, but Maria was relieved. The breakdown had saved her from making a troublesome decision, and she could see now that she wasn't all that far from work; she could walk from here. As she joined the line of disembarking passengers, she saw the American standing outside the door. He was asking everyone if they spoke English. Some probably did, but no one would admit it.

Maria was the last one to descend. He asked her, and she said yes, and he said "Thank God" and smiled at her. He explained that he'd just arrived on the island and had decided to do a little sightseeing, but he had no idea where he was. How was he going to get back to Fort Brooke? She smiled back and told him she could show him where to catch another bus, it was on her way.

They walked quickly, two strangers with a mission. He told her she spoke English very well. Maria laughed and told him she grew up in New York City. He asked what a nice girl like her was doing out alone at night, and she said she was late for work. He asked if the neighborhood was dangerous after dark, and she laughed again. In those days you could go out all night in Santurce and leave your doors unlocked, and no one would bother you or steal you blind.

She took him to a bus stop on a brightly lit thoroughfare and told him the bus would take him into the heart of San Juan, he could walk to the base from there. He thanked her and insisted on walking her to work before he caught his bus. "You're not going to walk by yourself late at night," he said.

Maria didn't know what to do. She would rather walk alone than with a strange man. But he was determined to repay the favor, and they were walking down major streets now, bright lights and people all around them, what could he do? By the time they reached the phone company she knew that her companion was Richard Jahnke from Chicago, that he had done his basic training at Fort Knox, that he was working at the hospital at Fort Brooke, and that he had the biggest blue eyes she had ever seen.

She surprised him by taking his hand and shaking it very hard, saying thank you very much, it was nice meeting you, good-bye, and then she rushed inside before he could say another word.

The next day was Saturday, her day off. On Sunday evening she caught the bus an hour early. The American was leaning against the wall outside the entrance of the telephone company. He was wearing the same freshly washed white pants and black shirt, and he smiled broadly when he saw her. He told her he had waited for her yesterday, but she hadn't come. He wanted to thank her properly for her courtesy. Did she have time for a cup of coffee or a Coke?

They went across the street to a cafe frequented by the telephone workers and ordered Cokes. She asked him about his work but scarcely heard his answers. Every few moments they were interrupted by one or another of Maria's friends nudging her and whispering in her ear, *"¡Qué guapo!"* or *"¿A propósito, quién es este gringo?"*

After she had introduced him to several people, including the owner of the cafe, they were left in peace. He smiled at her and said casually, as if talking about the weather, "You know, I am going to marry you."

She blushed, pretended she didn't hear him, and started talking about something else. He let the subject drop, but when it was time for her to go, he told her he wanted to take her out—with her parents' permission, of course; he wanted to do everything right. She didn't say anything. When he asked her again, she gave him her phone number and said, call me, I'll think about it.

For the rest of the night she wondered if she should have been so friendly. It wasn't that she didn't know how to say no. She wanted to see the American. He seemed very nice and clean, and *guapo,* of course. But it was clear that he was looking for a proper girl with proper parents, and she didn't know how to explain about herself.

In those days her name was Maria de Lourdes Rodriguez. She had a different name when she was born (on December 13, 1942, in Santurce) but her parents separated when she was nine months old. Her mother reclaimed her maiden name, Virginia Rodriguez, and took her daughter to New York City.

Maria never saw her father again. She knew little about him, except that he worked in a bank and once served in the U.S. Army. His family was well-to-do, and it is possible that the marriage failed because he had married below his station; Virginia Rodriguez was from a good family, but he married her without the proper arrangements and approval, wounding the pride of both families and prompting intervention from older, wiser heads. Maria was five years old when the divorce became official. Her father never came to see her, and Virginia said that she would accept nothing from him. Her own family was proud and stubborn, not the type to discuss its problems openly—as Maria later put it, *you knew better than to ask.* All that remained of the vanished father was a small picture in a locket his daughter would always carry with her.

Virginia worked at a series of factory jobs in New York, making eyeglasses, sweaters, candy—tedious work, but readily available during the war. Her daughter was an asthmatic, sickly child who wore leg braces to correct severe bowleggedness until she was five. Maria's earliest memories have to do with taking large doses of vile medicine and being pushed down the sidewalk in a baby carriage long after she was big enough to walk because she moved too slowly and awkwardly to suit her mother.

As she grew older and stronger, Maria became responsible for the household chores. She was expected to come straight home from school, clean the apartment, and have dinner ready for her mother when she came home from work. She had few friends in their Italian-Jewish-Puerto Rican neighborhood in Queens. Virginia liked to go out in the evenings to local parties and dances, but Maria was supposed to stay home, the Cinderella of Long Island City, waiting for her ducktailed prince. She would later tell people that if she didn't do her chores correctly—if, for instance, Virginia's favorite white gloves weren't properly cleaned and laid out for her when she was ready to go out—then her mother would slap her or beat her with her high-heeled shoes.

"I had a horrible childhood," she said. "I guess my mother blamed me for her life, for what happened to her marriage. And I was just there, barely existing. I wasn't allowed to do much. I was never allowed to speak English at home, so when I went to school I used to live in the library.

"I always had a fascination for dancing, and I had a talent for dancing. She used to discourage it. She never wanted me to do anything creative. I used to see my girlfriends, how lovely their mothers were treating them; they'd go to ballet and tap dancing and all sorts of activities, and I was never allowed to. She didn't even want me to graduate from high school. She wanted me to get out and work.

"She was very strict, and she didn't want me to grow, for some reason—she liked me right there. In some ways, my mother was more of a child and I was the mother. But at the same time, I didn't have the rights a mother has towards a child. I was the one who used to get it when she came home. It was always like that, as far back as I can remember. If the day didn't go like she wanted it to, I was her target. Oh yes, I was her punching bag."

School was her escape. Virginia was eager to leave New York, but Maria persuaded her to wait until she had finished high school. After graduation she found a job as a clerk typist in a department store in Manhattan and rode the subway to work. Her dream was to save enough money to go to college and become a pediatrician. But then Virginia quit her job and told her they were going home. They had visited Santurce every summer, and now it was understood that Maria would find a job there and support her mother out of love and gratitude for Virginia's long years of toil, when she had been saddled with a sick and useless child.

They returned to Puerto Rico in December of 1960. Maria's

uncle, her father's brother, a retired U.S. Army colonel, helped her find work with the telephone company. Virginia, still attractive in her early forties, eased into a retirement filled with male admirers. But Maria was beginning to blossom, too; she had discovered fashion and makeup and the bouffant hairdo. It would have been a blind suitor indeed who came to visit Virginia and failed to notice her dark, buxom teenage daughter, the one with the round face, pouting lips, and merry eyes, swathed in the heavy mask of makeup typical of Latin girls. More than one visitor to their house noted a certain tension between mother and daughter, which Maria blamed on her mother's "jealousy" of her.

At the time Maria met the American on the bus, she lived alone in a rented room in an old widow's house—a scandalous arrangement for a single girl in Puerto Rico, but Maria told friends that she had little choice. After two years of arguing with Virginia and enduring her "jealousy," she had informed her mother that she was tired of being treated like an animal. Her mother had replied, "There's the door—get out!"

She got out. She continued to send her mother a part of her paycheck, but she would not live with her.

When the American called her the next day, Maria had already decided to be honest with him. She told him that she didn't have proper parents, but she had an aunt and uncle who would take their place, and he could meet her at their house. He said he would be delighted to meet them.

Her uncle greeted the proposition with far less enthusiasm. A handsome young businessman of the island, a man of good family, had been courting Maria at family gatherings, and it was understood that in due time he would marry her. But Maria didn't care for him. He asked strange questions—"Do you consider yourself an affectionate person? How do you feel about my work?"—as if love were a quiz, and happiness lay in getting the answers right. She pleaded with her uncle to give the American a chance. The colonel gave his consent reluctantly, convinced that she was going to bring a hoodlum into his home.

Richard arrived with flowers and fine words and a firm handshake for the suspicious uncle. The colonel had never met an enlisted man with such good manners. When the American asked to take Maria into San Juan for dinner, there were no objections.

They walked all over town that night, from the tourist strip known as the Condado, down the winding streets of Old San Juan, with its stately clay-roofed buildings, all the way to the beach. It was the type of evening they would often have together in the months to come; sometimes they would go to parties on the base or at the house of one of Maria's friends, but mostly they would walk and talk. Maria soon realized that was just about all Richard Jahnke could afford to do. He always wore the familiar white pants—no doubt he had few clothes aside from his uniform—but Maria didn't care. The pants always looked as if they had been washed that day, and he smelled wonderful: like an ocean breeze scouring the peninsula, fresh and masculine.

On their walks together he displayed a sharp sense of humor and a curiosity about life in Puerto Rico that she was eager to satisfy. He told her stories about football and Chicago bullies and the stupidity of his superiors. Over time she was able to piece together his version of himself.

His father was also named Richard Jahnke, a good German name. His mother, Theresa Zielinski, was of Polish descent. They were both native Chicagoans, had met in a local school-supply store run by Theresa's family, and had married young. Shortly after Richard Chester Jahnke was born, his father went off to fight the Japanese and was wounded on the island of Leyte. Richard Senior still suffered from dozens of shrapnel fragments in his leg.

Richard Junior grew up on West Fifty-first Street in Chicago, in a neighborhood full of German and Polish families like his own. He attended Catholic schools (a welcome bit of information to Maria) until his love of football led him to defect to a public high school. He had a younger sister and brother back home.

Maria asked him why he hadn't gone to college instead of joining the army, surely he was smart enough. He said something about money and family obligations and the need to get out of Chicago as soon as possible. She sensed some deep frustration or resentment in him, a feeling of something missing back home; a suggestion, perhaps, that his life had been as difficult as hers. Far from alarming her, the thought made her feel more at ease with him. At some point he mentioned he'd seen the hit movie *West Side Story* and loved the song "Maria." Maybe, she thought, they could flee the darkness of their respective families, just like the couple in the movie, but with a happier ending.

But he didn't dwell on whatever it was he had left behind. He liked to talk about his plans, the grand life he was slowly but surely carving for himself out of his arduous time in the service. He was only a private, but already he had an important job as a bookkeeper at the hospital at Fort Brooke. He was learning a great deal about accounting and finance, and he figured the army would be his ticket to a good career in one of those fields. When he had made his pile, he would buy a farm and live there with his family and raise chickens. The happiest times in his own boyhood, he said, were the summers he had spent on his grandmother's farm in Missouri.

Maria loved to hear him talk. He talked as if he had his life worked out, already waiting for him; he merely had to live it. And although he didn't repeat his vow to marry her, the way he looked at her made her feel that she had been accounted for in his head, figured into his dreams.

At the end of their first date, as he walked her back to her uncle's house, he began to talk quickly. He said he wanted to learn Spanish and he hoped she would help him. He described the view of the sea from his barracks: how he could see the big white ships heading for the harbor, and the water rushing over the rocks. He would look at the ocean and think of her and feel at peace. And he told her he wanted to see her every day, if that was all right, even if it was only to walk her home from work. If she got off work late at night or early in the morning, that was okay, he would still walk her home, provided his duties didn't keep him tied down at the base.

He made this request with his usual smile and his large clear eyes fixed upon her. Maria didn't know whether to thank him for the compliment or rush inside. That he should want to see her every day was frightening. It was as if he was trying to own her. And yet . . . that he should care that much about her . . .

She told him she would think about it.

Of course, she still didn't know much about him. It would be weeks before she learned certain basic facts about him. His age, for example. From his manner and appearance, she thought he was in his early twenties. Months later she would learn that he was eighteen years old when they met, exactly thirteen months younger than she was. If she had known from the beginning that he was only a boy, she might have been less impressed with him. She might have considered that he had arrived in Puerto Rico only three weeks before he met her; that she was probably the first girl he had met since leaving home; that his vow to marry her indicated an impulsive, even reckless nature that his casual manner couldn't entirely disguise.

By the time these things did occur to her, they seemed like such petty details, easily dismissed by a girl in love.

Richard Chester Jahnke always looked older than his age. Even in his sixth-grade class picture, he appears as a smiling, debonair, white-tied man of the world, a midget *bon vivant* traveling incognito among the boys and girls of St. Bruno School. His buddies at Fort Brooke tended to be four or five years older than he was, men who scorned the company of most raw recruits. But Private Jahnke didn't look like a kid and didn't act like one. He had a quick mind and a talent for needling people, regardless of size or rank. He wasn't loath to respectfully remind officers who walked into the payroll office of Rodriguez U.S. Army Hospital to remove their hats.

He loved to talk. His stories relied heavily on exaggeration, but they were funny. Even if they weren't, he told them as if they were. If you had to leave in the middle of one, he would turn to whatever audience was available—a bewildered passerby or even a piece of furniture—and continue: "Now, chair, as I was saying . . ."

At times the private's towering self-confidence could come in handy. One night a comrade-in-arms "tied one on in San Juan" and was stumbling home in the slim hours of the morning. Private Jahnke, who always drank in moderation, was assisting him when a pack of local youths surrounded them. The four or five boys seemed to think that rolling a couple of drunk dogfaces would be a swell way to start the day. Private Jahnke informed them that they would get the hell out of his way or he would stomp the hell out of all of them. He was only five-eight, no bigger than any of the attackers, but it didn't make any difference to him. The little guy had spunk. The boys must have realized this, for they departed quietly.

When Private Jahnke began to boast that he had met the prettiest girl on the island, this claim was met with the usual cheerful skepticism accorded to the pronouncements of Private Jahnke. Among his colleagues in the payroll office, Private Jahnke's reputation as a talker was well known. But those happy few who double-dated with the private found out he wasn't joking.

One of the private's friends would remember the young Maria de Lourdes Rodriguez as a "living doll." Five feet tall, with a big, round face and a striking figure, she must have been the product of some very adult toymaker. Her attractiveness was complicated by her giggly, squeaky, little girl's voice and a kind of bubbly innocence; when you spoke to her, her whole face lit up with childish delight.

It was hard to keep your eyes off her, but you had to be careful about that when Private Jahnke was around. And he was always around, hovering over her, glaring at anyone who seemed to be paying too much attention to her. Other GIs learned to avoid confrontations by concentrating on their own dates, leaving the private's wrath for perfect strangers. A hapless passenger on a bus might become entranced with the lovely vision sitting opposite him, only to be shaken from his reverie by the hot challenge of her companion: *What the hell are* YOU *looking at, pal?*

Even Maria's friends, island girls raised on the idea that the man you married became your lord and master, were amazed at the *gringo*'s possessiveness. He was with her practically every day and phoned her constantly when they were apart. He was running her life, and Maria didn't seem to mind at all. She sat in his lap, stroked the back of his bull neck, and devoured him with her eyes. Everyone knew she had it bad, *se enamoró locamente de su gringo*. It was only a matter of time.

The time came in May of 1963, six months after their first meeting. Private Jahnke had just returned from two weeks in Chicago on leave; he was waiting for Maria when she got off work. He insisted on taking a taxi. Once they were safely on their way, he handed her a box of Cracker Jacks.

The gift was a regular joke of theirs. Not having much money, he liked to make a big production out of presenting her with the little prize wrapped in paper, and she fussed over the picture books, puzzles, and trinkets as if they were pearls. But tonight Maria couldn't find a prize in the box. He took her left hand and slipped a sparkling solitaire on the third finger, whispering, "Is this what you were looking for?"

The engagement stretched over thirteen months. They had to save enough money for a big wedding; that was every island girl's dream, and Maria's most of all. The private (by now private first class and on his way up) put himself on a strict allowance and handed his $325-a-month paycheck to his fiancée. During the long betrothal they had a scene or two—when he objected to her dancing with her cousin's friend, a man she had known for years, Maria threw the diamond ring at Private Jahnke and told him they were through—but they made up easily. Everyone agreed that they were made for each other. A few days before the wedding, Virginia allowed Maria to come home so that she could "come out of her house" in the proper manner.

They were married on June 6, 1964, in the Church of Santa Teresita in Santurce. It had rained in the morning, and the air was still cool and fresh when the colonel led his niece down the aisle that evening. The bride wore a mail-order gown (*"La novia lució una creación de* Bride's Magazine, *y estaba radiante de belleza,"* noted the local newspaper). She was twenty-one years old ("practically an old maid by local standards," Maria would later recall) but looked seventeen, and the groom was twenty but looked thirty. The groom joked afterward that he wasn't sure he was married, since the priest had jabbered in Spanish. None of the groom's family was able to attend.

At the crowded reception the groom drank little and said less. He waited patiently as the new Maria Jahnke laughed and cried and danced and hugged all her girlfriends, who had given her a total of forty-six nightgowns at her bridal shower. Shortly after one in the morning the couple made their escape in a new Cadillac borrowed from friends.

They told their friends they were going to Jamaica for their honeymoon. Instead, they spent a week in an inexpensive beach town on the southern side of Puerto Rico. When they returned, Private Jahnke was full of stories about the wonders of Jamaica in general and Montego Bay in particular. His wife backed him up in this, having agreed to tell no one that they had changed their plans. Maria didn't like to lie, but it seemed harmless enough at the time. Richard was so proud; if he couldn't yet give her everything she deserved, it was important that the rest of the world believe that he could. To do otherwise, to admit that they had never left the island, would tempt people to wonder if their marriage was really as magical as it seemed. She would much rather keep "our little secret," even if it drove a wedge between her and her old friends.

In the years that followed she discovered that she was good at keeping secrets.

* * *

Their first home in Santurce was a small, topsy-turvy apartment above a garage. The refrigerator was next to the bed, and the kitchen sink was out on the patio; a mango tree hovered over the bedroom. Maria woke up to find the dishes soaking in the rain and her husband leaning off the balcony to snatch mangos from the tree. He bellowed like Tarzan and brought the fruit back to bed. She laughed until her sides ached.

By midsummer she was pregnant. They found a roomier place on Calle Loiza, not far from the bus lines. Throughout their marriage, each home would be bigger and more expensive than the last. Richard Chester Jahnke had promised his wife that his family would always have the best, no matter what it cost.

Maria continued to work at the telephone company until she was eight months along. Days went by when she and her husband scarcely saw each other. Then Richard shooed away her girlfriends and insisted that she stay at home by the telephone. He had never approved of her working after they got married—"I hate coming home to an empty house," he said—but he had allowed it because they needed the money. Now her condition bound her to him. Every night he rushed in and demanded, "Where's that baby?"

He took her to a private hospital in the Condado district on the afternoon of March 16, 1965. It was a difficult birth, but Private Jahnke stayed at his post in the maternity ward until his daughter arrived safely. In keeping with local custom and Maria's wishes, they pierced the baby's ears and put earrings on her for her first baby picture, taken on the morning of Saint Patrick's Day.

They called her Deborah Ann—Deborah after Maria's favorite actress, Deborah Kerr, and Ann because it sounded right. Deborah Ann was a chameleon: she had fiery red hair that would later darken to rich chestnut, and large, watery, blue-gray eyes that would turn a deep green.

When the baby was exactly one month old, Richard signed his reenlistment papers. He had been in the service for almost three years, and he told Maria that he hated signing his life away for another six. But he was getting excellent evaluations, and opportunities were opening up for him. Besides, they would surely have another mouth to feed soon. Maria wanted three children. He'd settle for two, but he wanted a boy.

In the fall Maria discovered that she was pregnant again. The news was followed by Richard's exuberant announcement that they would be moving to California after the first of the year. He had been reassigned to the payroll office at Fort Ord, outside Monterey.

Maria didn't question the reassignment. She had known when she married him that they would eventually leave Puerto Rico and go someplace she had never been before. But in the following months she began to feel the accelerating pressures of family life—the presence of one restless infant already shrinking the walls of their stifling apartment, with the prospect of a new home and a new baby on the way—and she and her husband had the first memorable argument of their marriage, with a howling Deborah as witness.

Maria couldn't remember how it began, but her husband became quite angry. He shook her and unleashed his acid wit on her for the first time. He made some tasteless joke about her not being a virgin when he married her, an accusation that stung her like a slap in the face. She had saved herself for him, and he knew it. She grew hysterical and cried, and then she raged at him, as she had when he tried to stop her from dancing with her cousin's friend. The next day he bought her a huge fleecy stuffed bear as a peace offering. She would later say that she never felt as passionate with him after those ugly words, but she took the bear with her to California. It was bigger than Deborah and dyed a warm peach color, the same color as the flowers he would bring her the last night of his life.

They left Puerto Rico in late February. Richard rented one of the newer houses at Fort Ord, a one-story bungalow with a white stucco finish and sliding glass doors. Aside from one neighboring housewife she met while hanging laundry in the backyard, Maria knew no one within thousands of miles. She and her husband went for drives to Pebble Beach, Carmel, and San Francisco, but he didn't seem particularly anxious to make friends on base. Most of the time she sat at home with Deborah and her swelling belly, like an egg waiting to hatch.

One clear summer morning, June 27, 1966, they started out on a drive to Los Angeles, only to have to rush back to the base when Maria felt the first labor pains coming on. The child was the fat, healthy, blue-eyed boy his father had requested. Richard Chester Jahnke had never cared for his own middle name, so they named the baby Richard John Jahnke, after his grandfather. But the boy was clearly his father's son. He had his father's eyes.

4

Officer Raymond Lovelace was making his usual Tuesday night patrol, heading north on Ridge Road in one of the baby-blue cruisers of the Cheyenne Police Department, when he spotted the skinny kid outside the 7-11 store at the intersection of Ridge and Dell Range Boulevard. Lovelace eased to a stop at the light and glanced over his shoulder. The teenager was standing beside a telephone pole across the parking lot from the store, with his hands jammed inside the pockets of his gray down parka. He wasn't waiting for the light to change. He wasn't doing anything, except staring at the patrol car.

For the past hour Lovelace had been hearing radio reports of a homicide north of Cheyenne. The more recent dispatches had included a description of the suspect: white male, sixteen years old, five-eight, medium build, dark brown medium-length hair.

When the light changed, Lovelace headed slowly up the street, turned around, and drove back to the 7-11. The kid had disappeared. Lovelace turned into the parking lot and saw a flash of white emerge from behind the store. He grabbed his radio mike and informed dispatch that a possible homicide suspect had just crossed Dell Range on foot, heading north.

He managed to fix his spotlight on the fleeing figure for a moment before he ran behind a garden supply store. By the time Lovelace could reach the store, the teenager was gone again. Lovelace told dispatch the suspect appeared to be heading toward the trailer park a couple of blocks away.

As the lights drew nearer, Richard John Jahnke hugged himself tightly and clenched his teeth to keep them from chattering. If he could only will his body not to shiver, he told himself, he would be in good shape.

He was lying on his back beneath a camper trailer among the maze of trailers and mobile homes that lined both sides of the dead-end road known as Gregg Way. The ground was hard and cold, getting colder all the time. He had lost track of how long he had been there. An hour? Two hours? Long enough to freeze his ass off, anyway.

The police were shining their lights everywhere, but it really didn't matter. Every cadet knew that using a flashlight at night distorted what you saw. If the light was bright enough and the surrounding darkness dark enough, then all you could detect was movement. As long as he lay still, there was a good chance they could flash right on him and not see him. One heavy-footed officer had already checked his hiding place and missed him completely.

He could hear voices in the distance and dogs barking. It was as if they knew he would show up here: first the sirens, then the helicopters and the foot patrols, now dogs. He wondered if the dogs had his scent. How could they have known he would come to see Donna? He hadn't known it himself two hours ago.

When he ran into the house from the garage, his mother's screams pursuing him, he didn't know where he was going. All he wanted was to get away before Mom saw him; he couldn't stand the idea of her seeing him, pointing her finger at him. Deborah was standing in the hallway, asking a lot of dumb questions. He had to practically push her ahead of him—*I did it, let's get the fuck out of here*. He punched out the screen in Mom's bedroom, crawled out first, and waited for her. It seemed like she took forever to climb out, and then she couldn't keep up with him after that.

At the top of the next hill he paused to look back. The house looked so still and peaceful now that he could no longer hear Mom yelling. Deborah was nowhere in sight. He felt bad about leaving her behind, but hell, he'd done what he could. He figured he had about an hour before they caught him.

He had to tell someone. He started across the prairie toward town, but that meant wading through miles of knee-deep snow in his tennis shoes, so he turned to the road and followed the back streets and alleys to Michael Brinkman's apartment. Brinkman was one of his closest friends in ROTC. He was also one of the cadets pulling duty at the open house at Central High School tonight, a fact that eluded Richard until he reached the apartment house and saw that Brinkman's car was gone.

He walked to the Frontier Mall and roamed its warm, Muzak-lined concourse, telling himself, *This is the last time I will ever walk through the mall.* He saw a girl from his health occupations class, a girl he didn't like at all. He made sure that she saw him. When she hears the news tomorrow, she'll freak out, he told himself.

It wasn't until after he left the mall that he decided to go see Donna Haese. He didn't know her very well—she was just a freshman he'd been seeing recently, one of the ROTC freshmen girls he'd befriended when he was command sergeant major—but he had to tell someone. Fighting off the chill with every brisk step, he walked another two miles to the trailer park where she lived. He came up to the front window of the old wooden bungalow tucked among the mobile homes and saw Donna and her family sitting around the dinner table. He decided not to go in. They looked too happy.

He walked to the 7-11 on Ridge Road. He and Donna used to hang out under the familiar red roof, drinking colas and playing video games. It was the only source of entertainment within walking distance of her house—but that was in another life, and the game they liked to play was no longer there. He stood outside, wondering what to do next. Then the cop saw him.

He could have buried himself in a mound of dirt and dead leaves behind the store, but he ran into the street instead. He made it back to the trailer park before the sirens drove him under the camper. He had stayed there while the thickening hordes of local law enforcement went from house to house.

Now he heard more voices, the thud of car doors slamming, the crunch of tires moving slowly across the gravel surface of Gregg Way. They were leaving at last, or maybe just pretending to leave in order to trap him. He knew he was halfway to a good case of hypothermia; he ought to get up and move around. But he waited another few minutes—five? ten?—until the sounds died away. Then he shed his light-colored parka and crawled from beneath the camper.

He knocked softly at the back door of Donna's house. When no one answered, he knocked louder. Clarence Ketcham, Donna's tall, lean stepfather, opened the door. Richard liked Ketcham, a forty-four-year-old, easygoing cook; the man had always treated him decently. Tonight, though, Ketcham seemed terribly jumpy. Richard knew why even before he spoke.

"What's wrong?" Ketcham asked. "What did you do?"

"I'm in a lot of trouble," he said. "Can I see Donna?"

Ketcham stood aside to let him into the house. In the light he could see that the boy's face was deathly pale. His hands had turned beet-red from the cold, and dead leaves and grass were stuck to the front of his turtleneck. Ketcham took him to a bedroom at the back of the house and closed the door. Richard sat on the bed.

"What did you do?" Ketcham asked again.

"I shot my dad," Richard said quietly.

"What'd you do that for?"

"For revenge," he said.

Ketcham told him to wait there and left the room. He returned a few moments later with a towel and his wife, Hazel Mae. Ketcham started rubbing Richard's hands with the towel. Richard knew what was coming next. He wasn't going to have a chance to talk to Donna; Donna was probably fetching help at this very moment. He heard footsteps outside and then a knock at the door. The Ketchams moved away from him.

"Richard, this is the police. We're coming in."

Hazel Mae opened the door. Half a dozen Cheyenne police officers were in the hallway, their guns drawn. The ones nearest the door had their guns pointed directly at him. Richard stood up slowly and put his hands on his head.

He couldn't believe the number of cops who flooded into the room. Who would have thought a jerkwater town like Cheyenne had so many of them? They patted him down, slipped the handcuffs on him gingerly, as if he were booby-trapped, and then hurled questions at him. They wanted to know exactly where he'd left his jacket. They didn't seem to want to believe that he was unarmed. (Later he learned that a photograph of him wearing his ROTC Ranger camouflage outfit, which made him look and feel like one mean son of a bitch, had been supplied to the sheriff's office. The men who arrested him must have seen it and thought he was a one-man army, like the crazed Vietnam veteran in *First Blood* or the trigger-happy cadet in *Taps*, two of his favorite movies.)

He waited quietly while his captors discussed the problem of transporting him to the county jail. The homicide was being handled by the sheriff's office, but he was in the jurisdiction of the city police at the moment. Officers of both departments were present, and at length it was decided that a city police cruiser would take him downtown and hand him over to detectives from the sheriff's office for questioning.

Sergeant William Null and Officer Robert "Charlie" Hidalgo, the arresting officers of record, led him past Donna and her bewildered little brothers and sisters. Outside, Null read him his rights. Hidalgo read them again in the patrol car. Null started the engine. Once they were moving, the pair seemed to relax.

"Richard, our butts are really on the line," Hidalgo said, in an almost apologetic tone of voice. "Maybe you could help us out."

"Sure," Richard replied.

They asked him what school he went to, what grade he was in, his age, height, and so on. He answered every question. They chatted about how cold it was, and he told them a thing or two about hypothermia. Then, with the same offhandedness afforded the other questions, Null asked, "Why did you shoot him?"

"For past things," Richard said.

Hidalgo picked up the questioning from there. "When did you get the shotgun?" he asked.

"When I got home from school."

"Where'd you get it?"

"From my dad's bedroom."

"Did you load it?"

"No, it was already loaded. It's always kept that way."

"Where did you wait for your dad?"

"In the garage. I waited in the garage."

"Did you see him when you shot him, or were you firing blind?"

"When I saw his shadow, I was like watching a movie," Richard said. "I don't remember any more."

"Did you have any guns on you when you left the house?" Null asked.

"No. I didn't want to hurt anybody else."

Hidalgo was impressed. Although he must have been scared, the youth seemed bright, and his answers were calm and to the point. They were drawing close to their destination now, a complex of buildings in downtown Cheyenne that housed police headquarters, the county jail and courthouse, and the Laramie County Sheriff's Office. With so little time left, it didn't occur to Hidalgo to ask Richard Jahnke about the "past things" that had led him to shoot his father. It was enough that the suspect had confessed that he did shoot him. Hidalgo would let the sheriff's boys take it from there and see if they could do better.

At the sheriff's office a detective gave him a cup of coffee and a printed form titled "Your Constitutional Rights." Richard drank the coffee and indicated on the form that he didn't want to talk to the detective. A sheriff's deputy took him to the cell block and gave him blue prison clothes and flimsy thongs to wear. A man in a dark suit tested his breath, smeared a sticky solution on his hands, then studied his palms and fingertips under an ultraviolet light. Under the light his hands appeared to be stained a deep purple.

Other sheriff's officers took him to Memorial Hospital for more tests. As they signed him into the emergency room, he glanced at the ledger. His father's name was entered a few lines above his own, with a star beside it.

They took him into a small consulting room. A nurse drew blood from his arm. He was too nervous to give a urine sample. The doctor giggled and urged him to keep trying. As he tried to command his bladder to work, he heard voices from the hallway. It sounded like a couple of doctors discussing some X rays.

He couldn't catch all of it, but they were saying something about the slug entering *here,* fracturing a couple of ribs, severing the aorta or arterial something or other, tearing up the esophagus, hitting another rib, and winding up back *there*—yeah, that was probably the one that finished him, nobody could live with that kind of damage.

As he listened, a powerful calm stole over him, as if he had been running for hours and finally collapsed, the weariness sinking into his very bones. Until now no one had told him anything about his father's condition, and he hadn't asked. Now he knew. He didn't feel grief, exactly, but he didn't feel like dancing, either. It was difficult to say what he felt.

But at least he knew he'd done his job.

5

At the hospital a sheriff's deputy named Richard Hillegas took Maria aside for further questioning. The interview began at eight o'clock, forty minutes after Richard Chester Jahnke had been pronounced dead. Afterward Hillegas drove Maria to the sheriff's office. At ten o'clock Hillegas was joined by Detective Tim Greene, and the questioning resumed. At first Greene and Hillegas asked Maria the same questions that had been posed by the first officers on the scene and again by Hillegas at the hospital. But as the night wore on, the two men pressed her to describe the "argument" she said had occurred between her son and her husband earlier that day. They wanted to know how Richie felt about his father.

"Oh, I guess like every kid," Maria said. "When they become of age they resent their parents no matter how good you are to them. You're always wrong and they're right."

"Any hard feelings between the two of them over anything that might have happened?" Greene asked.

"Well, they've been mad at each other. . . . I guess Richard didn't like the way Richie was behaving. And Richie didn't like his father, you know, talking to him and telling him how he's behaving."

"During the time that they were arguing tonight, was the argument loud enough for you to hear?"

"Yes. It was loud."

"Did you hear any threats exchanged?"

"No. I didn't hear any threats—what do you mean? About killing somebody or something? No, I didn't hear any threats at all."

"Have there been any confrontations recently where threats were exchanged between them?"

"There haven't. Only once did Richie, and we landed up here."

The questions ran on and on, and Maria answered them in a

41

soft, hesitant, childlike voice. She was starting to believe she'd spend the rest of her life answering questions. Then the two officers stepped out of the room to confer in private. She wondered if they would let her go now. There was so much to do: relatives to call, a funeral to arrange, and nobody had told her anything about where Richie and Deborah were. She felt like she was losing her mind.

A sickly sweet odor, like that of overripe peaches, tugged at her nostrils. She had noticed the smell for some time, but it seemed to be getting stronger. She looked down and saw that the beige nylon jacket she was wearing was sticky with drying and crusted blood—Richard's blood, from the long moments she'd hugged him in the driveway, trying to keep him warm. She had been walking around all night like a refugee from a slaughterhouse and didn't even know it.

She fought off the urge to retch and went looking for a place to wash her blood-streaked hands. In the hallway were people she knew from somewhere. They offered their sympathies and she replied, but she didn't really pay attention to what was being said. She felt as if she were floating, detached from her own body. At the far end of the hallway she saw Richie.

He was crossing the corridor, from one door to another, in the company of several deputies. He had on strange blue clothes and handcuffs. Maria gazed at him dully. Was that Richie? Were they questioning him, too? What was he doing in pajamas and slippers? Didn't they know he'd catch cold?

The apparition glanced in her direction but said nothing. Then he was gone.

When she returned from the washroom, a deputy told her she was free to leave. But she couldn't go home, he added, because the officers were still there, gathering evidence. The deputy said he would drive her back to Cowboy Country, where some neighbors had offered to put her up for the night.

"What neighbors?" she asked. "I don't want to be a burden to anyone."

"People who live across the road from you," the deputy said. "The Hains. They called to say you could stay with them."

"But I don't know them," Maria said.

The shooting of Richard Chester Jahnke was the first homicide in six months in Cheyenne and only the fifth in three years. In a town where the antics of a runaway steer on a downtown street is front-page news, the crime was an event of cataclysmic proportions. KYCU, Cheyenne's only local commercial television station, opened its ten o'clock news that night with a sketchy account of the slaying. The report omitted the name of the victim and the suspects in the case. It is unlikely that any of KYCU's viewers (or anyone in the studio, for that matter) could have anticipated that the shooting on Cowpoke Road would soon be making national headlines. But even the bare details that crept into Cheyenne's two newspapers, the morning *Wyoming Eagle* and afternoon *Wyoming State Tribune*, over the next twenty-four hours—IRS agent slain outside home, juvenile sought, son arrested!—were tantalizing enough to suggest that the alleged parricide would be the talk of Cheyenne for weeks or months to come.

Before the media or public opinion got mixed up in it, the case had already captured the imagination of local law enforcement. Minutes after Maria's call for help, 8736 Cowpoke was festooned with more flashing lights than a flying saucer in a Steven Spielberg movie. Over the next twelve hours no less than twenty-four members of the Laramie County Sheriff's Office visited the crime scene, including deputies Olsen, Anderson, Bomar, and Hillegas, Sheriff Dennis Flynn, and the euphoniously named Sergeant Sargent.

Many of the officers were engaged in the tedious process of documenting and collecting evidence within and around the house. A few surely came to gossip and to gawk, to take their own measure of the bullet-riddled garage door and the bloodstains on the pavement. A shotgun blast to the heart from an enemy you couldn't see—that was not the way people died in Cheyenne.

The merely curious stayed only a few minutes, but others worked through the night. They chronicled the placement of the guns throughout the house with photographs, drawings, and videotape. They dusted the garage for fingerprints. They removed the perforated panel of the garage door, the ruptured white blind, and the shards of the glass pane. They retrieved the empty shotgun shells from beneath the cars in the garage and scraps of shell wadding from the glass-strewn driveway. They recorded the serial number of every gun in the house and carted all the guns downtown.

In their insatiable quest for evidence, they also seized six cassette tapes from young Richard's room and a suspicious-looking cardboard box from the family room. The tapes turned out to be compilations of rock-and-roll tunes. The box was full of canned goods and presents Maria planned to send to her mother in Puerto Rico for Christmas.

From the front window of a large white house across the road, Maria watched the patrol cars entering and leaving her driveway. It was hard to make out what they were taking from the house—except for the guns, of course, those damn guns; she should get a receipt, they're worth a fortune—but she kept returning to the window anyway. The longer she watched, the more upset she became.

"I wish they would let me go home," she said. "How can they keep a person out of her own home? I have rights, don't I?"

George and Sandy Hain sat quietly in the living room behind her. A tall, bespectacled, white-haired man with piercing blue eyes, George Hain was one of Cheyenne's most prominent businessmen, the operator of a string of Burger Kings in southern Wyoming. He stifled a yawn and exchanged a perplexed glance with Sandy, his slender, auburn-haired wife of twenty-two years. The couple had been trying for hours to persuade Maria to go to bed, without any success.

"What are they doing all this time?" Maria went on. "They should be out looking for Deborah. I don't understand any of this."

"They'll find her," George said. "You really ought to get some rest now, Maria. You'll need your strength."

"How can I sleep? This is all so terrible," she replied.

The Hains had moved out to Cowboy Country four years ago. At that time the house across the road was still under construction. It had remained vacant until the Jahnkes arrived in early 1981. The house was so secluded, George hadn't seen anyone moving around outside the place until two months later, when he spotted the father and son working in the garage with the door open.

He walked over that afternoon and rang the front doorbell. It took a long time for anyone to answer. Then the door opened abruptly, and the father—a short, obese man with a sour face—peered out from behind it. Hain introduced himself, explained that he lived across the way, and asked if they needed help with anything.

"Not interested," the man said. He slammed the door inches from Hain's face.

Hain was dumbfounded. The man couldn't have been ruder to a brush salesman. Still, if that was the way he wanted it . . . The Hains had moved out of the city for the same reasons everyone else did: to get away from the neighbor's ringing phone, obnoxious stereo, barking dogs, and complaints about *your* dogs and your son's basketball practice—in a word, privacy. Here was a family that really wanted to be left *alone*, he decided, so let them be.

He never did meet the rest of the family. Hain's two teenage daughters, Valerie and Wendy, rode the school bus to Central High School on occasion; they reported that the new kids across the street were "really weird." One time the father came out and threatened Wendy with some dire punishment if she continued to turn her bicycle around in his driveway. That was the extent of the Hains' contact with the Jahnkes until tonight. As far as George knew, no one else in the neighborhood knew anything about them, either.

The gunshots changed all that. After the ambulance arrived, Hain went over and saw Maria Jahnke standing over her dead husband in the driveway. He asked her if there was anything he could do. She looked through him and said, "No, someone just shot my husband." Although she was clearly in shock, Hain also got the impression—damned peculiar—that she was *relieved* somehow, as if the weight of the world had just been lifted off her shoulders.

The police shooed him away before he could say anything else. Then Deputy Bomar visited the Hains and took their statements. He also used their phone, and George heard him say something about child abuse.

After Bomar left, George and Sandy started talking about the horrible screams they used to hear in the summer evenings. Sandy had heard them first while working in the yard. It was a cat; no, a kid crying his head off, a kid being beat up by other kids; no, someone sobbing loudly and inconsolably, someone who's already taken his punishment. On several occasions the couple had gone driving in search of the source of these ghastly concerts, but the wind was always blowing and they couldn't figure out which direction the sounds were coming from. Now they asked each other: Could the screams have come from the house across the road?

They watched the ten o'clock news eagerly but didn't learn anything new. Maria arrived after eleven. She was exhausted from her ordeal at the sheriff's office, embarrassed to be in the home of strangers, and too upset to go to sleep. From what she said, the Hains gathered that her son had been arrested, but she didn't seem to know why. Her daughter was still missing.

In her anxiety she leaped from thought to thought: where could Deborah have gone, what if some burglar kidnapped her, why didn't they let her go home?

The Hains attempted to console her, but she was immune to their words. She told them again and again that her husband was a wonderful man. He loved his children. He had worked so hard to provide them with a good home. He had brought her flowers for their anniversary that night. He was a wonderful man, a wonderful man, a wonderful man . . .

Shortly after three in the morning her hosts showed Maria to the spare bedroom and excused themselves. When the Hains were alone, George remarked how odd it was that Maria went on about her husband like that. He supposed the poor woman thought it was expected of her; like all widows fresh in their grief, she felt obliged to convince the rest of the world that her husband was a great guy.

Sandy told him that wasn't it at all. The way Maria was talking, she said, it sounded like she was trying to convince herself.

The deputies had told Maria that they would be through with her house by six in the morning. Unable to sleep, she waited at the Hains' as the deadline passed and no one came across the road to fetch her. At six-thirty she walked over and found the last few officers taking their equipment to their car.

She slipped quickly past them. It felt good to be back in her own home, but she was horrified at what she saw. The place was filthy! It might as well have been ransacked. The deputies hadn't thrown clothes and papers around the way burglars did in the movies, but everything was different. They had gone through drawers and put everything back wrong. They had moved furniture. They had stomped all over the place in their big cop boots and left dirt on the carpets.

She started straightening up the place and discovered that the lovely peach carnations Richard had brought her last night had vanished. She was conducting a frantic search for them when the doorbell rang. It was one of the deputies who had just left.

"I just heard it on my radio," he said. "They found your daughter. She's okay."

6

Deputy Gerald Luce was one of the last investigators to leave the Jahnke home that morning. After assisting in the collection of evidence for almost twelve hours, Luce was on his way back to the sheriff's office when he heard over his radio that a female matching Deborah Jahnke's description had been spotted entering Lions Park, a spacious public park opposite the airport in north Cheyenne. Luce, who was in plainclothes and driving an unmarked car, pulled up near a softball diamond and waited. Ten minutes later he saw a small figure walking beneath the bare trees on the other side of the playing field. She was wearing a dark stadium coat and a long, flowing purple scarf, and her hair had been tousled by the wind. She didn't run when Luce approached her.

"Are you Debbie?" he asked.

"Deborah," she said.

Luce showed her his badge and explained that some other officers wanted to question her.

"Did they find my brother?" she asked.

Luce told her they had. She nodded. "I read about it in the paper," she said.

She had read about it while huddled in the warmth of a stairwell in an apartment complex near Central High School. She had seen the paper boy delivering the *Wyoming Eagle*, and after he'd left she had picked one up from someone's front door. The story was at the top of the front page:

A Cheyenne man was shot to death yesterday evening while opening his garage door. A juvenile suspect was taken into custody late last night.

That was about all the story had to offer, except for Sheriff Flynn's opinion that the man had died instantly. Deborah's atten-

48

tion was drawn to the picture that appeared on the same page—a photo of a tall, square-jawed woman watching a bearded young man work on a clay bust at Central High's open house last night. The woman was identified in the caption as a "Central parent," but Deborah recognized her ceramics teacher, Eve Whitcomb.

To see Eve's face next to this story about her father was too ironic for words. Eve was one of the people she had tried to tell about Dad, one of the few who would listen. Only yesterday Eve had taken her to see a school counselor; Deborah had kicked off her shoes, told Eve and the counselor about how terrible things were getting, and they had actually listened. And last night, after losing sight of Richard right outside the house, running like hell, climbing over barbed-wire fences, getting all turned around, feeling her stomach lurch inside her until she finally vomited, she had gone in search of Eve's house. If anyone could help her, she figured, Eve could.

But she didn't find Eve (although Eve, she later discovered, was out looking for her, too). Instead, Deputy Luce found her. Luce asked her if she had a weapon, which she thought was an awfully strange question. She told him she was sleepy. She waited quietly in the back of Luce's car for the other officers to arrive.

By the morning of November 17, Tim Greene had emerged as the chief investigator on the Jahnke homicide. Although many other sheriff's officers were engaged in some aspect of the investigation, Greene had been assigned by the sergeant of detectives to question Maria Jahnke in detail and to spearhead the search for Richard and Deborah Jahnke.

This was no accident. Around the Laramie County Sheriff's Office, where he had toiled for five years, Greene was known as one of the most dedicated, tenacious detectives. A big, broad-shouldered, bull-necked man in his thirties, with a wisp of a mustache, closely cropped dark hair, and a weakness for tinted glasses, Greene was a thorough legman and a brisk interrogator. He could be as sympathetic as a genial older brother or as imposing as a drill sergeant, depending on the type of confessor required by the suspect at hand.

In the course of his interview with Maria Jahnke, Greene had asked her for any information that might help him locate her daughter. Maria didn't appear to know much about Deborah's friends, but she did give him permission to return to the house in search of clues to her whereabouts. Greene and his partner, Detective Jess Fresquez, found a substantial cache of writings in Deborah's room, including diaries, short stories, unfinished letters, a datebook, and an address book containing names and phone numbers. They started dialing numbers. Acting on a lead developed by another officer, at two in the morning they contacted a Central High student named Chris Lawrence, who had seen Deborah less than four hours after the shooting.

Lawrence said that he and another Central student, Ken Kwiecinski, had been riding their bicycles at roughly ten in the evening when they passed Deborah on a street in north Cheyenne. She was on foot, and they didn't see her at first. She called them over and told them her brother had shot her father. She seemed upset, distracted, perhaps hysterical—at one point she laughed nervously. Lawrence said he hadn't known whether to believe her or not. He told Greene he didn't know where she was now, but he assumed she would be in school the next morning to clear herself.

Greene made a promise to himself to question Lawrence in more detail at the earliest opportunity. The fact that Deborah was roaming freely about the city but had made no effort to contact the authorities changed the character of the case. In Greene's eyes, Deborah Jahnke was transformed from a possible witness of the homicide to a strong suspect.

Upon her arrival at the sheriff's office, Deborah was taken upstairs to the patrol room, an office overlooking the alley that separates the sheriff's office from the city police department. Greene brought her a cup of coffee and sat down at the patrol lieutenant's desk opposite her. They chatted about her studies and the gray, brisk weather. He detected what he took to be an English accent and asked her where she got it. She laughed and told him he was the one with the accent. He smiled.

Detective Fresquez entered the room and took a chair at Greene's right. Greene handed Deborah a constitutional rights waiver form, the same type of form her brother had been given nine hours earlier. She waived her right to have a lawyer present during questioning, and the two men went to work.

They questioned her for almost an hour. She had a tendency to wander away from the question and dive into things that had happened years ago, when the family lived in Arizona, but the detectives steered her back on course without difficulty. She seemed alert and cooperative, even analytical, in her responses, although her speech was punctuated with "you know" and "like" and "kind of" to a dizzying degree. She shifted rapidly from subject to subject, sometimes in midsentence, as if what she needed to say had to come out at once or not at all.

At eight-twenty they took a break. Greene returned with a tape recorder. He turned it on and recited her rights for the second time that morning. Then he asked her to tell it all over again, from the time she arrived home yesterday afternoon.

"Okay," she said. "I came home from school on the bus. I walked through the door and threw all my garbage in my room and put on some scrubby clothes. And my mother, she just started nagging me about something. That really doesn't upset me because it happens every day. It's routine. So I just kind of ignored her. And then a bit later, my brother came home, and she started nitpicking at him. And it got worse and worse and worse, and we had a really early dinner. My mother, at this point she was hysterical, she was screaming her head off—about, you know, just very, very trivial things—her feelings that she's not appreciated enough, that we don't pay enough attention to her, that we're takers and not givers. . . .

"And my brother, he didn't say anything, you know, hurtful, or anything to provoke her. He just said, leave me alone, enough of this, I don't want to talk about this anymore, stuff like this. And she wouldn't let up. So he just shouted, in words I've never heard him use before, he stomped his fists on the table and he said, shut up, leave me alone. And she threw some things at him, like my mother was getting pretty physical about it. I'm just watching all of this. A nonparticipant."

"She threw some things at him?" Fresquez echoed.

"Yeah, she threw a candle, and she threw some dog food at him. Basically, whatever she could get hold of, and he went to his room, and I was sitting around going, oh my God, this is just ludicrous, this is really stupid. And she says, 'I suppose you're against me, too.' I go, 'I'm not against anyone, leave me alone.' And she went away, and I went [to] my room again. That's where I live.

"And I heard all this commotion, and then I heard my father screaming and yelling, and things being thrown around and punches being thrown. . . . I opened the door and saw them. He was just, you know, threatening to get rid of my brother, he just—''

"Okay, now, who is he? Is that your father?" Greene asked.

"My father. My brother did not strike back. He wasn't hitting him back or anything, just kind of avoiding things. And he said, 'Well, I don't know how we're going to do it, but I will get rid of you, we don't want you here, you're a fucking asshole' —quote, unquote—and I said very simply to him, 'You get rid of him, wherever he's going, I'm going as well. I don't want to stay here without my brother.' And he said, well, you—you're such a, you know, shut your mouth, you know, fucking asshole, and you slut, etc., etc. Then, you know, he was just—my mother just goes, oh boo-hoo, boo-hoo, you know, oh these kids, I mean, they're just so terrible to me, and, you know, my father just, yes, yes, I know, they're just a couple of bastards, you know. And we really, you know, got cheated—or something like that . . . so all of a sudden he goes stomp, stomp, stomp, stomp to my brother's room, you know, and bangs on the door, like bang, bang, bang, you know, like the wrath of Hades or something like that. And it just starts up again. I think it was even worse than the first time. I wasn't there; I did not see it. I was pretty scared.''

She started to explain about the places on the body her father preferred to strike: the back of the head, between the shoulder blades, the lower back. "My brother, with him, he hits him every place," she said. The subject had come up during the earlier, untaped interview, and the detectives were eager to move on.

"Okay," Fresquez said. "Now would you relate as to the occurrence of events"—Fresquez was fond of convoluted phrases such as "would you relate" and "at this point in time"—"during the period of time that your parents were gone?"

"I just came out of my room and, you know, I asked him what happened—"

"This is your brother Richard?" Greene asked.

"This is my brother Richard and me talking, and he—and another thing is that Mom, she made a lot of accusations. She said a lot of things to my father that my brother never even said. And I thought that was particularly cruel. . . . I mean, she saw my brother getting the stuffing beat out of him, and she didn't say anything, she just made matters worse and worse by inventing more shit, so he could get into more and more trouble. I thought that was really, really ugly, and very vindictive of her.''

Greene asked her if she was mad at her father.

"Yes," she said quickly, "to me he doesn't seem to be like a real person. . . . I've never seen him draw anything or write anything or be kind to other people or give anybody a hug, show any emotion. I've never seen him really laugh, you know, or really cry or anything. To me those are all the things that make an individual human. It's like I've been living with an automaton, literally. Anyway, I'm getting so off track here . . .''

She said that Richard told her, "I can't stand this anymore." He asked her if she wanted to get out of the house, "and I said okay, because I was frightened, I didn't know what was going to go on." Then he asked her if she would help him, and she said, "Yeah, I'm going to help you. I'm not going to leave you alone."

"How do you interpret that?" Greene asked. "Help him do what?"

"Help him do what—oh, it's hard. Just staying, staying with him. Being a backup, you know, with Murphy's Law—whatever can go wrong will go wrong—just for insurance.''

She told them Richard brought out the guns, and she selected the rifle that "kicks the least." Fresquez asked her if she was "fully aware" of her brother's intentions at that point.

"I knew what his intentions were," she said. "But I thought it would just be a scare tactic. Or he would chicken out or something. I had no idea that he would actually do it. I don't think he did. Because after it happened, he came in, and that's what he said. He goes, 'My God, I can't believe I did it, but I did'—and something to the effect of, 'Let's get out of here.' I asked about Mom, and he said that she was okay. You know, even though she was an awful pain in the ass and an awful bitch sometimes, there is no way in the world that my brother or me ever wanted to hurt her, ever.''

Fresquez asked her what her intentions were.

"I'm not a violent person," she said. "The only time I would ever strike anybody or do anything like that [would be] either in self-defense or to defend somebody else. My father, in the past, extensively carried a firearm with him almost wherever he went—like he would have something in the glove compartment of his car. That was my concern, because my father has a very, very short temper, he's very irrational. He would get hysterical and beat up on all three of us—my mother, my brother, and me—just over the teeniest things, because he just had a bad day at work. I thought, oh my God, what if he's armed? What if he pulls it out on my brother, what if he shoots him? What if he goes after me? At that point, definitely, yes, I would have shot him. But only as a last resort.''

"You said that Richard stated something to the effect that 'I have to do this,' " Greene said. " 'I can't take this.' Did he ever elaborate on what that meant?''

"No. But I know him well enough to know what he means.''

"What did you think that he meant?''

"I interpret it as, well, he's going to do something,'' she said. "He's going to be active, he's actually going to do something. I didn't think that he would just, you know, blow my father away, but simply that this was something that was bothering him intensely. Like, I remember conversations, you know, he'd just bring back all these really bad memories of things that I'd blocked out or just chose not to remember, for whatever reasons. My brother always felt really, really bad and guilty because my father used to beat up on me. And he used to get sexual with me, too. And I couldn't defend myself, and he was younger than me, he couldn't defend me, you know. And it got to the point that he just couldn't take it anymore.''

Her latest digression didn't give them a moment's pause. They weren't particularly interested in the bad things she chose not to remember or whether her father "used to get sexual" with her, whatever she meant by that. They wanted to know what else her brother had said last night and if he seemed angry.

"I think I was more angry than he was,'' she said.

Twice they asked her about the word "execution," which had come up in the earlier interview. Was that her "assessment" of what Richard was going to do? She said it was, and she added that Richard didn't use that word.

She said it was Richard's idea to subject their father to "night blindness" by turning on all the lights in the house; if he rushed into the house from outdoors, he wouldn't be able to see until his eyes adjusted to the light. However, she said it was her idea not to turn on certain lights outside the house, in order to provide a way of escape. It was her suggestion, too, she said, to put the dogs and cats in the basement so they would be out of the line of fire. And it was her copy of *The Portable Jung* that the deputies had found outside the window; she had picked up the book with her coat and dropped it on the way out.

Fresquez asked her where she was when she heard the shots.

"I was in the family room, right in front of the fireplace and the couch. Just looking at the clock. And then all of a sudden I heard bang, bang, bang, bang, in quick succession. And I thought, oh my God, the weapon isn't in my hand . . . I think I leaned it against the fireplace. I thought, oh my God, should I pick it up, or what am I going to do?"

"How did you leave the house?" Fresquez asked.

"My brother went into the master bedroom. He opened up the window and removed the screen, and I just turned off the stereo and I grabbed my coat, put it on really fast and went through. We heard my mother shriek about four times, and we didn't know where she was."

"Would you at this time tell me why it was," Fresquez said, "that you did not want to be picked up?"

"I didn't want to be there at that time to say my brother did it. I didn't want to say, 'My brother did it, I didn't do anything, I'm innocent,' because that would be betraying him. I felt very strongly about that."

"Did you relate to anyone what had happened?"

"No, I just wandered around."

"Did you meet anybody that you knew?" Greene asked.

"No," she said. "You know, cars, they just zipped by me."

Greene decided to play his trump card.

"You didn't talk with Chris Lawrence at all?"

Deborah's face tightened, then froze. He had startled her, but she was trying hard not to show it. "I did," she said.

"How about Ken?" Greene was rolling now.

"And Ken."

"And who else?"

"That's it," she said.

Greene noted aloud that it was 9:34 in the morning. They had been at it for two hours. Fresquez asked her why she didn't try to contact her mother.

"I didn't want to confront her. Whenever she got angry with my brother and me, she was just screaming and yelling. Whenever he wasn't around, you know, she was always [saying], 'Oh, he's such a bastard; oh, he's terrible.' I just hated that, because my brother isn't any of that, you know. My brother is not a deviant, he is not a monstrosity. He got out of control.''

"Did you feel like you were in control?" Greene asked.

"Physically, yes. Mentally, no. Emotionally, yes. Although I got scared. . . . I really couldn't prepare for anything because I didn't know how it was going to come out.''

"Would it be fair," Greene asked, "to say that you and your brother agreed, then, this had to be done?''

"No. We agreed that *something* had to be done. . . . I just felt like, well, I'm going to get away from here, I'm never going to see my father's face again, I'll never contact him. He's going to be one lonely person. And he's just missed out on a very enriching relationship . . . I don't dwell on, you know, bad things that have happened to me. As I see it, nobody in the world will ever be able to hurt me as much as my father has—I mean psychologically, physically, in virtually every way. He's always taught my brother and me that the world was out to get us. That's not true. That's something I've concluded by myself.''

They pushed on, the questions circling in hard grooves: what did she know about the arranging of the lights, the guns, her brother's intentions. Greene asked her why she didn't just leave.

"The reason I ask that, Deborah," he added, "is because I guess I don't understand why you would feel guilty, leaving him there to face whatever it was that you—''

"Danger," she said.

"Okay," Greene said.

"I've always been protective of my brother, especially recently. I remember, there were these kids—we were really little, going to grammar school—they used to tease my brother. They would beat him up. I'd be there flinging them off because I was bigger than they were, you know?''

"Sounds like my sister," Greene said.

"That's great, that's great, you know," Deborah said, a warm note rising in her voice.

"The stories I could tell you about my sister," Greene said.

The questioning continued in a friendly vein for several more minutes, but Deborah's responses were getting shorter. In a final burst of energy, she expressed her concern that the officers might think her brother was "playing soldier boy": "He doesn't freak out. He wasn't brainwashed by ROTC. I think ROTC's been very good for him. He's not an authoritative person, he's a leader and he's a teacher. Richard's a very vulnerable person. He's very sensitive, very caring."

Finally Greene declared that he thought they'd covered everything. Did Deborah have anything else to add?

"Sure," she said. "Like, Chris Lawrence—I don't know, maybe that wasn't very bright, lying about it. But I just felt badly about involving anybody else."

"I understand that," Greene said. "It's one of my ways to do a check and a balance, okay?"

"Okay."

"I've got to inform you you failed, okay?" In a softer tone, he went on, "But you cleaned right up on it, so we'll call it even. I can understand that you don't want to get Chris involved. The unfortunate fact is that Chris is involved, and we're going to have to talk with him."

"Okay."

"But we're nice guys," Greene added. "So, you know, he'll love us to death when we're through with him. You're sure you have nothing further you want to add to this?"

"I don't know," she said. "It's just, I can't believe that this is real, you know."

They took the tape recorder and left her alone for a few minutes in the patrol room. She sat with her hands in her lap and a sinking feeling in the pit of her stomach that she had failed more than one of Detective Greene's "checks and balances." She wondered what the detectives thought of her; Greene had winced, she noticed, when she called her mother a bitch. She hoped they would let her see Richard now.

A familiar notebook cover on the lieutenant's desk caught her eye. She leaned forward for a closer look. That was her datebook . . . and Richard's tapes . . . and—Jesus! her journals! They had her journals! How could they just take all this stuff? The thought of the detectives leafing through her journals, pawing the most private, intimate secrets of her life, reading aloud some choice passages to the rest of the cops . . . it was a violation, an atrocity, like rape.

Detectives Greene and Fresquez reappeared with a uniformed officer. In a flat, official voice, Greene informed her that she was under arrest. She was being charged with aiding and abetting first-degree murder and with being an accessory before the fact of

first-degree murder. After she was booked into the county jail, he
explained, she would be allowed to make one phone call.

"Don't worry about the consequences just now," Greene said.
"Just follow this man and do what he tells you."

The official complaint, signed by Laramie County Attorney
Tom Carroll and filed the next day, charged Richard Jahnke
with first-degree murder and Deborah Jahnke with aiding and
abetting first-degree murder. Both were also charged with conspiracy to commit first-degree murder. The complaint alleged,
not quite accurately, that "Richard J. Jahnke . . . stated to
Cheyenne Police Department Sergeant Null and Officer C. Hidalgo
that, 'I shot my father for revenge.' "

As for Deborah Jahnke, "she and her brother decided to
'execute' Richard C. Jahnke. In furtherance of this agreement,
they placed several loaded firearms throughout the house, each
selected a weapon they would use, and the family dogs were
placed in the basement. . . . Deborah Jahnke positioned herself
in the living room with a .30 caliber carbine. . . . After Richard
J. Jahnke executed his father as he approached the garage, both
fled the house through a window in the master bedroom."

At the time, Wyoming was one of thirteen states whose courts
operated under concurrent jurisdiction. Wyoming juveniles accused
of felonies could be charged in either juvenile or adult court,
based solely on the "discretion" of the local prosecutor. It
was Tom Carroll's policy, when dealing with juveniles accused
of homicides, to file charges in adult criminal court. That was his
rule, hard and fast. Although he'd never had what he called the
"grievous problem" of charging a twelve- or thirteen-year-old
offender in that manner, Carroll had filed adult charges against
defendants as young as fifteen. The "execution" of Richard
Chester Jahnke was no exception; the charges against sixteen-
year-old Richard and seventeen-year-old Deborah Jahnke were
filed in the First District Court of Cheyenne.

Carroll announced that he would not seek the death penalty. In
Wyoming, the only other penalty for committing first-degree
murder is life imprisonment in an adult penitentiary.

PART TWO

THE PROGRAM

You have to keep a firm hand on boys these days, Ward. My Clarence answered back to me the other day, and I smacked him right in the mouth. None of that psychology for me.

—FRED RUTHERFORD
to Ward Cleaver in the
television series
Leave It to Beaver

7

"**W**hen did it start?"

People wanted to know. All sorts of people: reporters, lawyers, doctors, neighbors, police, the rest of Cheyenne. They asked the children, but the children didn't know.

"How long has this been going on?" they asked.

"As far back as we can remember," the children said.

So they asked the mother.

"Mrs. Jahnke, when did it start?"

Maria learned to dread that question. It seemed simple enough, but it led to so many others. Do you remember the first time your husband beat you? The first time he beat the children? At what precise moment in the history of your marriage did your husband turn into a baby-thumping maniac? What was it like? What did you do about it? You mean this went on for *years?* Why didn't you leave him the first time he raised his hand to you?

That last question really got to her. *Why didn't you leave? What's wrong with you, woman?* Yes, it was all so terribly clear now: she should have thrown away her marriage at the first sign of trouble. She should have divorced Richard, bundled up the babies, hitchhiked back to Puerto Rico and collapsed penniless on her mother's doorstep. She should have learned Chinese or whatever it is they speak in Tibet and gone to the Himalayas. People didn't understand. They didn't know anything about her fear, her shame. Her hopes.

"When did it start?"

They thought there was a point, a line somewhere; you crossed over it and you were damned. One day you opened a door with a big banner above it: WELCOME TO HELL. You read it, and then you walked right in.

"When did it start?"

She'd like to know, too. Did it start the day she was born? Maybe she carried the seed of tragedy within her all those years, marked for suffering the way other people are marked for good fortune. Maybe the fatal moment came that night on the bus, when the American asked if she spoke English and she said yes.

Maybe the moment came and went when she failed to heed the "warning signs" that surfaced over the next few months: Richard's impulsiveness, his jealousy, his need to control her—the telltale spoor of an abusive mate, so apparent to all the experts in their perfect hindsight. Maybe the point of no return was the day of her wedding.

"When did it start?"

At times she was tempted to give a simple answer. She longed for the reassurance of one spare, tidy reply, an answer that would stave off all the other simpleminded questions about her actions or inaction; one that would absolve everyone of blame and give the entire ordeal the purity of a natural disaster: "One day my husband was hit on the head by a large hailstone, and he was never the same again."

She knew it wasn't that easy. Yet she felt compelled to make a distinction between the man she married and the man who hurt her—Dr. Jekyll and Mr. Hyde, she called them. Early in her marriage Dr. Jekyll went away, she explained, and when he came back he was Mr. Hyde. But sometimes he was Dr. Jekyll again; that's what made it so confusing. Maybe Mr. Hyde had been there all along, too.

"When did it start?"

Korea, she said. It started when her husband came back from Korea.

In November of 1966 Richard Chester Jahnke began a thirteen-month tour of duty in Uijongbu, South Korea, fifteen miles north of Seoul and thirty miles from the 1953 Demarcation Line. The exact nature of his assignment is unclear, but it involved a security clearance—possibly so he could prepare financial records for army intelligence operations in the Far East. Before he left, he saw that his wife and children were settled comfortably in the basement of his parents' house in Chicago. At the time his son was less than six months old.

Maria never knew why her husband wound up in Korea. He talked about the assignment as if he had little choice. It was a desk job, "better than going to Vietnam," he noted. She suspected, though, that he may have volunteered for an overseas post. In the last few weeks of their stay in California, he had become increasingly restless and short-tempered. He screamed at Deborah and told his wife he was fed up with the noise and diapers and late-night alarms. Maria put aside any notion of having a third child.

He wrote often. The letters have been lost, but Maria remembers the first ones as charged with excitement and curiosity about his surroundings. He was reading up on the exotic culture and bloody history of the Hermit Kingdom, making friends in his unit, and working hard. But he dearly missed his wife—his Mousy, his Ziggy, he called her—and the children.

The letters were a great consolation to Maria. She was terribly lonely in Chicago. She had met Richard's parents for the first time a few months earlier, when Dick and Theresa Jahnke came to California to see their new grandson; Maria had found them polite but reserved. Now she was living in their basement with two babies in diapers, while the senior Jahnkes' own children—Robert and Donna, her husband's younger brother and sister—still lived upstairs. The Chicago winter wore Maria down, and Richie and Deborah were often sick; they traded childhood sniffles and viruses with their aunt and uncle the way other kids swapped marbles. Theresa wouldn't accept a penny in rent, and everyone seemed nice enough, but Maria couldn't escape the feeling that she was simply a tolerated presence, stranded thousands of miles from where she belonged. No one complained, but she would have felt better if they had. She sensed in her hosts' long silences some Teutonic form of disapproval. After six months she couldn't stand it any longer. She took the children to stay with her mother.

In Puerto Rico the babies got fat and healthy. For Maria, living with her mother was as difficult as ever, but Virginia adored the children. Maria paraded the pair through Santurce in a double-decker baby carriage. It was awkward running into old friends; they all had husbands at home.

Each letter she received increased her anxiety. Korea was full of crooks, her husband reported—crooks and ass-kissers. An honest man didn't stand a chance. He was sick to death of all of them. His only escape was to slip off somewhere and sleep. He slept whenever he could, more than he ever had before. Maria didn't like the sound of that.

He lived in a Quonset hut that was so cold in the winter he had to stuff paper in his boots. In the summer the humidity knocked him flat and a strange fungus erupted in his clothes—what clothes he had left, that is; the houseboy took what he pleased. The natives seemed to think that poverty justified anything, from petty theft to murder. You could get your throat cut in the sinkhole bars, if you didn't go crazy first from hearing "Purple Haze," the goddam Korean national anthem; the local musicians considered Jimi Hendrix to be Number One Joe. After parties on the base the Koreans quietly made off with all the empty beer cans, which they cut in half and flattened to make roofs for their houses. A doctor told him that the army had a problem with people throwing their children in front of oncoming military vehicles in order to collect compensation from the U.S. government.

Such atrocities were easy to condemn, but his repugnance was a personal one. He sounded genuinely betrayed by Korea. It had promised him something—adventure, perhaps, the mysteries of the Orient—and delivered tedium and ugliness. Years later, in a tone of outrage and wonder, he urged his son to imagine what it was like to encounter a Korean beauty on the street, a real looker: almond eyes, high cheekbones, that delicate feline way of walking Oriental girls have. You admire her. You draw nearer. She pulls up her skirt and pisses on the street in front of you. Savages, son, the people are savages.

He told Maria he tried to lose himself in his work, but the people he worked with were star-studded assholes. He had access to documents marked SECRET, and he knew more about what was going on than his superiors, who were a bunch of lazy, ignorant, corrupt brown-nosers, but what was the use. The only good thing to come out of the gruesome experience was a promotion to staff sergeant, and he deserved that long ago.

Sergeant Jahnke finished his tour two weeks before Christmas of 1967 and summoned Maria and the children back to Chicago. They wouldn't be there long, he assured his wife; he already had quarters for them at Fort Benjamin Harrison outside Indianapolis.

He met their flight at O'Hare International Airport. He had lost weight. He seemed distant, too; perhaps that was inevitable after a year's separation, Maria thought. They talked for hours during the drive from Chicago to Indianapolis, trying to catch up on everything at once, but at day's end Maria didn't feel any closer to him.

They moved into a two-story brick house on base. Both chil-

dren were walking now and favored the tumble-and-yell approach
to locomotion. Their father put gates at both ends of the stairs.
Richie and Deborah fell down elsewhere.

For the first few weeks Sergeant Jahnke was too busy to pay
them any attention. Then he found some time for child-rearing
among his other duties and decided to do something about the
noise. The noise bothered him, the crying most of all. He shook
the offender vigorously and explained the necessity of quiet. This
resulted in more howls, which resulted in a slap or a spanking
and an unambiguous but unheeded order to shut the fuck up.

Maria told him that the children were too young to be treated
that way. He ignored her. He knew they weren't too young, she
just treated them as if they were too young; that was the whole
problem. They were getting spoiled, especially his son. After his
second birthday, Richie graduated from spankings to whacks on
the back of the head. Maria attempted to intervene again, and it
occurred to Sergeant Jahnke that his training wasn't working
because she kept getting in the way; the kids knew that if they
howled long enough, Mommy would tell him to lay off. Finally
he'd had enough. The next time she started to say something
about his methods, he slapped her jaw shut for her.

She blinked back the tears. She was too angry to feel the pain;
that would come in a moment, along with the fear pinching at her
spine. But first came the anger, a raging disbelief: *How dare he!*
She said she was going to call the MPs.

"Go ahead," he said, his face turning crimson. "You do that,
and I'll tell them what a rotten mother you are. You're a fat,
stupid little spic, and nobody gives a shit what you think."

He slapped her again, but the words hurt worse. She felt like a
child in braces again, crippled and exposed. It wasn't just the
words *"fat spic"* (although that would become one of his favorite names for her). It was the other business: *"nobody gives a
shit what you think."* Of course the MPs would believe him, not
her. Worse than that, he might even be right. Maybe she was a
rotten mother. It was the worst thing in the world you could be.
She knew all about that, her own rotten mother had always told
her she was good for nothing. And now the man she married was
telling her the same thing.

She didn't want to find out if they were right. The anger she
felt was swallowed whole, lost in the deepening fear. *So this is*

the way it is going to be. You must be very careful from now on,
you have so much to learn, don't you, señora?

Sergeant Jahnke came back from Korea with a shining letter of
recommendation from an infantry colonel, who singled out his
"unusual personal sense of direction and acceptance of responsibility." The letter made clear its bearer's desire to skip the
folderol of Officers Candidate School and seek a direct commission.

He worked hard in Indiana. He taught classes in finance at Fort
Harrison's Army Finance School while pulling administrative
duties in the accounting department and taking a variety of
classes himself—everything from "Land Mine Warfare" to "Bud-
geting for Executives." He wanted to give the army no choice
but to promote him.

In March of 1968 he complained to a base physician of nosebleeds, dizziness, severe headaches, and weight loss over the
past several weeks. The doctor believed the symptoms to be
stress-related. He prescribed Librium (an anti-anxiety sedative)
and a powerful muscle relaxant for the headaches. The headaches
went away, but the nosebleeds persisted. They flowered during
the worst of Sergeant Jahnke's domestic rages and sometimes for
no reason at all. Eventually he was diagnosed as having high
blood pressure.

His hard work won him "the coveted Finance School instructor's badge" and a certificate of achievement that cited his "great
stamina" and "long hours of overtime . . . an example truly
worthy of emulation by his contemporaries." The promotion
eluded him.

But at least he ruled his own house.

The children learned to be quiet when Daddy came home.
Daddy was so tired. Daddy wanted to eat his meals in peace.
And he wanted his children to eat properly. If Richie didn't eat
all the food on his plate, then Daddy would give him more. If
Richie didn't eat all his food in the right manner—taking bites
from each serving in turn, instead of eating all of one item before
starting another—then Daddy would hit him. The children would
sit up straight, chew with their mouths closed, and finish every
goddam bit of food put in front of them, or they would be sorry.
Sometimes the food ended up in unusual places—the spaghetti
sauce splashed all over Maria's new olive-green drapes, the
chocolate cake crumpled in the trash, the Thanksgiving turkey

skidding across the floor like a warped, greasy bowling ball—
because the children hadn't learned. But Maria was learning.

She learned to be quick with a camera. Those special moments
when the children looked the way you wanted them to for a
family album came along too rarely. If they were smiling and
having a good time, chances were it wouldn't last long.

She learned that, as a rule, small children cannot eat soup
without slurping or dragging the spoons along the bottom of the
bowl. But if you gave them big plastic spoons, the kind they use
in Japanese restaurants, the noise was kept to a tolerable level—
tolerable, that is, to Daddy.

She learned that after a bad day her children could still go out
and play, provided they wore the right clothes. Long sleeves
were essential for bruised arms; so were turtlenecks for pinched
necks. People were less likely to notice skinned knees and the
like; just about the only thing you couldn't disguise was the red
tracing of a palm print on a well-slapped face. After her own
bouts—which escalated from slaps to punches, chokings, pulled
hair, and a growing familiarity with the hard corners of most of
the furniture in the house—she preferred to stay indoors. No one
missed her because almost no one knew her; as in California, she
had only one regular acquaintance, a neighboring housewife.

She learned that hitting back made Daddy hit harder.

She learned that Daddy could be as capricious as a Greek god.
Some of the things the children did that she thought deserved a
spanking—such as the clogging of the toilet with towels by
Deborah Jahnke, aided and abetted by Richie, which flooded the
bathroom and ruined the kitchen ceiling—were greeted with great
amusement. But Richie's habit of toddling around with his mouth
open infuriated his father. Richie had thick lips, nigger lips,
nothing he could do about that, he got them from his fat spic
mama, but the least he could do was keep his fucking mouth
closed, he looked like a goddam nigger-lipped moron, didn't he?

"You're going to ruin their minds, talking like that," Maria
told him.

He told the bitch-swine-asshole to mind her own fucking business. She tried, but there was so much to learn.

She learned it was possible to do things right. For a while,
perhaps for a week or two, you could do things right and life was
good, Dr. Jekyll was back in town. He brought her pearls and
jade earrings, stuffed animals, and flowers—so many flowers!—to

atone for their past misunderstandings. He complimented her on her cooking and took her out for dessert. He played Mr. Spider with the children, walking to the bathroom with his arms under Deborah's arms and hers under Richie's, and they all washed each other's hands. He stretched out on the floor and pretended to be asleep so the kids could cover him with blankets and toy jewelry; Deborah, who was fond of dressing up in funny clothes, particularly loved this game. But Maria never knew how long the calm would last.

Most of all, she learned she must not assume anything. The rules were subject to change without notice. She could get it right, but only for a while. Then it changed. Whatever she learned might have to be unlearned. And she was always wrong.

Fourteen months in Indiana were followed by two years in Frankfurt, West Germany, where Sergeant Jahnke served as chief accountant for the European headquarters of the U.S. Army Security Agency. The job required a thorough background check, but the sergeant's record was virtually spotless. He scored in the excellent-to-outstanding range on the standard evaluations. His security clearance was upgraded from SECRET to TOP SECRET, allowing him access to cryptographic materials dealing with the budget and management of USASA operations in Europe.

This time he took his family with him. Maria was tired of their nomadic existence, but she didn't want to be left behind again. Besides, Germany wasn't Korea, it was the land of Richard's ancestors. The German people were his kind of people, and German food was his favorite. He started to put on weight. By the time he left Frankfurt his five-eight frame would be carrying more than two hundred pounds.

Maria quickly discovered that the shopkeepers of Frankfurt had something against Americans—something against a bronze-skinned American housewife looking for good cuts of meat for her serviceman, anyway. They were rude, sometimes openly hostile, and they charged a fortune. People in the countryside were nicer, but she rarely got out of town.

Most of the time she stayed at home, "home" being temporary quarters in an inexpensive hotel in Frankfurt, and later, an apartment on the Platen Strasse. She met other army wives at the playground beside the apartment house, but in most cases she barely got to know them before they smiled the brave smile of GI

Josephine and shipped out for another station, same duties. For reliable companions Richie and Deborah had only each other, but they didn't seem to mind. They filled each other's empty places, the way a brother and sister can for a time. Deborah (never Debbie, she was always trying so hard to be grown-up) was restless, playful, crackling with words and schemes and wild stories. Richie was small for his age, unnervingly silent, and wide-eyed with wonder at every unfamiliar animal or machine. He was the captive audience Deborah demanded, and she provided the sort of spectacle with running commentary he required.

The children were old enough now, at four and five years old, to understand that when Daddy came home, they were supposed to go to their rooms. But Daddy's program for better children had expanded. Each new responsibility they assumed, from dressing and washing themselves to caring for their toys, came with a new set of instructions. Meals were still a sore point—when she could, Maria fed them before Daddy came home—and led to another problem: their teeth weren't white enough to pass inspection. Sometimes Daddy screamed at them and sent them back to the bathroom for another scrub. Sometimes he brushed their teeth for them, adding a vigorous, painful gum massage for good measure.

The worst times tended to be holidays, especially Easter, Thanksgiving, and Christmas. Each one had the logic of a recurrent nightmare. For days the children squirmed with excitement and anticipation; Maria spent hours baking, basting, and braising, filling the house with the odors of fresh bread and roasted meat, smells as sacred as the heady cloud of incense in church. Richard gave the feast the hearty blessing of a king at his board; then the scene dissolved into a few minutes of anxious chewing, followed by a roaring disaster. The children weren't eating enough to suit him, the slabs of meat and mounds of potatoes he'd heaped upon their plates were going to waste, or they were eating too fast, what pigs you're raising, Maria, listen to them. . . .

At Christmas he spent freely on gifts for the children, complaining all the while that it was more than they deserved and certainly more than he ever had as a child. The gifts were opened Christmas morning. Few lasted until the end of the day. He took away the toys and dolls or smashed them on the spot. They just didn't appreciate them enough, he said. It was difficult to tell what he expected; a thank-you was never enough. If he wasn't infuriated by their initial reaction, then wait a bit. He would go back to bed after the presents were opened, only to be disturbed by the little bastards playing with their toys. The way to get some rest was to confiscate the noisemaker, terminate it with extreme prejudice. You like this? You can't have it. You're going to cry now? Okay, you fucking crybaby, I'll really give you something to cry about.

He gave Richie an arsenal of toy guns and legions of toy soldiers, but he almost never played with him. One year he seized a wooden musket from Richie and split it in two over his knee, then tossed the pieces back to his astonished son. Richie never learned why his new gun had to be destroyed, but it may have had something to do with the way he was holding it or where he was pointing it. The first time he ever trained one of his cap pistols on Dad, the enraged target sent him flying across the room.

"Don't you *ever* do that again," he said.

The sergeant's own gun collection began with a .22 plinking rifle purchased in Monterey. In Frankfurt he made a few modest purchases. Guns frightened Maria, yet she saw in his hobby an opening of sorts. While doing laundry in the basement of their apartment house she had met two other wives whose husbands had the gun bug. She persuaded Richard to put aside his loathing of all social engagements for one night, long enough to play cards and talk guns with one of the couples. He surprised himself by having a good time. Soon they were taking turns hosting Monopoly and pinochle games twice a week. It wasn't much, but it was a few hours a week away from their lonely bedlam, the first semblance of a social life since their wedding. Those precious evenings with Gary and Martha and Jim and Judy loomed large in Maria's memories of Germany.

The card games ended with Sergeant Jahnke's military service in April of 1971. Although he had served the full six years of his second term, certain obligations of his work in Germany apparently weren't met. He signed a statement acknowledging that "as a result of my failure to fulfill my overseas commitment I will be barred from reenlistment in the United States Army."

No doubt he signed with pleasure. For months he'd been telling Maria that he could do much better on the outside, the hell with the whole fucking army. He wasn't blind, however, to the generous consideration Uncle Sam gave to veterans seeking employment elsewhere in the government. In the nine years since he'd first confided in her, his plans for a career in finance had crystallized. He was going to join the Internal Revenue Service and use his training in the byzantine world of military accounting to catch tax cheats. It wasn't a job for a man who wanted to be loved, but he was more interested in respect. An IRS investigator carried a gun, a Treasury Department badge, and the dread power of the federal tax laws wherever he went. Pushers, grafters, mobsters, and corporate cheats wet their pants when they saw one coming. And Special Agent Jahnke would give them reason to be afraid.

Once again the family moved into the basement of Dick and Theresa Jahnke's house in Chicago. Richard landed a job immediately with an insurance company—as good a place as any to wait out his application to the IRS. He and Maria went house-hunting at night. After a few weeks they found a two-bedroom house for rent in Riverdale, a quiet community just south of the city proper.

Turning civilian didn't alter the basic dynamics of family life. A distant relative who visited the apartment in Riverdale after they had lived there several weeks was surprised to hear from Maria that he was their "first company." Surely he didn't hear right, the visitor replied; didn't Dick and Theresa visit often? Maria insisted that he was the first.

Another visitor, one of her husband's aunts, thought Maria looked troubled and asked her what was the matter. Maria broke into tears and took the woman to her bedroom. The wooden headboard of the bed was cracked and lopsided. Richard had pulled her hair, Maria said, and thrown her into the headboard. She had grabbed a crucifix from the wall and thrown it at him but missed. She could have killed him, she said, she was so angry; now she didn't know what to do. Neither did her visitor.

She was usually more resourceful than that, offering to others and herself hopeful theories about her husband's "temper." It was all this moving around, she said; the army soured him, and selling insurance was even worse; as soon as he got the job he wanted, things would get better. He worked so hard, he didn't have any time to get to know the children; how was he supposed to understand what lovely children they really were, what a good wife and mother she was, when he was gone half the time? As soon as his plans fell into place they could start being a real family.

In early 1972 Richard Chester Jahnke swore an oath to support and defend the Constitution of the United States "against all enemies, foreign and domestic," and flew to Washington, D.C., for several weeks of training as a criminal investigator for the Internal Revenue Service. He requested and received assignment to the Chicago office, General Enforcement Branch. The starting salary was far from handsome, scarcely more than nine thousand dollars a year, but he approached the job with the same expansive faith in his ability to rise through the ranks that Maria had seen in the young private ten years earlier.

The government paid for his family to stay with him in Washington for a month that summer while he took more training courses. For Maria the trip became an orgy of sightseeing in the swampish heat of the capital: snapshots of the kids in front of the dazzling white stone of famous monuments, long hours in the Smithsonian, and a special trip to the National Zoo to see the pandas that had just arrived from China. The trip was one of the best times of all—excluding one dark afternoon, when Dad came home to the apartment in Arlington, Virginia, and discovered that the inflatable boat he had bought six-year-old Richie to use in the apartment house swimming pool had been ruined.

"Where's that little bastard?" he asked, slamming the door behind him.

Maria pushed Richie into the closet and stood in front of the door. Her husband struck at her with his fists, yanked the boy from his hiding place, and whipped him with his belt. It was all over within minutes. Maria tried to put the incident out of her mind just as quickly. What's done is done, she told herself, why ruin a vacation over one bad day. But her son never forgot it: couldn't, wouldn't, must not forget the howling pain of the strap descending; and worse, the dull, pathetic gasps of his mother being hit while he stood in mute terror and shame in the dark closet, letting her take the blows that were meant for him—and which he would get anyway. Dad always finished what he started.

At the end of the summer Special Agent Jahnke received word that the IRS had completed its routine inquiries regarding his "good character and high personal integrity." He had been "accepted as meeting the Security and character requirements of

Executive Order 10450 and Treasury Department Order #82, revised." His virtue was now certified.

The family returned to the house in Riverdale. Within months they were on the move again. That winter a slot opened up in the Phoenix office, and Special Agent Jahnke jumped at it. The job didn't pay any better, but it was bound to be an improvement over Chicago. He outlined the advantages to his wife: lower cost of living, better opportunities for advancement, desert nearby for hikes and hunting and the outdoor life, sunshine year-round—just like home, you'd like that, wouldn't you, Mousy? Besides, they had just learned that Richie had asthma; that's probably why the little bastard walked around with his mouth open all the time. The desert air would do him good.

They had lived in a dozen different apartments and rented houses in the past nine years, never in one place for more than a year or so. Dad promised this would be their last move, a chance to develop roots, join the community, and raise a family. He flew to Arizona ahead of the rest of them, looked at a model of a one-story, three-bedroom frame house that was being cloned for a new subdivision in Scottsdale, and picked out a site on the edge of town. He ordered a lush green lawn (not one of those rock-garden-and-desert-landscaping jobs most of the other houses had), a swimming pool, and a modest fruit grove—melons, oranges, peaches, grapefruit, a lemon tree.

During the three months the house was under construction, the family stayed in an apartment in Tempe. Richard commuted to his office in Phoenix. Maria couldn't wait until their new house was ready and everyone could relax. Toward the end of their vigil Richie did something that stirred his father's wrath, some-thing at least as heinous as the destruction of the inflatable boat. The belt was produced—a long, wide leather monster, indicative of its owner's increasing girth—and Richie, meek as Isaac, was led into the bathroom. This time Maria followed them and attempted to take the belt away from her husband. Within mo-ments she was pinned against the tub, her face scraping the floor tiles, while the strap lashed at her shoulders and spine. The brass buckle hit her on the back of the head.

She screamed and screamed. At least she thought she did; hard to say if her shrieks ever reached his ears. At a time of his choosing, perhaps out of simple weariness, he finished and stomped off to the bedroom for a nap. She picked herself off the floor, gingerly removed her clothes, and slipped into the tub. She moaned as the stinging hot water rushed over her body. The welts rose quickly.

A few weeks later they moved into their brand-new house at 5049 East Poinsettia Drive in Scottsdale, their first real home. He picked her up and carried her over the threshold.

8

In the beginning she had only her feelings to guide her. The words to describe the feelings came later. Sometimes the words came from watching television and movies or from listening to the way other people talked. But Deborah found most of the words for what she was feeling in books.

One of her earliest memories of her father dates back to the family's stay in Germany. It is 1969; she is four years old. She has just received an ornate wooden dollhouse for Christmas. The dollhouse has many rooms, but her dolls are too big to live there. So a bunch of make-believe people live in the house—the castle, she calls it. Sometimes she lives there, too. So do Richie and Mommy. It is a very safe place.

One day it is no longer safe. Perhaps she isn't playing quietly enough. Perhaps the people in the castle talk too much. Whatever the reason, Daddy bursts into her room. He rips her toy telephone off the wall and hurls it onto the floor. The plastic splinters fly like shrapnel.

"Shut up!" Daddy yells.

She starts to cry. This is exactly what Daddy told her not to do. He stomps over to the castle. He looks at her. She cries louder; she knows she mustn't, but she can't help it. He puts his foot through the roof. Only one wing is left standing; the walls shiver perilously over her friends in the last rooms. She kneels over the castle and reaches out to prop up the ceiling, to evacuate the survivors. Daddy's foot crashes down again and flattens the place.

At the time Deborah was too shocked to do anything but cry. The words came later, years later, when she saw an old movie on television about a giant ape who smashed cars and planes as if they were toys. She had learned a new name for Daddy: King Kong. She thought of herself as Fay Wray.

When she was eight years old she read her first grown-up book, *Jane Eyre* by Charlotte Brontë. It took her a month to finish it. She felt an immediate kinship with young Jane and cried at the death of Jane's childhood friend, Helen Burns. Jane's experience in the orphanage seemed as sad as her own life. That was only part of the story, of course, but it was a start. The notion that other people suffered and wrote about it was a great revelation. Deborah began to read as much as she could, trying to match up her own life with the lives of the people in books.

That same year, their first in Arizona, her mother gave her a one-year diary for Christmas. Deborah didn't know what to write in it. She wasn't Charlotte Brontë; she didn't have any great story to tell. Even if she did, she wasn't sure she trusted the tiny lock that was supposed to keep her secrets from others' eyes. "I hope no one will find this diary!" she scrawled on the inside front cover. Then she embarked on a day-by-day rendering of her life. The words, often misspelled, trickled across the page in pencil and crayon. They formed a long, winding trail of the vital matters she supposed she should put down: the weather, what she had for dinner, what programs were on television that day.

In time her writing, like her reading, became a way of making sense of her life. But when she began, she didn't have the words. It was enough to record what happened. The first entry of the new year—January 1, 1974—betrayed a love of hard facts, such-and-such happened at such-and-such a time. She wanted to get it right:

It was a nice day but I got a very bad spanking Oh did it hurt I have been in my room till 4:15 to 7:00. boy when I was in my room I was crying. This morning I got up at almost 11 o'clock. I ate my breakfast and play awhile. my dad got up about 3:00 he was sleeping all that time . . .

Home was half her life. The other half was just as important and deserved a record, too:

[January 3] This morning I had to go to school. When I went on the bus I ask Sally and Anagela if they know the qeision it was Why did everybody hated me? They said I acted big . . .

Today is Wednesday January 30, 1974. It was a nice day to day. Everyone hates me but why? I don't give them a reasen too hate me. I don't like reaseses. Thay are so borring.

Becuase no one plays with me. So at reases time I stay in.
Once in a while Richie plays with me. But Richie has friends
too. I am going to sleep now.

For the next eight years Deborah filled various diaries, journals, and notebooks with reports on the chaos of home, the
hurtfulness of school. These were the twin themes of her life; she
had to make sense of them in order to answer the central question, asked in a thousand ways but never more succinctly than in
her earliest efforts: *Everyone hates me but why?*

She didn't see that the two miseries were related—not at first.
At first she was so unhappy at school that she scarcely thought
about anything else. Home was familiar; even King Kong was
familiar. She had no way to measure the chaos of her home
against that of other homes, no basis for comparison; she
accepted it without question. But school was different.

In Riverdale she had liked going to school. The trouble started
when the Jahnkes moved to Scottsdale and Deborah entered the
third grade at Cherokee Elementary School. She wore ribbons in
her long hair, frilly blouses with long sleeves, plaid skirts, long
dresses with tights, knee socks, and patent-leather shoes. The
kids at Cherokee wore designer jeans and suede tennies and shirts
with alligators on them. They talked about her behind her back.
Before long they were laughing in her face.

At school everyone was starring at me. Because I was dressed
beautifly. And most of the[m] said after starring at me, yuck,
how ugly. And few said without even knowing, you sure must
take a long time dressing. The[y] all are so jeales.

It was her mother who told her that the other children were
jealous. Ignore them, Mom said, they don't know a proper lady
when they see one. Deborah agreed. Most of the kids at school,
she decided, were "dominating and ragged little brats."

She preferred the company of her friends Reinhart and Anna.
They were twins with blond hair and brown eyes, a few years
older than she was. Anna had very white skin, and Reinhart was
full of mischief. No one could see them but her. Sometimes
when she sat down to dinner she would look in their direction
and talk to them in her head. Her parents never noticed, but
Richie knew. He would see her staring at some vacant corner of

the room, and right away he knew Deborah was talking to her invisible friends again.

She read *Wuthering Heights*, a book by Charlotte Brontë's sister Emily, and books by Jane Austen and Charles Dickens. England was such a wonderfully cultured place, not at all like Scottsdale. She loved the way people talked in English movies and television programs. Before long she was talking to Reinhart and Anna that way. Then she tried out her new accent at school. People who didn't know her asked if she was an exchange student. She had never been to England, but the plane that carried the family back from Germany had stopped in Ireland, and she and Dad had walked around Shannon Airport. She told them she was Irish. Tallyho!—that was Irish, wasn't it?

Some people were fooled. They treated her nicely for a change; it was curious how people forgave you for being different if they thought you were from another country. But some of the brats made fun of her worse than ever. "What country are you from today?" they asked. They called her the Actress, the Millionairess from Ireland. They tried to get her to say something in Irish, so they could laugh at her. If she didn't say anything, they pulled her hair.

Today is Thursday, January 30, 1975. It was a very nice day. Oh I feel so good inside. I had not gotten to go to school because I had not yet made a complete recovery from being sick and that is why I stayed home, back at school they would say yay Debra or Deb-bra a a a a a in there way. I have to face them practically every day. They are so mean.

She hated waiting for the school bus in the morning. The other kids at the bus stop said mean things to her. They even made fun of the dumb briefcases she and Richie carried, the ones Mom had bought for them. Richie picked fights with the boys and told the girls to shut up. After a while it seemed like they teased her in order to see her brother fight. Richie was so small; he always took a beating. The teachers became accustomed to seeing him with bruises all over his face.

Deborah knew Richie thought she was strange. But then, she thought he was pretty strange, too. Back in Riverdale they had slept in the same bedroom, and she'd sat up nights listening to him struggling to breathe. His asthma was terrible. He sounded

like a deep-sea diver. More than once she thought he was going
to die. Instead they came to Arizona and got their own rooms and
played together less and less. Dad didn't want Richie playing with
her. Dad said he was a mama's boy and a sissy. At times
Deborah thought so, too; Richie wasn't at all like other boys. But
at least he stuck up for her, even if he was too small to do any
good. Most of the time he was just another piece of the scenery,
a detail to be noted, like the dinner menu:

Today is Thursday August 8, 1974. It was a pretty nice day. I
did not do very much today. I went in our pool and mom and I
cleaned it. Richie did not help because he was so lazy but he
got clobbered. I sure had a lot of fun. I had pizza for dinner . . .

Her beat was local: family and school, school and family,
everyone hates me but why? She wrote more about school than
anything else, but the reports on her family were often illus-
trated. If it was good news she drew a happy face. If it was
bad news she drew an unhappy face. If it was very bad news,
such as the two passages below, she drew multiple crying and
frowning faces:

Today is Saturday, March 29, 1975. It was a fine day exept for
a fight mom and dad had, it was very bad. It started with dad
making comeplants about Richie. I hate that when they fight.

Today is Monday May 5, 1975. It was a rotten day. I'm
such an unhappy person. My mother has had it with me.
And I don't blame her! I know I'm an inconsitarate stupid spoild little brat. I make trouble. No one knows what
I go through not even my mother. She knows only what
goes on at home. But not all that happens at school. I'm
so unhappy!!!!! I'm a terrible brat that shouldent have ever
lived . . .

In her desperate need to make sense of it all, she accepted the
logic of her parents. If things were bad at home, it was because
she and Richie were lazy or spoiled. Or it was because of what
they had to go through at school. One day she and her father
went to the principal's office "and reported the kids that have
been hitting me and doing harm." On the way home Dad told her

the world was full of people out to hurt her. She was inclined to
believe him. Anna and Reinhart were a lot nicer than the brats at
school. They were also more reliable than any of the boys she
fell madly in love with; every one of her crushes soon rejected
her and was secretly denounced as a "pigheaded baboon" or
some other mutant.

In her 1975 diary she declared, "I have a lot of friends," and
listed more than a dozen. By the end of the year every one of the
names had been crossed out.

In the late summer of 1979, a few days before she entered
Chaparral High School as a thirteen-year-old freshman, Deborah
Jahnke wrote a memo to herself listing the "precautions" she
must take to avoid the "cruelty" of other students. She welcomed the opportunity to attend high school, she wrote, but
experience had taught her certain survival skills:

1. Do not attend any social events, such as dances and sports
   competitions.
2. Do not use the lockers.
3. Do not go off school campus under any circumstances.
4. Keep all school materials with me at all times.
5. Take different routes to classes.
6. Avoid using restrooms—except the Nurse's.
7. Do not leave class to buy a snack or for whatever reason.
8. During lunch go directly to the library.
9. In class, if at all possible, sit up front.
10. Have mom or dad drive me to and from school.
11. Do not join any groups (except maybe the Intellectu-
    als providing that they do not force you to do some-
    thing you don't wish to do).
12. Be extraordinarly perceptive!
13. Do not put too much faith in the teachers or other mem-
    bers of the faculty.
14. Do not lend work, or do any special favors.

As the list suggests, the teasing that had dogged her in elementary school had escalated in junior high school to a form of private
terrorism. No matter what she did, she was doomed to be different; even her own body had revolted against her. She had started
menstruating at the age of ten (an event recorded in her diary:

"Today I have the problem that every girl gets sooner or later. Yeuch, yick, fhoay!"). Her physical development soon outraced that of any girl in her class, making her more of a freak than ever.

At times her precocious sexuality pleased her. She felt like the lush heroine of a Gothic novel, perhaps the heroine of *Portrait of Evil,* a romance she began to write when she was twelve.

> I don't consider myself the average everyday twelve year old at the least. I have the physical appearance of an eighteen year old, the mind of an adult and the ambitions of a fame hungry fool . . . I have a terrific future in front of me!

But not being average had its price. Boys pinched her breasts to see if they were real. Girls could be even crueler. For reasons that remained unfathomable to her, they attacked her in restrooms and in gym classes. They taped Kotex to her locker, threw food at her in the lunchroom, and called her a lesbian. A male classmate remembers seeing more than a dozen girls chasing her around the playground during one lunch break in eighth grade. Deborah cried out earnestly for help, but the chase continued for several traumatic minutes before a teacher told the other girls to leave her alone.

Puberty had other terrors, too, far worse than anything her classmates could do to her. She didn't like most of the adults she knew, and the thought of growing up horrified her. What if she grew up ugly, what if no man wanted her? To her diary she confessed her envy of her best friend, who was "talented, pretty, intelligent, and popular":

> I only wish I had a fraction of the beauty she has. my face is covered with pimples, my nose is to[o] big, and no matter what I do I always seem to look terrible . . . Sometimes when I'm near her I feel like a shabby old dog! Maybe I am!

Yet she never despised herself for long. She crossed out the last three words of the passage above and wrote encouraging notes to herself. A year later, not long after her thirteenth birthday, she completely revised her song of herself, drowning out the whine of the shabby dog with a shameless hymn of self-love:

> I glance at the mirror and what do I see. The reflection is of a

young girl with a fair complection, thick chestnut hair and expressive blue-green eyes, well-emphasized with heavy brows. She is five feet, two 1/2 inches tall, 35-21-32, 102 pounds, and in perfect health—no allergies, asthma, or anything of that sort. In a public place she is often stared at by others, or whistled at (which she considers a compliment) and can be considered physically beautiful. She is also very intelligent, talented, charming, and kind. She is known as the "debornaire," or "intellectual" or the "prima donna." She speaks in a smooth, suave fashion, and is said to have somewhat of a British accent (Isn't that impressive?) and is known to use a large vocabulary. And dresses in a manner which always seems to emphasize her splendid physique. This is myself and no other!!!!

Her new attitude about herself wasn't all bravado. In the months between her dog days and the debut of the "prima donna," she had made a crucial discovery—thanks, in part, to her parents. Keenly aware of Deborah's all-too-healthy body and more "protective" than ever, Mom and Dad attempted to restrict her efforts at a social life. The usual adolescent tug-of-war had begun: the more they resisted, the more defiant she grew. But in Deborah's case the rebellion didn't just chafe; it burned, and burned deeply, as she found out they had tricked her all these years. Her popular best friend and others invited her to their homes for dinner, and she began to realize that other families didn't operate the way hers did. Other girls had boyfriends, and parties, and parents who didn't blame them for every little thing. She had Mom and Dad—and Richie, which was just as bad as having three parents, since he ratted on her when she tried to have fun.

She wasn't so terrible, it wasn't her fault, it was them! She was a prisoner, a Gothic heroine, the victim of a conspiracy! It was as if she had just discovered that the sun didn't revolve around the earth but vice versa. The corollary truths surfaced rapidly, and the implications were staggering:

[September 5, 1977] You know it is very odd how few friends I have. Well I just learned one reason why I don't. My brother never leaves me alone with them. He's always there nagging me . . . And another thing, I'm frightened to have my friends over while my father's here . . .

[September 10, 1977] When I get married or if I certainly don't want to end up like my parents. They practically hate each other. They're always arguing and degrading each other constantly! I don't know which is worse than the other. Mom nags and punishes me unjustly, but at least she takes me out places and likes me to be pretty, mature, intelligent and well mannered. My father doesn't nag me as much but he hates it when I look or act grown up. That's his own damn problem.

[December 24, 1977] I'm so damned bored of my "childhood" it ought to be proclaimed a sin. I have a housework fanatic who only complains about her housework and how worthless I am . . . and my "plain average American father" . . . he is also incredibly rude and mean to others as well as to me. and my brother who is probably going to grow up to be a homosexual because of his bizarre behavior! We have no friends—no family and we don't do anything *together*. My father is always locked up in his den, my mother is always too busy cleaning the house and my stupid immature brother is too busy trying to find something that I did wrong so he can tell "Mama" my god! . . . I don't want to be anything like them . . .

[June 8, 1978] My father . . . hates people, absolutely everyone, especially children . . . For no motive at all he will swat me on the ass (with immense strength) and comment on my bad breath. God—I'm not evil. I don't deserve this rubbish . . . Mom and Dad are always searching through my drawers, in my closet, under my bed . . . God I hate them more than anyone else on this earth. They beat me, humiliate me—and I'm not supposed to be upset in the least. I despise them! I've got to get out of this living hell before I lose my sanity . . . how could a thirteen year old girl like myself have such horrible, horrible, horrible luck?

[summer, 1978] I'm the only person fighting for myself, regardless of what anyone says . . . At times I think of swallowing a bottle of allergy pills or slitting my wrists or swallowing insecticide. That would put an end to everything now wouldn't it. But I've decided not to engage in suicide. I've too much ambition—dreams, by all means I must fulfill them.

[summer, 1978] I am continually being punished for absolutely nothing at all . . . For instance, my rotten father just beat the living daylights out of me for just a phone call . . . In a psychology encyclopedia a girl in my place would be on her way to an institution.

[fall, 1978] I wish I could pack up my belongings and get away from this bedlam. But that is impossible. First of all I haven't any money, second I haven't anywhere to go, and third I'm too young, I can't even get a social security card so I can't even get a job. So if I run away—even though the entire police force is searching for me (& not to mention my rotten parents) and if by some miracle I outsmart them, I will end up being a prostitute in Las Vegas. So that means I have to stay here until I am eighteen years old—My God, half a decade from now! How can I survive?

[fall, 1978] I think I would literally sell my soul for someone to love me . . . I haven't any friends—Mother won't permit me to have one, not one . . . "Never trust anybody—don't be intimate with any friend—the only person that will care about you is mother"—that's what she said . . . how horrible . . . Soon after I had cried in the Lady's room (we were going to the movies) because I experienced such a feeling of resentment, insecurity, and lack of hope. And of course Richie agreed with mother—then told her, "One person in my class wanted to tell me all his problems—and you know what I said? I said I didn't want to hear it and walked away." As if he were bragging—Lord God—I would never deny an ear to listen—I do encourage people to tell me their problems—it makes me feel that I'm not the only person alone suffering. I'm so angry at God—why does he punish me so damn much?

[fall, 1978] I really wish I could go off to a Catholic school. I'm not sure that I believe in God though. It seems as if he has abandoned everyone. The evil always live on and damn the innocent.

Chaparral High School turned out to be not as terrible a place as she had feared. Most of her classmates still shunned her, but at least no one assaulted her. A few of the students thought her weirdness was refreshing. They were intrigued by her exaggerated and indefinable accent, her wild accounts of herself, her odd clothes and manners. She was smart, too; assuming, of course, that she actually read those fat paperbacks she hauled out of her pack during lunch breaks, some trash and some classics, everything from Danielle Steel to Fyodor Dostoyevsky, Robin Cook to Henry James. Maybe she wasn't a geek after all. Maybe she was just cooler than anybody else.

Then again, maybe not. You never knew where you stood with her, or who she was. Did her father really work for the CIA? And what was this business about growing up in Ireland and being attacked by the IRA—or was it the CIA?—in Belfast? She said she was going to be an actress or a famous writer, but she wrote these dippy stories about dragons, maidens, knights, and stuff, a real fantasy kick. And those wool trousers she always wore to school—what the hell was wrong with jeans? And the long watch chain hanging from the pocket, wasn't that a bit much?

Even her name was suspect. She said Jahhhnkey (as in "donkey"); her goofy little brother said Jank-ee (rhymes with "Yankee"). How many families do you know who can't even agree on how to pronounce their name? She joined the staff of the school newspaper, the Chaparral *Ashes*, and when the staff posed for their yearbook photo she pulled her coat over her face. That was Deborah, all right—a mystery, a cipher.

No one got too close to her. Old-fashioned peer pressure may have been one reason; it was fashionable to ridicule her behind her back and to groan loudly whenever she got up in class to make one of her impassioned, off-the-wall statements about art and the necessity of suffering. She met a boy in the school drama club and kissed him once. But Richie found out about it and told Mom, and Deborah stopped going to the drama club meetings.

A far more interesting relationship developed between Deborah and Walter Headley, a guidance counselor at Chaparral. Contacted by investigators shortly after the shooting of Richard Chester Jahnke, Headley provided them with a seven-page account of his efforts to fathom one of the strangest students he'd ever encountered.

"Miss Jahnke 'felt me out,' as we say in counseling, during several contacts early in the 1979–80 school year," he wrote. "She was quite flamboyant in her manner and very melodramatic. She finally advised me that she had been testing me to see if I was sincere and if I would help her with her 'problem.'

"The problem turned out to be . . . her relationship with her parents. She was very upset and angry about the fact that her parents, and specifically her father, would not permit her to become involved in what she referred to as the normal things other high school kids do, such as attend school sporting events, school dances, go to movies. . . .

"Deborah painted a picture of the father as being extremely & unreasonably authoritarian, overbearing, and restrictive. . . . her mother was very passive and went along with the father's demands. She spoke of the mother with an attitude of disgust, contempt, and disdain.

"Deborah also indicated resentment at the fact that her brother was allowed to do more than she was just because he was a boy. This resentment was severe. She related that her parents did not want her associating with other children in the area because their behavior and standards were a 'bad moral influence.'

"On several occasions I approached Deborah about my contacting the parents and trying to act as a communicator. She totally rebelled against this and at one point, after my suggesting this, Deborah failed to come back to see me for more than a month (as opposed to 1–3 times a week as a normal rate of contact). . . . Her attitude was clearly FLIGHT as opposed to FIGHT. As a matter of fact, I was concerned . . . that there was potential for [Deborah to become a] run-away. . . .

"Deborah did a great deal of fantasizing and wrote poetry and short stories about her ideas. . . . It was as though she was creating a highly perfect and purely romantic world to compensate for the lack of satisfaction and peer relationships and family life in the real world. In this regard I can only refer to my perceptions and concerns. I am not a trained psychologist or psychiatrist. . . .

"Deborah related to Mrs. M_____ [another teacher] the fact that she was an orphan. Mrs. M_____ came to me very concerned over the girl's misfortune. When I assured Mrs. M_____ that Deborah's parents were very much alive, she was dumbfounded. . . . Deborah had related a very detailed

account of her being an orphan & did so in a most elaborate and
convincing way. As I recall, it was this specific event that
directly resulted in my referral of Deborah to the school psychologist. . . .

"Deborah's attitude continued to be one of seething anger
combined with a sleuth-like plotting of a 'way out' of her situation. On occasions, she made reference to the fact that her
brother was also very upset . . . that he would probably run away
some day. She referred to severe arguments between her brother
and father. . . .

"In perhaps January of 1981, she announced that her father
had been transferred to Wyoming, and she went into quite a
tirade about Phoenix being vulgar enough, let alone moving to
such a 'God Forsaken Hole' with cowboys and animals. She was
thoroughly disgusted over the thought of the move and kept
relating that she couldn't wait for the next two years to pass so
she could get away. She was, of course, referring to graduation. . . . I have never seen her since nor have had any contact
with her."

Headley never saw any bruises on Deborah; nor did she make
any explicit claim to him that her father physically abused her.
But the counselor was concerned enough about her behavior to
ask both male and female gym teachers at Chaparral to discreetly
examine Deborah and her brother while they were taking show-
ers. The gym teachers reported that they couldn't find any evidence that the Jahnkes were being beaten.

In his written statement, Headley conceded that Deborah "had
fabricated certain events to see what kind of reaction she could
get from me"—but, he added, "I was probably the only adult
she really trusted and related to, in spite of the fact that she
'tested' me on occasions."

Yet certain truths eluded her confidant, just as they eluded
everyone else. When the investigators contacted him, Headley
was still under the impression that his former pupil "had spent
some time in Ireland" and had attended private schools there,
which explained her "definite and pronounced Irish brogue." To
the school psychologist, whom Deborah saw only twice, she
confessed that she had never lived in the British Isles; she added
that Mr. Headley did not understand her.

But then, how could he? How could anyone? In many ways
she was still a mystery to herself. She had made sense of some of

the feelings, but not all; she had found some of the words for
what was happening, but others escaped her. She could tell
Walter Headley about the "arguments" at home, but not about
the other things. She could be painfully explicit about her father's
violence in her private writings—journals, as she now called them;
diaries were for little girls—but one topic never found its way
onto the page. She could report a beating and a pizza in the same
breath, produce pages of awkward pornography without blush-
ing, rage against her mother ("I would love to take a cleaver to
that Tyrant!") or her brother ("that impetuous ass . . . that
mongrel . . . he looks like a Peking duck") without a twinge of
conscience, but there was one secret she would not utter, not
even to her journals—not until after her father was dead. Those
who seek proof that the secret existed, that it was not one of her
dark fantasies or a later invention, must search for it among
several comments she made when she was thirteen and fourteen
years old.

She told one girl at Chaparral High that her father was a
pervert. The girl wasn't sure what she meant. On another occasion, Deborah told the same student she'd had some "traumatic"
sexual experiences. She didn't elaborate.

She told the boy she kissed that her father used to beat her,
"but that was years ago." She also told him she had slept with
an older man. She hinted that the man was a relative, possibly an
uncle.

She told her mother that she didn't like the way Dad hugged
her and put his hands all over her.

She told her brother that Dad felt her up sometimes, and she
was sick of it. She was going to tell him to stop it if Mom didn't.

But in those days she didn't tell anyone, not even her journals,
what she would later tell the lawyers, the doctors—the whole
world, if they cared to listen:

When she was six or seven her father used to take naps with
her. He would lie down beside her and pull up her nightie and
yank her flowered panties down around her ankles and finger her.
This happened over and over on Sunday afternoons, when Mom
was out shopping. Dad never talked about what he was doing to
her, and it wasn't *nasty,* exactly. It was just Dad being rude
again, taking charge of her body—not much different than the
times he tickled her, pulled down her pants and swatted her on
her bare bottom, or brushed her teeth for her.

Then the family moved to Arizona, she began to develop physically, and Dad would come into her room in the morning, before Mom was awake. He pressed himself against her on the bed, kissed her on the mouth, and felt her breasts. This happened once or twice a week, she said. Sometimes she could feel his erection against her thigh, but he never took his clothes off or penetrated her.

It was easy for him to slip into her room unnoticed. Her parents didn't sleep together anymore. When she was eleven or twelve years old, Dad rolled out a pallet in the den, among his guns and magazines, and slept there. (He had moved out of the bedroom at Mom's request, but Deborah didn't know that.)

"Don't you get tired of sleeping on the floor?" she asked.

"Good for the back," Dad said.

He tried to be nice to her. Oh, on occasion he still gripped her in a hammerlock and took her into the bathroom to brush her teeth or try to scrub the pimples off her face. But he didn't hit her nearly as much as he used to. And he called her "sweetheart" and "baby" when he came into her room in the mornings, instead of "bitch" and "asshole." Despite his efforts, Deborah didn't think it was so nice, really, to have fat old Dad slobbering on her. It was gross. But pretending to be asleep didn't work. She could only lie there, as still as a virgin in her tomb, with one eye fixed on the alarm clock on her dresser, while he pawed away at her.

"How are you this morning, baby?"

"Dad, I've got to get up now . . ."

"Not yet you don't."

She felt like his girlfriend, and she hated it. She never had any privacy; he came into the bathroom when she was in the shower to "check the pipes." His hands were always on her ass. On a few occasions he stuck his hand down her pants and groped around in front of Mom or Richie or both. Mom didn't seem to see it, and Deborah didn't know how to tell her. When she started to say something about Dad "touching" her, Mom marveled at his kindness.

"You should be glad," Mom said. "You're the only one he gets affectionate with."

(But Mom did talk to him once. She prepared a little speech: "Deborah is getting to that age where she's very fussy about people touching her. She doesn't even like me to hug her, so maybe you shouldn't either. She doesn't like it.'' Her husband's response was a long, silent, what-the-hell-are-you-babbling-about stare, a look of innocent bewilderment.)

It isn't clear just how or when it all ended. Perhaps it was something Mom said, or Deborah's increasing resistance. Finally she couldn't stand for Dad to lay a hand on her, even a so-called fatherly hand. When he tried, she cringed and yelped ''Don't!'' By the time she entered high school the whole business was over.

By then she had discovered the works of Jacqueline Susann and her father's stack of mainstream skin magazines: *Oui, Penthouse, Gallery, Playboy,* and the like. ''I have a tremendous knowledge about sex,'' she wrote in her journal. She had learned about the subject ''all by myself, by reading novels (all writers know that sex sells), magazines such as *Cosmopolitan* and *Penthouse,* encyclopedias, articles, and the college dictionary. And another thing—sex on the movie screen. All these recourses have been most efficient.''

She knew that sex was something adults did in all sorts of ways for all sorts of reasons. Young people could have sex, too, if they were particularly bold and free-spirited (and didn't have to be in bed by nine o'clock). But she didn't know that sex was something a father could use against his daughter.

Still, she had intimations of the ''part'' her father wanted her to play, a role she had questioned as far back as her childish vow to be ''different,'' to be nothing like the rest of her family. In late 1980, shortly before the family moved to Cheyenne, she wrote in her journal:

It is so very sad that I have to wait until I'm eighteen in order to have a good, interesting, meaningful relationship, and to go to a movie by myself, or just rush off to an art exhibit or a carnival at my leisure. I will really be able to fully appreciate my independence after playing the part of Richard C. Jahnke's social decoration or clever pet. . . . Thank Christ I don't love my father! It would completely destroy me.

9

For years he was afraid of the dark. That made him a baby, only babies are afraid of the dark, but he couldn't help it. When it was time to go to bed a blind panic seized him. He switched off the light, crawled quickly under the covers, buried himself under a pile of ragged stuffed animals and plastic soldiers, and wedged a pillow lengthwise on the edge of the bed, between his small, shivering body and the door. He squeezed up against the wall, and only then, when he was sealed off from the rest of the house and the world outside, did he feel safe.

Dad teased him for being afraid. It was one more thing he did wrong, like being small, having nigger lips, breathing through his mouth, walking pigeon-toed, letting the other kids bully him, crying when he got hit—you baby, you pussy, you faggot, you little shit-ass mama's boy, scared of the dark, what the hell is there to be scared about?

Yet Dad got jumpy at night, too. He prowled around the house, checking the locks on doors and windows, making sure the drapes and shades were drawn, putting guns out here and there like cookies for Santa Claus. If Mom or Deborah tried to look out the window he snapped at them to get the hell away, some maniac with a machete was probably eyeing them right now. If he heard the dogs barking, he would slip out to the darkened carport with his commando .45 in his hand and wait silently for some bastard to try something. He told Mom a man in his position couldn't be too careful.

But at least Dad didn't try to hide in his room under a pile of pillows and toys. That was plain pussy, and Dad wouldn't let him forget it. Sooner or later Dad would come into his room, stand him up against the wall, and hunker down in his face like a drill sergeant.

"Still sleeping with your bunny rabbit?" Dad asked.

He looked at his father's shoes, hard and shiny. The open hand caught him in the temple and sent his head crashing against the wall.

"Answer me, goddamit."

"Yes," he whispered.

"What the hell is wrong with you? You're going to be a faggot when you grow up, did you know that? A goddam fairy."

Sometimes he was beaten. Sometimes he had to listen to a recital of the horrible things in store for crybabies who were afraid of the dark. Sometimes Dad started screaming at Mom about the kind of mama's boy she was raising, and that was worst of all. He hated it when Mom got hit on account of him.

He had to do something. He couldn't help being small or some of the other things, but he could sure try not to be afraid. One day he swept all the baby stuff off his bed, put it away for good, and decided his name was Richard, not Richie. Mom still called him Richie, but he knew he was Richard.

He was seven years old.

It was hard being Richard. At the bus stop, for instance—Mom told him to turn the other cheek whenever anyone bothered him. But she also told him to stand up for his sister, so what was he supposed to do? Deborah was such a goof, talking funny and pretending she was English. What an act—the things she did to try to get people to like her. She drew trouble like a shit magnet. If he turned the other cheek, the teasing just got worse. So he learned to launch himself into his foes with briefcase flying. He didn't win many fights—he didn't know the important things, like when to stop—but anything was better than just taking it.

Mom yelled at him for getting into fights. Dad got pissed, too, but if he explained about how they were teasing Deborah, that usually made it okay. He was supposed to take care of the women. That was the last thing Dad said to him before he left on business trips; Dad stood in the doorway in his shiny black shoes and gray suit, a garment bag draped over one shoulder, and coolly surveyed his family from behind smoked sunglasses.

"You're the man of the house now, Richie," he said. "Take care of the women."

"Yes, sir," he said—and he felt so proud saying it! He ached for a chance to prove himself. Just let some thug try to bother Mom or Deborah, he'd stop him; and that went for the bullies at school, too. He'd die before he'd let any harm come to the women.

But no matter how many fights he got into at school, he never tried to fight back when Dad struck him. And that was hard, too, because the older he got, the more it seemed like Dad *wanted* him to fight back. For no reason at all Dad pushed him up against the wall and stuck his chin out.

"Go ahead, you get a free shot," Dad said.

"What?"

"Come on. Hard as you can. You scared or something?"

"I can't."

"What do you mean you can't? Come on, you little baby, just once."

He wanted to, but he never did. It would be a dumb thing to do; he saw what happened when Mom tried it. But there was something else that stopped him, not just the fear of getting hurt but a deep distrust of what it might mean, a fear of what he might become if he did. He couldn't explain it, he just knew he wouldn't be Richard anymore. So he stood there in mute refusal until his father grew angry and beat him or left in disgust.

Dad didn't give up. He staged wrestling matches in the swimming pool. At first Richard tried to play along—*don't show him you're scared,* he told himself—but each time Dad held him under a little longer. He had to fight and thrash his way to the surface; gasping and sputtering, he would burst into the air with the sound of his father's soft laughter in his ears. He had to climb quickly out of the pool or risk being dragged under again.

He couldn't figure it out. He knew this was some kind of test, Dad's way of toughening him for unseen ordeals that lay ahead. Dad even told him a Charles Atlas sort of parable about how, when he was young, this "older guy" used to whup on him after school. Dad got his weight up, went out for football, and finally confronted the son of a bitch and beat the hell out of him. Richard got the message, but he knew he couldn't do the same. He couldn't fight back—if for no other reason than that Dad wanted him to. That was Dad's way. He had to find another.

He heard kids at school brag about their fathers and what kind of work they did. He never said much. He wanted to tell them his father was a special agent who caught dope dealers and other crooks, but Dad didn't want the family discussing his work with anyone. What baffled him was how cool some of the other kids made their fathers sound.

"My dad hasn't hit me since I was five," one said.

"Yeah? My dad never even spanked me," said another.

He couldn't believe what he was hearing. They all had to be lying through their teeth.

At times he felt as invisible as Deborah's imaginary companions. He made a few friends at school, but since he wasn't athletic or popular, he had trouble keeping them. At his mother's insistence, he joined the Cub Scouts; he won a fistful of badges but no lasting loyalties. It seemed as if the only people who paid any attention to him or his sister were the kids who found them peculiar and thus suitable for teasing or fighting.

Yet it would be inaccurate to say that no one noticed, no one cared. Two children so painfully isolated from their classmates, so strange in their behavior, so erratic in their academic performance, often earning the most abysmal grades despite high scores on intelligence tests, were hard to ignore. From time to time the experts stepped in, determined to find out why Richie or Deborah was not achieving as expected. But in each instance the diagnosis revealed more about the doctor than the patient. The symptoms were obvious. It was the disease that was invisible.

He underwent his first major evaluation in the second grade. "Richie seemed pale," the learning disabilities specialist reported. "His mouth was open almost continuously. At times there seemed to be a very slight tremor in his writing hand. He wore a worried look. He said *smaw* for *small*. . . ."

The specialist suspected vision problems and "auditory sequencing problems." She recommended further testing and a parent conference. The testing went on for years, but inquiries concerning his home life never went further than unilluminating consultations with his mother, who routinely gave her permission for more tests. In 1978, when Richard was twelve, Maria consented to a psychological evaluation for her son. The school psychologist noted that he mumbled and appeared tense. The referral resulted in more tests and a greater emphasis on spelling and general comprehension skills.

His sister was supposed to receive a similar evaluation that same year, but for some reason it was never done. "Deborah did not respond well to my attempts to help her," one of her teachers reported. "She's quite remote and self-conscious." Her grades continued to fluctuate wildly, even though an aptitude test administered in her sophomore year of high school indicated that her writing abilities were superior to those of the average college freshman.

The strangeness of the Jahnke children was noticed by the neighbors on Poinsettia Drive, too, but most of them shunned any kind of diagnosis. They knew very little about the family. The Jahnkes kept their shades down and steered clear of any social functions on the block, declaring a love of privacy that was exceptional even in this most private of neighborhoods, where tall wooden fences sealed off the houses on three sides.

The truly curious knew that the father did some kind of government work and didn't talk to anybody. He spent entire weekends tending the citrus grove in the backyard, even though the frost defeated him every fall. The kids dressed awfully *old* for their age, carried briefcases, acted as if they were better than anybody else, and were picked on constantly at the bus stop. The mother could be pleasant but seemed overly protective; she waited outside for the bus to arrive after school and marched the kids right inside. Later she learned to drive (against her husband's wishes, but nobody knew that) so she could drive them to school and back, putting an end to the trouble on the bus. On quiet spring evenings, when it was cool enough to have the windows open, some families heard shouts and crying coming from the Jahnke house, but no one could make out what it was about. No one interfered.

Still, not even the Jahnkes could remain an island unto themselves. On at least two occasions Richard Chester Jahnke threatened the lives of neighbors who had offended him.

The first incident was the result of a long-standing feud with Roger and Jacqueline Carrel, who lived two doors west of the Jahnkes. The Carrels had a hyperactive son, one year younger than Richie. The boy was one of Deborah's chief tormentors at the bus stop. Maria complained angrily to the Carrels about their son's behavior. The Carrels told her she was overreacting. Shortly before Deborah was due to enter high school, Richard Chester Jahnke confronted Roger Carrel as he got out of his car after work. He told Carrel to keep his children away from Deborah.

"I've got a lot of guns, and I know how to use them," he said.

Carrel walked into his house without making a reply. Not long afterward, the Carrels put their son in a private school.

The date of the second incident can be fixed more precisely. On March 20, 1980, a man who lived directly behind the Jahnkes found a note in his mailbox politely requesting that he repair his fence. "Dogs have entered your yard through the holes in your fence and knocked boards off my fence which resulted in my dogs running away," the note explained. The note was signed "Rich Jahnke." The neighbor had never met Mr. Jahnke.

He met him a few hours later. Shortly after midnight Richard Chester Jahnke rang his doorbell and complained that his dogs had run away again. The neighbor refused to open his door. Jahnke kicked at the door, told him he was a "goddamned faggot," and announced that if the fence wasn't fixed soon, he'd kill him. The man called the police. They told him this was a neighborhood dispute and not a criminal matter.

The police did have a word with Mr. Jahnke, though. The next time the neighbor saw him, one day when they were both working in their backyards, Jahnke nodded and greeted him amiably across the fence. It was as if nothing had ever happened. The man who had come to his door at midnight screaming bloody murder must have been some other Richard Jahnke.

The best times were the times in the desert. Richard got up at first light and helped Dad load the guns in the Scout while Mom fixed them breakfast. Dad wore his floppy camouflage hat, a flannel shirt, khaki pants, and army boots; as soon as they were out of Phoenix, heading south past the Indian reservations, he lit up a Mena Petri Toscana. The heady smell of the cigar stayed with Richard all day, mixing with the acrid tang of gunpowder and the sharp scent of sage and baked earth. The smells were soothing somehow, like inhaling pure oxygen; Richard took deep breaths and felt at peace.

Dad took the back roads until he found a canyon desolate enough to suit him. Then they went looking for jackrabbits and snakes, or set up coffee cans and paper targets against a bank of soft dirt. Dad talked to him about balance and scoping and different types of bores, a lot of technical stuff about guns that he didn't understand. He didn't have to answer, he just had to listen; he might have been a dog for all it mattered. But he didn't mind. The talk was soothing, too. Dad seemed so calm in the desert.

Most of the time it was just the two of them. Deborah came
along a couple of times because Dad wanted to teach her how to
shoot. He started her out with his .357 magnum. The recoil
knocked her down. She tried other handguns, but it was no use.
The noise frightened her. She couldn't hit a thing, not even with
a .22. She didn't belong there.

Richard wasn't afraid of guns. He grew up with them. He
killed his first rabbit with a .38 when he was seven years old.
The gun leaped in his hands, and the rabbit flew sideways in a
cloud of red dust. The explosion echoed against the rocks and
finally faded, like the ringing in his ears, into a ghostly silence:
the sound of death.

Dad stood beside him with his hands upon his hips, his eyes
hidden behind the smoked glasses. "Nice shot," he said.

Dad took good care of his guns. He was always stripping them
down and cleaning them in front of the television. (His favorite
television fare included John Wayne movies, Clint Eastwood
movies, and the Charles Bronson movie *Death Wish;* after seeing
Dirty Harry, he bought a .44 magnum.) He took his commando
.45 with him to the bathroom the way another man might take a
book. He carried a gun at work, too, a Smith and Wesson .38
revolver, and if he was doing surveillance work he brought it
home with him. Not that he needed it; he had a rack of guns he
kept loaded and waiting for any son of a bitch who was dumb
enough to try to break in. The most impressive—to his son, at
least—was a sawed-off, pump-action Smith and Wesson 12-gauge
shotgun. Dad called it his "riot gun." He kept it loaded with a
"candy cane" mixture of birdshot, buckshot, and lead slugs.

One night, after everyone else had gone to bed, Dad accidentally blew a hole in the wall of the den with the riot gun. Mom
gave him hell about it, but he just laughed it off.

"Somebody's going to get killed," Mom said.

"You don't know what you're talking about," Dad said. "I
know what I'm doing."

Richard figured that Dad did know what he was doing—most
of the time, anyway. The women just didn't understand. Dad told
him stories about the kind of guys he had to go up against, like
the ex-wrestler whose wrists were so big Dad couldn't get his
handcuffs on them. You never knew when one of those bastards
might get out of jail and come after you. You had to be ready for
them, and a gun was the great equalizer. It was like that line in

The Godfather: "Women and children can afford to be careless, but not men." Richard pictured his father defending the house against a horde of vicious thugs, taking out the last one with a blast from the riot gun before collapsing himself, bleeding from a dozen wounds. It seemed like a fine way to die.

One night, shortly after he had subdued his fear of the dark, Richard padded into the kitchen around two in the morning for a snack. Suddenly the light snapped on, and he spun around to find Dad pointing his .45 at him. Dad yelled at him something awful: what was he doing up, he knew better than that, he was lucky to be alive.

But even then, it wasn't the gun that scared him, it was Dad. Richard lay awake for hours thinking about it. Surely Dad knew it was him, even in the dark. Then why did he do that?

In the desert, things took on their proper shape again. Richard learned to shoot quickly and well, and Dad was pleased. But at times he walked clumsily, or the asthma took hold of him like a big hand gripping his chest, pushing out the air in wet gasps, and he was no good for anything. Then Dad cursed him and went off on his own. When he breathed quietly, stalked well, and squeezed off a few good shots, Dad was proud of him, and said so—and Richard was proud, too. It felt so good to do it right.

The women just didn't understand. He tried to tell Deborah once what it felt like to kill a rabbit, how he gave him a warning shot and then picked him off on the run, what aim—and his sister started crying. She thought he was terrible for killing helpless "bunnies." She called him a malicious monster. Well, what did he expect? After that, he and Dad agreed that what happened in the desert was just between them.

One afternoon in the desert, around the time Dad told the Carrels he had a lot of guns and knew how to use them, Richard and his father climbed to the top of a ridge and spotted two other hunters on the plain below. The two men were walking toward them, several yards apart. Dad got down on his belly and told him to do the same. Dad watched the men until he was satisfied they hadn't seen him. Then he fired his .30-06, kicking up dirt halfway between the pair. The men hit the ground.

"Don't shoot!" they yelled.

Dad grinned. "Come on, let's get out of here before they see us," he said.

They ran down the ridge to the car and drove off. Dad was quiet for a while. Then he began to laugh. What assholes!

Richard didn't tell anyone about it—not for years. What happened in the desert was just between them.

It was hard being Richard, hard even when he did it right, harder and harder as the years went by.

Somehow even the best times went wrong. On the way home after a perfectly fine day in the desert, someone would cut them off in traffic, and Dad would go nuts. Richard hated driving with Dad; everyone did. Dad tailgated and honked and sped up whenever somebody tried to pass. He flipped people off, too. A couple of times guys caught up with him at stoplights and tried to start fights. Dad waved a gun at them and floored it. Assholes!

He liked to make jokes about the other drivers, calling them niggers or spics or queers. He wasn't prejudiced; he hated everybody. If he didn't like the looks of the driver of a big car, he wrote down the license plate number for future reference, on the general proposition that most people who were rich enough to drive big cars were probably cheating on their taxes.

When they stopped at a convenience store for Cokes to wash away the gritty taste of the desert, Dad would ogle the women, if there were any around. He would nudge his son and say, look at the knockers on that one, how about *that* . . . he was so obvious about it, God, he even *whistled*. Shut up, Richard thought, why couldn't he just shut up—God, make him shut up. But no, it just went on and on. Hot shame and loathing coursed through him from his toes to his bright red eartips.

But it was worse when Dad didn't act like that. You could get all the way home and think everything was going fine. You'd be feeling pretty good, thinking Dad could be pretty cool after all. You wanted to tell him you loved him, tell Mom what a great time you had today, and *then* something would go wrong. Dad would get pissed, he'd call Mom a fat spic or Deborah a little slut or slap you around because you spent too much time in the bathroom. You'd want to cry, but you didn't dare. Then you'd remember that this was always what happened; you never should have trusted the good times, they never lasted.

When Dad was through hurting someone in one part of the house, he went out to the others and acted as if nothing had happened. He told jokes, made faces, tried to get them to laugh, to ignore the sobs. Richard grew to hate that. If he was going to be Richard instead of Richie, he had to stop playing that game. Mom and Deb could play along, maybe they were afraid not to, but he wouldn't. He would sit there and scowl, accusing Dad with his eyes.

But it didn't make him feel any better to scowl. He just heard the screaming and crying more clearly. He didn't mind so much getting hit himself. He had learned how to take a licking and not cry about it. But the women—why did Dad have to go after the women? More to the point, why did he have to go after Mom?

His sister's case didn't seem nearly as serious to him. Dad wasn't hitting Deborah that much anymore. When he did, she didn't make a big deal out of it; she went into her room and wrote in her diary. As far as Richard could see, she was developing her own defenses, weird but effective—like leaving used Kotex around for Dad to find when he went rummaging through her drawers, looking for dope or love letters or whatever. And she was getting good at sneaking out on her own. She wouldn't listen to Richard about anything, not after he told Mom about the boy she kissed. She just scratched his face the next time he tried to stop her from going out when Mom and Dad weren't around. Richard decided it was pretty hard to feel sorry for someone who hated your guts.

But Mom, Mom was a different matter. Richard remembered all the times Mom tried to keep Dad from hitting them. She couldn't help it if she wasn't as strong as he was, if she just gave up after a while. It tore him up to see her try so hard to keep things together, put on a big smile and pretend everything was wonderful—and wind up getting beat anyway. Sometimes after Dad went to work she would stay where he had left her, on the floor of her room, moaning softly to herself. Or she would pound the floor and break into a torrent of tears and wailing you could hear all over the house.

"That bastard!" she would shriek. "God, make him die! Please, God! I hope he rots in hell!"

On several occasions she threatened to leave. Richard hoped she would. When he came home from school one day and found her packing a suitcase, he felt dizzy with relief.

"I've got to get out of here," she said. "Don't worry, I'll come back for you and Deborah as soon as I'm settled."

"Go ahead, Mom," he said. "We'll be okay."

She was gone by the time her husband came home. Dad tried to make a joke of it. He took them out for hamburgers and then to a drive-in movie. Deborah sat in the front seat and joked around with Dad. Richard sat in the back and despised them both for pretending it didn't matter that Mom had left. When we get home, he vowed, I'll pack my bag, too . . .

But when they came home, Mom was there. Mom and Dad kissed and hugged like a couple of teenagers. It was wrong to hope, Richard told himself, you should have known it was too good to be true.

Within days Mom and Dad were back to screaming and cursing each other. It was a cycle as predictable as the seasons. Every fight led to a truce and ultimately to another fight again, and each one was less tolerable to him than the last. Deborah knew how to handle it, she closed her door and wrote, but he couldn't. The pathetic sounds of their battle followed him everywhere.

When he was twelve the sounds finally drew him out of his room and down the hall. His mother was lying on the floor of the kitchen. His father was sitting on her chest. She was slobbering and crying. Dad was slapping her face and calling her names. Richard clenched his fists tightly and walked up behind them.

"Leave my mother alone, you big fat jerk."

Dad stood up. Richard ran. Dad caught up with him in the living room, pulled him down, and hit him in the back with his fists. Richard didn't hit back. Then Dad went away, and Mom was standing over him. She was smiling. Her eyes shined damply at him.

"I want to shake your hand, young man," she said. "You are the only one who has ever helped me."

Young man! At that moment he knew he had finally found his way. He didn't care about his bruised back; he didn't care if he had to play the role of a human punching bag for years. He wasn't a baby anymore. He was a young man. He was Richard.

In his seven years of service in the Phoenix office of the IRS, Richard Chester Jahnke divided his time between two distinct investigative teams: Group Three, which focused on the lucrative activities of organized crime, such as drug trafficking; and Group One, which dealt with general enforcement of tax laws concerning corporations and individuals. During that time his salary more than doubled, from $10,154 to $26,349 a year, and he earned a reputation around the office as a relentless, highly motivated agent, a man who really loved his work—every tax evader's worst nightmare.

His colleagues knew that he worked hard, but some questioned his methods. They thought he had a tendency to rely on instinct in a case, sometimes at the expense of common sense. If he *knew* someone was guilty, he'd spend countless hours trying to prove it, regardless of the evidence. He breathed fresh life into the ancient art of the vendetta. He wasn't just another G-man, he was an avenging angel: Harry Callahan with a Treasury badge, Chuck Bronson armed with the tax code. He pursued one prominent county official for years, producing complaints of harassment from the man's lawyer but no conviction. He ridiculed other agents who were more likely to write off a case or turn it over to the "civilians" down the hall for a routine audit. He called one agent "Backoff John," apparently because the man's work wasn't thorough enough to suit him.

One coworker regarded Special Agent Jahnke as a bloated version of Don Rickles; he had a sour word for just about everybody and everything. Occasionally he got a laugh, but he was too unpredictable to laugh with for long. He could be abrasive, demeaning, profane, confrontational. He took advice rarely, and criticism almost never. He liked to work alone.

The people he worked with knew little about his family. A few agents who carpooled with Jahnke had met the wife and kids—a quiet bunch, nothing remarkable. He talked about them on occasion, in the usual fatherly grunts of pride or concern—my boy went shooting with me, some creeps are bugging my daughter at school—again, nothing special. But he never invited anyone home to dinner or brought his family to any of the office parties.

By the same token, his family knew little about his work. They knew about his investigation of the local official because it made the pages of the *Arizona Republic,* the Phoenix morning newspaper. They also knew that, during the 1976 presidential campaign, Special Agent Jahnke was "on loan" to the Secret Service and guarded Betty Ford briefly when she came to Phoenix to speak to a Republican women's group. (The First Lady looked much older, he reported, without her makeup.) Aside from such scraps of information about his most public assignments, he brought nothing home from work but his abysmal suspicion of the outside world, his mania for locked doors, drawn shades, and loaded guns. So his wife and children had very little warning of his discontent before he announced, in early 1980, that he was applying for a transfer to Cheyenne, Wyoming.

Maria was told that the Cheyenne job was the break he'd been waiting for. He was tired of being passed over for promotion in Phoenix, tired of watching assholes get credit for his work. If he went to Cheyenne he'd be promoted to grade 13, he'd be the senior investigator in a small office. That meant more money (an increase of almost $10,000 in his annual pay over the next two and a half years). He would also be next in line for the job of group manager. Of course, there were other considerations, too: in the seven years since they arrived in Scottsdale, their modest little subdivision had been swallowed in a frenzy of suburban sprawl. The city had pollution, traffic, murder, rape, dope fiends— might as well be back in Chicago, this was no place to raise kids. Wyoming was God's country, everyone knew that. Plenty of hunting and fishing, cleanest air in the whole goddam country. Low cost of living, too.

Maria remained unconvinced. He'd *promised* they wouldn't move again. He told her there was no point in arguing about it. The papers were already filled out. In June he moved into a Cheyenne motel and started work, leaving his family in Phoenix to dispose of the house. Two months later he summoned Maria to Cheyenne to inspect the house he'd found for sale on Cowpoke Road. The asking price was $145,000, but he was confident that he could get it for $115,000. Maria stood at the front door, looking out upon the bare hillside opposite them, and a wave of loneliness swept over her.

"My God, where are the trees?" Maria asked. "There are no trees."

"We'll get some," he said.

When she first heard the news, Deborah cried. A few days later she went shopping with Mom at the local mall. A security guard stopped them as they were leaving the Sears store and demanded the barrettes Deborah had taken from a display stand. As promised on signs posted throughout the store, Sears prosecuted her for shoplifting. Dad had to take time off from work to meet with the Sears security manager. As they were leaving the store, Dad slapped Deborah on the back of the head.

Richard thought moving to Cheyenne sounded just fine. He was fourteen years old, entering his freshman year at Chaparral

High School that fall—and he hated it. He had finally passed his sister in height, but the bullies he had contended with all through school were still bigger, and they had a host of cute names for him now: Zitface, Wimp, Leather Lips. In Cheyenne no one would know him. He could start over. Maybe he could be somebody. Like his father, he longed to swim upstream, against the usual American social currents, to smaller and more obscure places. He thought about what it would be like to live in the Rockies, where everything was fresh and clean and the water was alpine cold, where the mountains towered over you, gave you something to live for.

"Mountains!" Deborah jeered. "Richard, I take geography, you know. Cheyenne, it's just this cowtown, this hole in the wall. There aren't any mountains. Cheyenne sucks."

"You don't know that," he said.

The house on Poinsettia Drive stayed on the market for months, a reflection of the housing slump and high interest rates across the country that year; Maria wasn't able to close with a buyer until early 1981. On February 3, shortly after noon, Richard and a friend were ambushed at their school lockers by two large and familiar adversaries, the class bullies. His friend suffered a broken jaw. Richard took a blow to the head that left him glassy-eyed and confused the rest of the day. His mother drove him to the emergency room of a local hospital, where he was diagnosed as having received a mild concussion.

It was his last day at Chaparral High School. Eleven days later—Valentine's Day, 1981—the Jahnke family arrived in Cheyenne.

PART THREE

THE GOOD SON

Wyoming is a land of opportunity. Few questions are asked the newcomer concerning his past or his ancestry. It is not altogether rhetoric to say that a man is accepted for what he is and for what he can do. He must be resourceful and self-reliant to a high degree.

—*Wyoming: A Guide to Its History, Highways, and People* (1941)

10

Dad drove the Scout, with Richard beside him to keep him company—"riding shotgun," Dad called it. Mom and Deborah followed in the Chevrolet Laguna station wagon. They drove east to Albuquerque, New Mexico, then north through Colorado, where the highway runs parallel to the Front Range, splitting the view into a running diptych: parched yellow grasslands on their right, the foothills and blue-and-white spine of the Rockies on their left. They made few stops; Dad had to get back to work. As far as Maria was concerned, the trip was pure hell, buster, try keeping up with that man for a thousand miles . . . you lose him in the traffic and five miles later he's waiting for you by the side of the road, bellowing: what the hell's the matter with you, don't you know how to drive?

North of Fort Collins, Colorado, the mountains began to recede from view, tugged west by a whim of the Continental Divide. Within minutes the high plains closed in on them, and the highway became a narrow ribbon of hope twisting up, down, and around rolling hills. Broad signs for motels and gas stations lined their way, a gauntlet of bright colors and promises. At the state line they were greeted by the silhouette of a cowboy riding a bucking bronco beneath an enormous setting sun. HOWDY!, the sign said. YOU'RE IN BIG WYOMING.

In minutes Cheyenne surfaced from the prairie: a sprawling, wide-laned, low-rise town, scoured by the wind. The signs offering food, lodging, and other comforts multiplied. The cowboy motif was all around them; every motel, restaurant, and liquor store in town seemed to be named Frontier, Horseshoe, Maverick, Roundup, Plains, or Pioneer. The Jahnke caravan exited at Little America, a vast motel-and-gas-pump complex at the junction of I-25 and I-80, one of a chain of "resorts" for motorists in the intermountain West named, aptly enough, after Richard Byrd's base camp in Antarctica.

The family stayed at Little America for several weeks while

interior work was completed on the house on Cowpoke. To save money, they shared one room: Mom and Deborah in one bed, Dad and Richard in the other. It was an uncomfortable arrangement at best, a teeth-gnashing exercise in communal misery the rest of the time. The only place to find any privacy was the bathroom. Deborah and Richard took turns soaking and reading in the tub. Maria drove them to school down gray, snow-lined streets. She told the children, as she'd told herself in Tempe eight years before, just a few more days, a few more days and we'll be in our own house, and everything will be all right.

The night after they arrived, Dad drove them out to Cowboy Country to see their new home. They had already seen Dad's pictures of the house, the same snapshots he had passed around the office with considerable pride and commentary. (Before returning to Arizona to help his family move, he had even persuaded another Cheyenne IRS agent to drive out for a firsthand look at the property. "This place is a present to my wife," he explained, "for putting up with me all these years.")

The moon was high, bathing the house's white trim and the patches of snow around it in a pale blue light. Dad pulled into the driveway, and the four of them got out and walked around to the front door, past the darkened windows of the empty front rooms. Deborah looked back at the dimly lit dirt road.

"What happens when we get blizzards?" she asked. "Will we get stranded out here?"

"I can think of worse things," Dad said. "Like being stuck in Little America."

"God, there's nothing out here," Deborah said.

"That's right. Nothing but quiet. Pretty nice, huh?"

She waited until Dad was inside, then whispered to Richard, "This looks like that house on *Dallas*—the funeral house."

Moving to Cheyenne was supposed to be a way to start over. Starting over, Maria figured, would take a little time. Rome wasn't built in a day, my friend, you can't wipe out thirteen years of bad luck and bad temper just like that. So moving is difficult, what are you supposed to do? Give up and die on the side of the road like an animal? God, you need a little patience, moving is hard on everyone. And Little America, okay, who could be happy living like that, a month crammed into one room in Little America isn't anybody's idea of a good time. Things can only get better, it's all up from here. A person can only hope.

New town, new job, new school, new house, it takes time to get used to it all. Everybody gets a little upset, and they start pulling on Maria: Mom, fix this; Maria, take care of that. Maria has to be strong.

Maria has to be strong because Deborah, Little Miss Know-it-all, can't abide with brown and white and beige, the basic color scheme of the new house. She wants a sky-blue shag rug in her room. The poor girl is so unhappy about leaving Arizona, Mom has to make it up to her. So even though Dad wants to sock some sense into her, Mom talks him out of it. Let the poor girl have what she wants, Mom says. Now Deborah spends all her time in her room, reading her books and dreaming her dreams.

Maria has to be strong because Dad says he can't sleep in the nice big bedroom with her. (Not that they have actually slept *together* for years; these are the twin beds from Arizona. One day Maria simply told him, "I just can't anymore"—who could, she wanted to know, with someone who's hurting you all the time? —and instead of throttling her for failing to perform her marital duties, he got up and said quietly, "I'll wait until you feel like it again." That was three years ago.) No, Dad can't sleep; too much noise. If Richie coughs or Deborah sneezes, Dad hears it right through the wall. Maria can't hear a thing. The walls look pretty solid to her, but don't argue, just fix it. She finds a deal on what they call a daybed, and it just fits in the laundry room and he's so much happier there. Let him sleep at the other end of the house with his guns and his silly gun magazines like *Soldier of Fortune* ("The Journal of Professional Adventurers"—that's him, all right!). Let him sleep alone and let him eat alone, too; it's not so hard to fix him up a tray so he can eat cross-legged on the floor of the family room, in front of the television, while the rest of the family sits at the kitchen table and eats like human beings. It's a lot easier that way. A body can have some peace.

And Maria has to be strong because of Richie, too. Richie is changing so fast. Richie, who was always so kind and good-natured, the best son a mother could have, Richie is getting as particular and demanding as everybody else. Richie has acne—not as bad as Deborah's, but he thinks it's the end of the world. Poor kid turns off the light every time he goes into the bathroom so he won't have to look at himself in the mirror. Scrubs five, six times a day with the latest teenage miracle paste, until his face is beet-red with chemicals. He insists it's all this greasy food in his diet. He won't eat; makes faces, as if Mom were trying to poison him or something; gets as thin as a scarecrow. Maria starts cooking special meals for him, lean meats and fish and no fat (although once in a while she butters the bottom side of a waffle for him, the kid is so thin). Maria doesn't mind, really; that's what mothers are for, to fix it. But Dad has a fit. It's the blue-shag rug battle all over again, he's screaming about all the extra work and expense, what kind of little pizza-faced bastard makes his mother fix dinner twice—and guess who's caught in the middle again, buster, you think it's easy being Mom?

One day Mom made a mistake. Mom went out shopping with Deborah and left a meatloaf in the oven for Dad and Richie. Dad cut the meatloaf in half and put one half on Richie's plate, one half on his own.

"Dad, I can't eat that," Richie said.

"You'll eat it," Dad said. "We don't waste food around here."

"I can't. It makes me sick just looking at it."

"You'll eat it or you'll take a licking."

"I'll take the licking," Richie said. He stood up and waited patiently for his father to strike him. Dad just stared at him. When Maria came home, Dad told her that her son was crazy.

But Dad said that about everybody. Everybody was wrong, everybody was crazy. If you tried to tell him it was dangerous for him to sit there in front of the television cleaning his guns, pointing one at the screen every once in a while, like a little boy playing John Wayne—what if one of them went off, bye-bye TV . . . if you brought it up, he told you that you didn't know what you were talking about. If you asked him why he banged on the door of the bathroom and yelled "Time's up!" when Richie or Deborah was in there—the house has three bathrooms, what's the problem; if you asked him why he had to ride the kids so much, why he had to stand sideways in the narrow hallway and nudge Richie every time he passed by . . . if you asked him, he looked at you as if you were absolutely demented. You're losing it, lady. You're seeing things. You're crazy. Nuts. Bonkers. Loco.

Well, maybe she was. A person would have to be crazy to put up with so much *tumulto* in her own home.

Of course, it wasn't always so bad. Dr. Jekyll still put in an appearance on occasion; he brought his wife flowers for no reason at all and became perfectly charming when her mother visited. And he never beat Maria anymore, not since the day Richie came to her rescue in Arizona. Oh, he still screamed at her, maybe even slapped her when Richie wasn't around to see it, but it was nothing like before. He even went to church now, which astonished her. In Arizona going to church had become such a chore that they had become twice-a-year Catholics, braving mass at Christmas and Easter, if at all. It just wasn't worth the trouble; waiting for the kids to get ready always put him in a terrible mood, and the drive to and from the church made things worse. But now he went to mass at least once a week. He even dropped in at Saint Mary's Cathedral during his lunch hour, just to get a whiff of the place and be alone with his thoughts and his God. Surely that was a good sign, Maria told herself. If only he could bring the Prince of Peace home with him and leave Mr. Hyde in the pew . . . if only Deborah wasn't so hostile to the Church and anything Maria tried to tell her . . . if only Richie wasn't brooding so much all the time . . .

After a few weeks in the new house it occurred to Maria that things weren't getting any better. If anything, they were worse. Instead of having one unhappy person to deal with, she had three—and they all *blamed* her for their unhappiness. She was supposed to fix it. Get us out of here, Mom, this place sucks. Tell the wind to lay off. Bring back the swimming pool. It's your fault my face looks like a pizza; your fault Dad brought us here; your fault Dad acts the way he does; your fault we're broke, Maria, where does the money go, do you have to spend it all on those little bastards; your fault if they act like the world owes them a favor; your fault if they get bad grades. It was hard to figure out how the arguments started, but they always ended up with her being found guilty as charged. Mothers, Maria learned, are always guilty.

One Sunday morning she argued bitterly with her husband about money, food, children, and who was to blame for the misery of the entire western hemisphere. He stomped outside, screamed names at her from the driveway, and drove off. Richie and Deborah watched her pack two suitcases and take them to the garage. She was back inside in minutes.

"The car won't start," she said.

Dad telephoned from a drugstore. He had "done something"

to the car, he explained, because he didn't want her to leave him. Maria listened as he apologized—gravely, sincerely, and at length—for all the trouble he had caused her. He said he loved her; and he said it in a voice she had almost forgotten, the voice of the young private—bold dreamer, adoring lover—who had courted her on long walks through the streets of Santurce.

When he came home that day, Richie and Deborah didn't go to their rooms, as they usually did after an argument in the house. Instead they sat in the family room, pretending to read the newspaper, with defiant and amused looks on their faces. Never mind. Maria got a kiss and flowers, and nothing more was said. Not yet.

Later that day Dad took her back to the laundry room. It was his favorite place for discussing family business; he always had Maria come to his room and pull up a chair next to the bed when he felt like talking or playing chess or gin rummy. He closed the door and told her he had finally seen the light. He was wrong to treat her the way he did, he said. He loved her. He didn't want to lose her, no matter what. Anyway, it wasn't her fault that things went wrong, he knew that now.

He knew what the problem was. It wasn't her. It was the children. The children were in the way.

Of Cheyenne's three public high schools, Central High is reputed among many parents to be the most desirable. It is the oldest of the three schools, but its facilities are practically new, housed in an imposing, monolithic red-brick complex built in 1976 to replace the old Central. It draws many of its 1300 students from the city's affluent north side, yet retains a measure of "diversity" in its representation of minorities. It has a strong suit of pragmatic, vocation-oriented programs for the forty percent of its graduates who won't go on to college, and ample parking for those students who can afford cars and college.

Deborah Jahnke entered Central High as an anonymous sophomore transfer student in February of 1981. Central, she discovered, was at least a third smaller than Chaparral High in Scottsdale and not nearly as *advanced*. My God, they even talked about *school spirit* here, as if kissing ass to get on the football team or the debate team was the only way to get your existence validated. In English class they made her read Steinbeck and Hemingway and other boring second-raters, ground she'd cov-

ered long ago. How was she supposed to stay awake? She
finished the semester with a B in English, a C in journalism, a D
in Spanish, and Fs in biology and algebra.

Richard had a few months of ninth grade left when he arrived
in Wyoming. That made him a "senior" at McCormick Junior
High School, a demotion from his big-league status as a freshman at Chaparral High. He signed up for wood and metal shop
classes, social studies, English, algebra, and science courses.
That left one hole in his schedule and two classes to choose from:
vocal music or ROTC.

And what, he asked, is ROTC?

Reserve Officer Training Corps, his classmates told him. Army
stuff.

Does that mean, he asked, you have to join the army when you
get out of school?

Nah. It means you go over to Central one hour a day and
march around and shoot rifles and stuff. You get gym credit for
it, but you've got to wear a uniform and salute and all that crap.

He considered. One, he hated gym classes worse than anything, except maybe meatloaf; in Arizona he had asked his gym
teachers to let him pump air into balls or count towels, anything,
just don't put him out on the floor with those sweaty, smelly
animals. Two, he was pretty good at shooting rifles. Three,
wearing a uniform didn't bother him; he grew up with more toy
soldiers than the babes in Toyland. Four, an hour a day out of
McCormick was, well, an hour a day. It took him about ten
seconds to decide to sign up for ROTC.

The program he entered at Central claims to be the second
oldest ROTC program in the country, offering military education
to the youth of Cheyenne since 1903, when it was known as the
National Cadet Corps. As one might expect, the program has
drawn its strongest breath in times of patriotic fever and gasped
for survival when the young grew restless and disaffected. At one
point every boy at Central High was required to take ROTC. By
the time Richard Jahnke joined the cause, it was just another
elective, one that had lost the sinister air of military indoctrina-
tion that had dogged ROTC offerings at schools across the country during the Vietnam War. The advent of the volunteer army,
and a need to make ROTC "relevant" in new ways in order for it
to survive, had changed all that. The instructors at Central were
still retired U.S. Army personnel—an NCO for the ninth-grade

cadets, an officer for the upper-classmen—and the troops still performed their drills at basketball games and military funerals. But the notion of ROTC as preparation for a military career had been replaced with a vague Boy Scout rhetoric stressing the virtues of "youth development," "leadership," "self-confidence," and, of course, discipline. The program was coed and actually had a handful of female recruits.

The change in labels had done little to alter the popular perception of the program at Central, which, by 1981, was quite abysmal. ROTC, everyone agreed, had an "image problem"; many students regarded the cadets as belonging to another species. Why would anyone want to spend half their time in high school—*high school,* man! time to party hearty!—shining shoes and marching up and down the halls in a brown suit, saying yes, sir, no, sir? Unless, of course, you happened to be a goon, a geek, a straitlaced "strat" (a nickname, sometimes derogatory, for Strategic Air Command personnel at Warren Air Force Base)—in short, a nerd. Central students concerned with being politically correct, or at least hip by the community standards of hipness, shunned the ROTC students as if they were traitors to the cause of youth, spies from the parental camp.

The one day a week he wore his uniform, Private Jahnke came in for his share of ostracism and harassment from other students, both at McCormick and at Central. It didn't bother him that much. He didn't figure to become *popular* by joining ROTC. His own sister had let him know she disapproved, and Dad had greeted the whole affair with mild amusement. ("Say, maybe you'd like to go to one of those military schools where they really straighten kids out," he said.) But what disappointed him those first few weeks was the sheer dullness of the military routine. He learned to march and to take orders—is that all there is? he wondered. Taking orders from a bunch of wimps, hanging in there until it's your turn to give orders to another bunch of wimps? As he saw it, "youth development" was some kind of code for pointless paperwork and mindless attention to detail. His ROTC class was little more than a glorified study hall.

He had almost made up his mind to quit at the end of the semester when he heard that a new chief instructor was coming in to shake things up. Enrollment was down; if it got any lower than 100 students, the army would put the entire program on probation. The new man was a veteran of Nam. Green Beret. Hard-ass. Had some new ideas. Name's Robert Vegvary. *Major* Vegvary to you, Private.

Robert Vegvary arrived in June, shortly before the scheduled four-day ROTC summer camp. He proved to be a short, muscular man with a round face, dun-colored hair, and ramrod posture. He was fresh out of the service and still talked in the clipped, formal tone of a superior accustomed to being obeyed. His first official act was to gather the faithful and invite them to voice their grievances. A few cadets hesitantly aired their displeasure with the uniforms, the type of training, the harassment from other students—the whole "image problem," and more. Vegvary listened expressionlessly and then launched into his pitch.

Things were going to be different, he said. The uniforms would be changed. Promotions would be a matter of merit rather than longevity in the program. And there would be new opportunities for merit, new activities to give the cadet a sense of pride in himself. Other students would see that ROTC wasn't a collection of Sad Sacks and Beetle Baileys. The program would diversify and become something everyone could respect. For example, Vegvary wanted to revive Central's Ranger program. The Rangers would have special uniforms, learn a variety of outdoor skills, and assist state and county agencies in mountain search-and-rescue operations. This would involve a substantial investment of time and energy, and only the most academically stable cadets need apply.

Richard listened with growing fascination. It wasn't just the warning about "substantial investment of time," which he instantly computed as time away from home. It was the way Vegvary used words like "pride" and "respect." Richard was familiar with the words, but he had always heard them used in a different way: *Show some respect, you son of a bitch! I'll bet you're real proud of yourself, aren't you?* Here was a man—not just a desk man like Dad, but a real soldier—who talked about pride and respect as if nothing else mattered. Well, he ought to know. He had been there. He knew the true meaning of the words, the manly sacraments they contained. Richard felt as if he were hearing the words for the first time.

Pride. Respect. Saving lives in the mountains.

He was going to be a Ranger. The best Ranger of them all.

11

After twenty-one years of active duty, retirement did not come easily to Major Robert Vegvary. Some men have a vocation for the priesthood or politics, a "calling," as they say, which cannot be denied. Vegvary's calling was the United States Army. He grew up in Ohio, attended Kent State University on an ROTC scholarship, and joined the army upon graduation. His career spanned a wide range of assignments: infantry and staff officer, instructor, a Ranger in the Army Airborne, Special Forces (Green Berets) captain, three tours of duty in Vietnam between 1962 and 1970. At the age of forty-two, having been a soldier half his life, Vegvary visited Cheyenne and decided he liked the town, and the kids at Central High. Assuming command of the local ROTC program seemed like a good way of easing into the civilian world.

He knew, of course, that he had his work cut out for him. The program was on its knees. The faculty and school administration welcomed him warmly, but he sensed that, in many cases, their encouragement was merely lip service to a hoary tradition; athletics at Central enjoyed more obvious support. Given the indifference of the faculty, the contempt oozing from other students, and the defensive, us-versus-them mentality of the cadets, it was no surprise that morale within the unit was so atrociously low.

As Vegvary saw it, the first order of business was a swift course in attitude adjustment. The cadets needed to feel that they were achieving something. They needed to work for their medals and promotions, so the finest among them would rise to the top. Most of all, the divisiveness had to stop; he had to find ways to integrate ROTC with existing school activities and establish new ones. He had to bring in new blood, not only to boost enrollment but to gain more of the "quality" students at Central.

He ordered new uniforms, replacing the dreary brown outfits with light green ones. He gave the girls permission to wear slacks on uniform days, same as the boys. He encouraged the color guard to develop a snappier flag-raising and offered the drill team red berets. For the Rangers, his pet project, he came up with a commandolike ensemble—camouflage fatigues, black berets, and black boots—and a rigorous, outdoors-oriented training program. He wanted the Rangers to stand out from the rest of ROTC as an elite search-and-rescue team, in much the same way that the Green Berets could never be mistaken for regular army joes.

He tried to temper his innovations with an equal emphasis on the fundamentals. Shoes still had to gleam, trousers had to boast a sharp crease. And, although courses in military tactics and history had been abandoned years ago, rudimentary weapons training was still required of all cadets. At his first ROTC summer camp, at the National Guard's Camp Guernsey, north of Cheyenne, Vegvary supervised the cadets' efforts with M-16s on the firing range. A few of his charges also tried out one of the Guard's M-60 light machine guns.

Vegvary himself had been a small-bore shooter as far back as college; his personal gun collection included an M-1A semiautomatic rifle. When he came to Cheyenne, he volunteered as a reserve deputy sheriff, which entitled him to carry a badge, handcuffs, and a loaded revolver in his car. He wasn't loath to share his firsthand knowledge of firearms and combat with cadets in informal chats, away from the range or the classroom. But for most of the cadets—excluding those who went through the hunter safety program and the handful of marksmen who made up the rifle team—summer camp was the only occasion they handled live ammunition. The chrome-plated rifles used for drills were completely nonfunctional; the rifles used by the ceremonial detachment, usually for twenty-one-gun salutes at the funerals of military veterans, fired only blanks.

By the fall Vegvary felt he had made significant progress. Enrollment was up, morale was improving, and the Ranger team was starting to take shape. He had made one tactical error: for the ROTC display table during school registration that fall, he'd had the cadets bring in radios, backpacks—and rifles. The rifles weren't loaded, of course, but they seemed to scare kids away rather than intrigue them. He vowed to soft-pedal the firepower the next time around; after all, the objective was to persuade his troops and the rest of Central High that ROTC wasn't strictly a military training program, that it could be as challenging as Outward Bound or as much fun as a dance class.

Yet as the semester wore on, he began to realize that he was wrestling with more than a morale problem, more than an image problem. It took him a few months to accept it—twenty years in the army had in no way prepared him for it—but the truth was that some of his cadets were in the program because they had nowhere else to go. Vegvary knew that ROTC, like every branch of the service, had always been a haven for the down-and-outers, the kids nobody wants, life's losers—the old Foreign Legion syndrome. But the situation at Central struck him as exceptional. This wasn't high school as he had known it in Ohio in the fifties; maybe they did things differently in Cheyenne, or maybe the civilian world had changed more than he had dreamed. In any case, he couldn't believe the number of kids who had drug problems, alcohol problems, emotional problems, family problems—family problems most of all.

He had kids he suspected of using marijuana, amphetamines, and other drugs, but this was difficult to prove. He was more concerned about the widespread use of alcohol, the drug of choice among many "straight" cadets. He had kids who came to class blind drunk and one girl who had spent three years as a sophomore, in between suspensions from school and alcohol treatment programs. He had kids with a range of behavior problems—mysterious fits of anger, depression, withdrawal—that could be attributed to substance abuse but were probably something else.

A surprising number of cadets lived with a stepmother or stepfather, a single parent, or no parent at all. One boy made a point of informing other students that he was a bastard; he tried to interest the others in the occult. A freshman girl approached Vegvary in tears, fearful that she was pregnant by her boyfriend. There were no school funds available to pay for a pregnancy test, so Vegvary raided the ROTC petty cashbox. He urged another cadet to put her baby up for adoption, which she eventually did; the birth was the result of a rape that the girl had refused to report for fear of retaliation.

Vegvary soon found himself spending as much time counseling students on an informal basis as he did in the classroom. He felt uneasy in the role, as if he were putting out random brush fires while other, more dangerous fires smoldered underground. From stray comments the cadets made, he came to the conclusion that several were encountering serious difficulties at home; maybe not physical abuse, but some form of neglect. One student returned from a weekend outing and called his mother for a ride home from school; from the conversation, which he overheard, the major gathered that the boy's mother hadn't even known he was gone. Vegvary was appalled. How many of his problem cadets, he wondered, were potential runaways or suicides?

He couldn't get over it. Years later, when asked to reflect on his experiences at Central High, he managed a wan smile.

"Let me tell you something," he said. "Conservatively speaking, in the first year and a half I was there, I saw more human misery up close than in any ten years of military service—including a combat tour of Vietnam."

But not every cadet he came across fit some stereotype of the troubled adolescent. While family problems seemed to be the rule rather than the exception, Vegvary was impressed by the number of stable, capable, hardworking cadets in the program. They could be enthusiastic if you gave them something to be enthusiastic about. During his first eighteen months on the job, one of the most impressive was Richard Jahnke.

Vegvary first became aware of Richard during the summer session at Camp Guernsey. Actually, it was a case of noticing Richard and his "twin," Greg Porter, for the two were inseparable. Porter had been in the program for his entire freshman year, while Jahnke was practically a new arrival, but the two had become fast friends. They were both short, skinny, attentive, eager to prove themselves, both at that awkward, self-conscious stage of midadolescence—boys struggling to be men, searching, with exaggerated seriousness, for somewhere to belong.

Vegvary had a score of incoming sophomores who were determined to become Rangers, but Porter and Jahnke were easily the best athletes of the class. They were the first to pass the Ranger qualifying tests: a three-mile run, thirty minutes floating in a swimming pool, tests of mountaineering, first aid, and winter survival skills. They seemed to be competing for the black berets against each other more than anyone else. Vegvary had a hunch that in two years one or the other would wear the saber of the battalion commander, the senior student officer in charge of the entire program; it was going to be interesting to see which one would prevail.

Of the pair, Jahnke was the more demonstrative cadet. Porter was the strong, silent type; he had a way of fading into the background. Jahnke always seemed to be around, practically at Vegvary's elbow half the time, handing him a compass or a canteen. One of the first things Vegvary noticed about him was that his hands shook. During camping trips, he had a habit of staying up night after night, staring into the campfire. When Vegvary asked him if he was having trouble sleeping, Richard shook his head. He said he did his best thinking at night.

At times Vegvary fretted that Private Jahnke might be a little too gung-ho for his own good. In his sophomore year, Richard spent so much time on various ROTC activities that his grades in other classes suffered, something Vegvary had warned the Rangers to guard against. He also had a way of carrying himself, particularly when he wore his Ranger fatigues, that provoked comments from other students, along the lines of "Who the fuck do you think you are, strat?" Instead of ignoring the taunts, Richard replied in kind. Worse, he had a tendency to bluff; Vegvary heard that he had tried to scare off one attacker by telling him he knew karate. It didn't work.

Vegvary took him aside and lectured him about grades and honor, about not losing face, about not getting your butt ripped over something that isn't important. Richard turned crimson with embarrassment and promised to do better.

The major was confident that, with a little prodding and encouragement, Richard Jahnke would emerge as one of his finest senior officers. He was a bit raw and impetuous—but who wasn't at age fifteen? Compared to the more visibly troubled youngsters, he was a model of stability. He could be aggressive, but he didn't seem particularly interested in the macho aspects of soldiering that attracted some of the other boys. Oh, he joined the rifle team at one point—the sophomores volunteered for everything until they finally found their niche—and he learned to fire the .22s, the M-16, and a few handguns. But he didn't seem *obsessed* with firearms the way some of the others did. Huddled around the fire on camping trips, other students would brag about hunting trips they'd been on, or their latest exploits on the firing range; Vegvary would talk about night maneuvers and night blindness, hand-to-hand combat, or the big guns used in the war; a voice would call out of the darkness, asking what the major thought about the seven millimeter versus the .308. But Jahnke didn't show much interest. He might have been out there listening, but he didn't say anything.

So Vegvary was mildly surprised when another student told him that there were a lot of "interesting" guns over at Richard's house.

That winter, their first winter in Cheyenne, Dad kept the thermostat turned down to save money. He bought two electric space heaters, one for his room and one for Mom's room; Richard and Deborah piled extra blankets upon their beds. On the chilliest mornings, Richard awoke at dawn and rubbed his face until he could feel the warm blood rushing to his ears, his fingers, the tip of his nose. Then he got up, removed the heater from Mom's room, and took it into Deborah's room. If his sister was awake, he sat in her overstuffed reading chair in his pajamas, the heater toasting his feet, and talked to her with the door closed. They had a great deal to talk about.

In the past few months Deborah had revised her opinion of her brother considerably. She still resented the fact that he had more freedom than she did, that he could go camping or go to movies with his friends while she was expected to stay home, aloof and virginal; but she no longer blamed him for that. That was just Dad's twisted notion that some boy was going to rape her. Richard was entitled to have some fun if he could get away with it. And it was doing him some good: he came back from his camping trips looking lean and handsome. His complexion had improved. He was getting more assertive, too, and she liked that.

They still didn't have much in common. He didn't read books, he knew next to nothing about art; all he could talk about was ROTC and that swaggering major he idolized. She didn't think much of the military—it sure hadn't done anything for Dad—but at least Richard wasn't a dumb *soldier* like some of those other clowns. He was smart, funny, and sensitive, too. The tough-guy routine he went through every time he put on his Ranger fatigues was just a big act, Deborah decided. He was really quite thoughtful, or he wouldn't bring her the heater in the morning.

She felt like she was seeing him for the first time. She knew she could help him. He was discovering girls, and she could give him some advice about that. And he was beginning to share her sense of outrage about what was happening at home. That fall everyone at school was listening to Pat Benatar's *Crimes of Passion* album, and one song, "Hell Is for Children," had made a strong impression on Richard, particularly the lines:

You shouldn't have to pay for your love
With your bones and your flesh . . .

Well, God knows, she didn't have any argument with *that*. For years she'd been trying to tell Richard that there was no excuse for the way their parents behaved. As far as she was concerned, Mom and Dad were "psychic vampires"—which, as she explained in her journal, were "creatures who look at somebody who has something extraordinary, and they think it terribly, terribly unfair that he/she should enjoy it. They are so jealous. . . . [they] hate to see others who have more than they do, and feel justified to punish them for it as a way of compensating for their own inadequacies."

What was Mom's constant nagging but the frustration of a psychic vampire? What was Dad's ridicule of Richard's involvement in ROTC—"You'll never be good for anything but shining shoes," Dad said—but the jealousy of a psychic vampire? Richard could see half the equation, but not the other half.

"You're letting that psychology class go to your head," he said.

"Richard, you're so naive," Deborah replied.

"Mom's okay," he said. "She wouldn't be like that if Dad wasn't around."

"She's terrible," Deborah said. "Look how she treats me. Look what happens when Dad's out of town. She gets twice as bitchy, she won't let me do anything. She's so damn afraid we're going to take advantage of her."

"You could try being nice to her."

"Oh, Christ. I know what's going to happen. They're going to throw you out and keep me here until I go crazy."

Whenever she started to get upset, he tried to make her laugh. He could imitate Dad's voice, his pompous, blustering way of stomping around the house, so perfectly that she would burst into giggles. But he still tried to defend Mom, and that made her angry.

One night Deborah overheard her parents as they were playing cards in Dad's room. Dad was going on and on about the little brats they were raising, and Mom was saying, "I know, I know." Deborah told Richard about it, convinced that she finally had proof that she was right. Richard merely shrugged.

"Maybe she was afraid to disagree with him," he said.

She wondered if she was wasting her breath. But sometimes it seemed like Richard did understand. One morning he told her about an argument he'd had with Mom while Dad was on a business trip. Mom recited her usual list of recriminations: I don't get any respect, you don't appreciate me, you're no angel, it takes two to tango—and finally marched off to her room. Richard fetched a .38 revolver from the gun cabinet, put it outside her door, and knocked. She opened the door. He pointed at the gun at her feet.

"If that's the way you feel about it, why don't you just shoot me," he said. "Get it over with. I'm no damn good."

Mom blew up. "Oh, that's very nice. That's just great," she cried, and slammed the door.

Richard told the story in a low voice, but he was smiling. He thought it was a hilarious trick to pull on old Mom. Deborah laughed.

In the course of her junior year, Deborah became as much of a mystery girl at Central High as she had been at Chaparral. She wasn't widely noticed, but those who did notice her couldn't figure her out. In psychology class she engaged in spirited debates with the teacher on everything from homosexuality to atheism, quoting (or at least paraphrasing) Freud, Jung, Adler, and Laing. She may not have known what she was talking about, but she sure used a lot of big words. A few of her classmates tried to get to know her better.

That took some doing. She was risking a scene every time she borrowed the phone from the empty living room, hooked it up in her room, and called someone. Dad yelled at her for tying up the line and sometimes yanked the cord out of the jack in midsentence. She promised to join other students for a pizza or a midnight movie when her father was out of town on business, but few of these outings materialized. When she did manage a rendezvous, it was usually by getting her mother to drop her off at the public library; her friends would meet her there, go for a walk or a drive, and bring her back in time for her unsuspecting mother to pick her up. Or she would obtain grudging permission to sleep over at a girlfriend's house and then join a party in progress there.

Once she felt comfortable with a new acquaintance, she wasn't at all reluctant to talk about herself. She complained that she didn't get along with her mother, that her father hated her and didn't want her to grow up. She described her father as a "Nazi survivalist" who kept plenty of guns around the house and was intent on surviving a nuclear war. With one friend's mother, a woman who was everything her own mother was not—divorced, bohemian, artistic, and "liberated"—she was more explicit. Her father beat her, she said. He used to take advantage of her sexually, too.

Her friends responded with murmurs of concern, urging upon her the same panacea Ann Landers offers to millions of newspaper readers: why not get some counseling? Deborah resisted. She didn't need counseling, she said, her parents did, but they'd never agree to it. Why not talk to them about it? her friends asked. Deborah shook her head. Her friends didn't understand; most of the time, she had the sense they didn't even believe her. They were merely humoring her.

Perhaps it was easier not to believe her. After all, her tales of being a prisoner in her own home did sound rather Gothic. And her friends quickly discovered that Deborah had a talent for exaggeration, not to mention outright lies. For example, her clothes never fit; she accounted for her rapid gain and loss of weight by telling people that she was a diabetic. That prompted plenty of sympathy, until you happened to talk to her brother about it, or caught her gorging herself on Reese's peanut butter cups. She'd talk about a dear friend in Arizona who committed suicide, and you'd think, wow, how tragic, and later you'd find out the friend never existed. So what were you supposed to think about this Nazi-father business?

One friend who had difficulty believing her was Tim McNally, a thin, dark-haired, freckle-faced senior who was one of Central's resident math geniuses. One day after school in early 1982, Deborah declined to go for a drive with McNally because, she said, she was afraid her father might see them.

"Deborah, you can't be afraid of your father your whole life," McNally said.

"Well, if you lived with him and knew him the way I do, you'd be afraid of him, too," Deborah said.

McNally dropped by the Jahnke home to visit Deborah one evening around nine o'clock. The visit was not expected, and the door was opened by an irate Richard Chester Jahnke. McNally stammered something about coming to see Richard. Jahnke looked him over and coldly replied that Richard wasn't home. After McNally left, Jahnke boasted to his daughter that "some freak" had come to the door, but he had run him off the place.

The incident apparently upset Deborah far more than it did McNally. She told him her father had stayed up most of the night, patrolling inside and around the house with a gun in his hand. She wished her father was dead, she said. McNally made some fanciful suggestions: maybe she could feed him poison mushrooms, he said. They also talked about having a bunch of friends concentrate on Richard Chester Jahnke's heart and will it to stop beating. Deborah told McNally that she didn't think that would work.

On March 16, 1982, her seventeenth birthday, Deborah had a friend call the principal's office at Central, identify himself as Richard Chester Jahnke, and explain that Deborah had to be excused from classes today; he was taking her to an appointment with the orthodontist. The friend then took her to lunch. When she got home, her father was waiting for her in the driveway.

"The school called me," he said. "I understand you went to the orthodontist today."

He grabbed her by the arm, pulled her into the garage, and threw her against the wall. With his hands wrapped around her neck, he screamed at her so loudly and angrily that she could hardly understand what he was saying. He sent her to her room.

Richard went out after dinner to run some errands and buy his birthday present for Deborah. His father told him to be home by eleven. Richard made it back to Cowpoke Road at eleven-fifteen. The garage door was down and locked. He banged on the door like a good sport; he knew Dad had to be waiting up for him.

Several minutes passed before the light snapped on and the door went up. Dad was standing in front of him, blocking his path to the house.

"You're late," he said. "Your mother was worried about you."

"Sorry," Richard said. He held up a shopping bag and tried to smile. "Look at these records I got for Deborah."

"I said, you're *late!*"

The bag went flying across the garage. Richard was propelled into the house by a series of swats and shoves. He felt like a donkey.

"Knock it off," he said.

"Don't you talk back to me," Dad said.

Richard ran to his room. Dad caught up with him there, dragged him to the floor, and began pounding on him with his fists. Richard covered his face with his hands. He was wearing a heavy denim jacket with a sheepskin lining; if he shifted his body just right, he could barely feel the blows through the padding.

"Do you like this?" he hissed.

"Shut up," Dad said.

"I'll bet you loved doing this when I was a little kid," he said. "Did you enjoy beating me up, Dad? Huh? Did you?"

"Shut the fuck up," Dad said, his voice rising.

"Leave him alone!" Deborah stood in the doorway in her nightgown. "Leave him alone, you big bully!"

Dad turned and glared at her. Richard lifted his hands from his face to see what was going on.

"You get out of here," Dad said to Deborah. "Didn't you get enough yet today?"

"Oh, that's right, go after the women now," Richard said. "Go beat on the women, macho man."

"That's right, go ahead," Deborah said. "You goddam bully."

Dad ignored her and went to work on Richard again. Richard squirmed beneath him, trying to guide the punches to the best protected areas of his torso. After a few moments of struggle he was able to push his father's weight off him and roll away. Dad pulled himself to his feet. He was breathing heavily, and a trickle of crimson was spreading across his upper lip.

"Your nose is bleeding, big man," Richard said.

"Shut up, you asshole," Dad said. He abruptly turned his back on both of them and went into Mom's bathroom to tend to his nosebleed.

Richard stood up. He felt exhilarated—in control of the battle somehow, for the first time. He didn't want it to end. He could hear Mom telling Dad to calm down, and Dad screaming at her to shut up.

"Don't tell me, go tell that little bastard," Dad hollered. "He's a goddam pain in the ass."

"Oh, no you don't!" Richard hollered back. He rushed into his mother's bathroom. Dad was standing at the mirror, holding a crumpled Kleenex to his nose. Mom was beside him, wide-eyed.

"You shut up," Richard said. "I'm not going to let you

brainwash Mom anymore. Telling her all this crap about how it's our fault. Nope. No way. You're not going to get away with it. Just get out of here.''

Mom looked like she was going to throw up. Dad's face turned deeper and deeper colors of red; he looked like a fat, balding Indian with a Kleenex up his nose, an image so ridiculous that Richard wanted to laugh. How much can I push him, he wondered, before he pops a blood vessel? How much would it take to make him turn purple? To make him explode, his fat guts splattering all over the walls?

Dad pressed the tissue to his nose, saying nothing, until the color drained from his face. Then he pushed past his son and went down the hall to his room. Richard followed him.

"You know, you really blew it," Richard said. "It could have been great. But it's too late now. We're enemies."

Dad sat on the bed and stared at the wall. He said nothing.

Three weeks later, on the sixth day of April, Jimmy Chrisman hanged himself.

Chrisman, a seventeen-year-old senior at Central High School and a second lieutenant in the Central ROTC program, had been staying in a Cheyenne group home for troubled teenagers. The first reports of his death to reach the cadets at Central stated that Chrisman had "passed away" due to a "heart condition." When the truth became known, many reacted with more surprise than grief. Few knew him well. Jimmy Chrisman wasn't a very popular cadet.

Chrisman's death was the beginning of a wave of suicides in the Cheyenne school system—four in nineteen days. The second was an East High School junior, age seventeen, an athlete who, unlike Chrisman, was well known. The third was a thirteen-year-old girl at McCormick Junior High; she walked into a crowded school lavatory and fired a bullet from a .22 automatic into her mouth. The fourth was a twenty-three-year-old teacher's aide who worked at Hebard Elementary School. None of the victims knew each other.

The deaths stunned Cheyenne. They came out of nowhere, like a sudden plague that struck only the young. You couldn't begin to come to terms with one death before there was another . . . and another . . . each as baffling as the last. And no one knew what to do; the overwhelming sense of helplessness was as frightening as the deaths themselves. Calls for suicide prevention programs in the schools were countered with pleas not to give the kids any ideas. The local newspapers were criticized for "sensationalizing" the matter. A prominent psychologist was summoned from Denver to assess the situation. Dr. Byron Barry, the superintendent of the Cheyenne school system, suggested to a *Rocky Mountain News* reporter that the suicides could be due to "three factors: nerve-wracking winds as high as 70 mph that ripped across the plains daily during the spring; increased student use of drugs and alcohol; and a widespread social breakdown in respect, love and concern."

After the news of Chrisman's death, Major Vegvary assembled the entire battalion to discuss their loss. He was aware, he said, that Chrisman wasn't well liked by many of the cadets. But what happened to Chrisman didn't have to happen again.

"The next time you feel like giving somebody a hard time, or putting them down, or not showing them proper respect and courtesy, you better think about it," he said. "That may not be what went wrong here—but we are a team, and we should be helping each other through the rough times, not making them worse."

Everyone has problems, he said. If a cadet has a problem, he or she should talk to somebody about it—go to your folks, your friends, a guidance counselor, a teacher, anybody, but talk about it. No difficulty is so great that it can't be overcome; no teenager's predicament is so dire that it justifies the taking of a human life.

"My door is always open," he said. "Dismissed."

Jimmy Chrisman's parents requested that their son be buried in his ROTC uniform. Vegvary saw to it that he was.

12

For several weeks an undeclared truce prevailed in the Jahnke household. It was as if the anger that had flared on Deborah's birthday had been expended so prodigally that the combatants were left panting in their corners, too punch-drunk and bone-weary to go another round. So they made overtures of peace. Dad invited Richard to go target-shooting with him, and Richard accepted. The two had a reasonably good time and made plans to hunt elk together in the fall.

Yet everyone knew that the peace was illusory. There were too many silences, a dumb show of the rancor that pulsed beneath the skin. The bad blood wasn't exhausted; it had merely dropped in temperature. All you could do was wait until it boiled over again. And the waiting didn't lull you into thinking the peace was real. It put you on edge.

The truce lasted until May 2, 1982.

It was the first Sunday in May. On Saturday Richard was supposed to have cleaned the basement, one of the weekly chores for which he was occasionally paid an allowance of five dollars. Instead he had spent several hours helping out at the ROTC office at Central. At noon on Sunday he was puzzling over his algebra homework when Dad pounded on his door.

"I want you in the basement," Dad said.

"In a minute," Richard said.

"Now," Dad said. "You already got your allowance. Now do your job."

Richard opened the door and tried to move past him. Dad grabbed him by the hair, pulled him down the hall, and shoved him down the stairs. It was all Richard could do to keep from plunging headlong onto the concrete below.

"Take it easy," he said.

"Do your job," Dad said. Then he left.

The basement was a mess. Boxes had been overturned, their contents scattered beneath them. Sand and feces from the cat litter box were spread liberally over the floor. Richard knew the cats couldn't have been so methodical. This is what he got for not cleaning the room yesterday, before Dad decided to spruce it up.

He began to stack the boxes. He had just started, it seemed, when Dad reappeared on the stairs.

"What the hell are you doing?"

"Dad, I have to move the boxes before I can sweep," he said.

That was how it started. Dad accused him of goofing off; a few moments later Dad had him down on the floor. He punched him in the ribs. Richard groaned loudly, until Mom finally opened the basement door and called down.

"Please stop it!" she screeched. "Can't we have a Sunday in peace?"

Mom went away. Dad's nose started to bleed. He stood up and muttered, "You keep goofing off, and you can forget about that hunting trip."

Richard glared at him. "Don't you *dare* take me on that trip," he seethed. "You do and I'll kill you!"

Then Dad was on top of him again. He flailed away at Richard with fist and open hand, oblivious to the blood puddling in his mustache.

"You little bastard!" he yelled.

Dad released him, stood up, and wiped his nose. Then he reconsidered and went after him again. Richard ran up the stairs with his father chasing him, screaming at him to get out of the house. He grabbed his tennis shoes from his room but didn't have time to put them on. As he headed for the front door, he saw his mother sitting at the kitchen table. She looked up at him blankly.

He ran barefoot down the driveway. The rough gravel cut into the soles of his feet. He sat down, slipped into his shoes, and ran on. It was a hot, listless afternoon, but he ran for several minutes. He was putting miles between himself and Dad; he was free, he was free!

The beating he'd received began to catch up with him. He slowed to a dull, aching walk. He was wearing shorts and a T-shirt and had no money. Mom and Deborah were still in the house with that lunatic. The sun was scorching the back of his neck. Yes, sir, he was about as free as they come.

For hours he wandered through Cheyenne, seeking out the older section of town, where the pavement was dappled with bursts of cool shade from rows of cottonwoods and poplars. At length he came to Major Vegvary's house, where he had attended ROTC meetings and barbecues. Major's jeep was parked in the driveway. Richard stood on the sidewalk as if rooted there.

My door is always open, Major had said.

Yeah, but how would it look, he wondered. What would Major think? BAD-ASS RANGER RICHARD JAHNKE COMES CRYING TO MAJOR; SAYS DADDY BEAT HIM UP. Hell, no.

He wanted to ring the bell. He also wanted to make tracks out of there. He sat on the curb, sobbing softly to himself, waiting for something to happen.

Around four o'clock that afternoon Robert Vegvary left his house to attend to some paperwork at Central High School. He was accompanied by his fiancée, Betty Fulton. The couple got into Vegvary's jeep, rounded the hedge at the end of the driveway, and saw Richard Jahnke sitting on the curb. Vegvary pulled up beside him and asked him what he was doing there.

"I guess I'm in trouble," Richard said.

"What kind of trouble?"

"I had a fight with my dad."

"We're going to school," Vegvary said. "Hop in."

Richard climbed into the back seat. Vegvary noticed that he had a mark above his cheekbone and what appeared to be scratches on his knees and elbows. The major pulled away from the curb.

"What happened?" Vegvary asked.

"He—well, he kind of hit me," Richard said. His voice was low and shaky.

"Your dad?"

"Yeah."

"This ever happen before?"

"It's been going on for a long time. Maybe once a week, or once every other week, I guess," Richard said. "I hate his guts," he added hotly. "All he does is hurt us."

"He hits the rest of your family, too?"

"My mom, he used to. He still hits my sister sometimes."

"Your mom ever try to do something about it?"

"She blocks it out."

"What do you mean?"

"Well, I try to talk to her about it, and she acts like nothing's going on,'' Richard said. "She says, 'What are you talking about?' "

After they arrived at Central, Vegvary took Richard into his office and asked him to remove his T-shirt. He saw red marks on the boy's rib cage and shoulder—bruises too fresh to have turned blue—and more marks all over his back. Also on the back were two distinct palm prints, one high, one low, as if someone had pressed down on him forcefully with both hands.

Vegvary told him the bruises would have to be reported to the sheriff's office. Richard balked at the suggestion, but Vegvary held fast. It wasn't just the right thing to do, he said; it was the law. As a reserve deputy sheriff and as a teacher, he had an obligation to report such things.*

"What happens after you call them?" Richard asked.

"They'll take your statement," Vegvary said. "They can't do anything if you won't make a statement."

"I don't know if I should do that. My mom is really afraid of him. She doesn't want anybody to know about this."

Vegvary suggested that Richard call his mother first, ascertain that she was safe, and let her know the steps he was taking. The major stayed in the office with him as he dialed his home.

Deborah answered the phone. Richard asked her if she was all right.

"I'm fine," she said. "What's going on?"

"Put Mom on," he said.

Maria came on the line. "Where are you?" she asked. "I thought you were in your room."

Richard started to cry. He wanted to scream, *But you saw me leave! You heard Dad yelling at me to get out! Didn't you?*

"Mom, I can't take it anymore," he said. "I'm going to stop it."

"What?"

"I'm going to report Dad for child abuse."

---

*Every state requires that doctors, teachers, and other professionals report cases of suspected child abuse to the local authorities. Wyoming's child protection statute is stricter than most. It states that *any person* "who knows or has reasonable cause to believe . . . that a child has been abused or neglected . . . shall immediately report it. . . ." However, Wyoming's statute, like that of most states, doesn't specify how this "requirement" is to be enforced; it is rare that an individual is penalized for failing to report.

"What are you talking about?"

"I'm going to sign a statement at the sheriff's office. I'm going to tell them how he's been treating us. Somebody has to. I think you should, too."

"Hold on a minute," she said. "Your father's right here. He wants to come pick you up. Hold on, I'll put him on and you can tell him where—"

Richard hung up. He'd tell him where to go, all right.

Vegvary made the call to the sheriff's office. Deputy Robert Bomar came to Central and drove Richard to DePaul Hospital for a physical examination, then to the sheriff's office, where half a dozen photographs of his injuries were taken. When the photographer was through, Bomar interviewed Richard. Vegvary sat in on the session.

Bomar's interview style was strictly professional, so detached and unemotional as to suggest boredom. His laid-back, world-weary manner bothered Richard. It was as if he'd seen it all; nothing that Richard could say could possibly impress him. But then, Richard wasn't sure that what he had to say was of much importance, anyway. He told Bomar that his father was a "tyrant" who had beat up on the family for years. But when he tried to come up with specifics, he drew a blank. He had difficulty remembering what had happened only a few hours ago, let alone what happened on Deborah's birthday or for a dozen years before that. He kept thinking about the way Mom talked on the phone; what *was* he talking about, anyway? Was he "abused" or just a crybaby? Was he going crazy?

Bomar talked about the beating as a "one-time incident." Did that mean he didn't believe there were other times, or only that he couldn't prove them? Richard wasn't sure. He knew Bomar wasn't going to arrest Dad. If he'd been a little younger, five years old maybe, or if his injuries were more serious than a few tiny bruises on his back, it'd be different; sure, he could understand that. (In fact, under Wyoming law, Richard Jahnke barely qualified as a battered *child;* the statutory definition of "child" was "any person under the age of sixteen." Richard was two months shy of his sixteenth birthday.)

Yet it would be difficult to say what, in his own mind, Richard hoped the sheriff's office would do. He wanted to stop it. He wanted Bomar to . . . well, open a case . . . collect the evidence in secret . . . talk to Mom, talk to Deborah . . . then prosecute Dad for child abuse (wasn't that a felony?), throw him in jail if necessary, just so long as it all stopped forever. But he didn't tell Bomar that. He sat silently while Bomar was joined by a short, doll-like woman named Pat Sandoval, the Department of Public Assistance and Social Services (DPASS) employee on emergency call with the sheriff's office that afternoon. The deputy and the social worker began to explain Richard's "options" to him.

One, he could go home alone and think about what he wanted to do next. Bomar would drop him off out of sight of the house, and Dad didn't have to know he'd been to the sheriff's office. No report would be filed, no officers would call on the family until Richard contacted them again.

Two, Bomar could go home with him and tell Dad that if he ever got violent again, they'd "throw his ass in jail." This was the "fear of God" approach, which, in some cases, was sufficient to make the offender think twice before he or she struck again.

Three, they could initiate an official investigation right now. His family would be called down to the sheriff's office and interviewed. Then the case would probably be turned over to DPASS, which would send a social worker out to the house "within days" to talk to everyone and recommend appropriate action, such as family counseling.

Richard liked the idea of getting something on the record now. But, he asked, did his father have to be notified? Bomar and Sandoval insisted that he did; if they filed a report, Dad had to know about it. And if a report was filed, they said, Richard should consider staying in a foster home for a three-day "cooling-off period" before returning to the house.

The first two homes Sandoval called were full. Bomar told Richard not to worry; he could stay in the county jail, in his own private cell—unlocked, of course—if nothing else was available. Richard didn't see what staying in jail for three days would accomplish—he was the victim, wasn't he? And foster homes . . . Jimmy Chrisman hanged himself in one of those places. He told Sandoval not to bother calling a third facility. He'd go home to his family.

Did that mean he still wanted to make an official complaint?

"Go ahead and do it," he said, "but be sure you do it good."

*　　*　　*

This time Dad answered the phone. He listened patiently, said little, and hung up. He turned to his wife. He seemed amused.

"That was the sheriff's office," he said. "The little prick has reported me."

"What does that mean?" Maria asked.

"It means we're going down there," he said. "Get your coat. They'll want to see your *bruises,* come on, let's go. I swear, that kid's in his own fucking little world. I'm gonna have a talk with that son of a bitch major."

He saw Deborah staring at him and scowled.

"Come on," he said, "you're coming, too."

Dad showed Bomar his Treasury Department badge and sat down to talk with him as one lawman to another. He explained that he had "spanked" Richard because he was "acting like a little boy," but then his son had threatened to kill him, and, well, he lost his temper. He complained to Vegvary that his son was spending too much time on ROTC, staying up late to shine his shoes while neglecting his chores and homework. Vegvary assured him that he didn't want any "professional cadets" in his corps. The major promised to speak with Richard about meeting his other obligations.

No one asked Maria any questions. She avoided meeting any-one's eyes and started crying when Sandoval mentioned the possibility of placing Richard in a foster home. Richard himself seemed acutely embarrassed by the idea. Deborah was asked if she'd had "any problems" with her father that day. She said she hadn't.

Bomar summarized his observations in his report:

1. Excessive force was used in the corporal punishment of Richard John Jahnke by his father.

2. His father admits that he "probably" used too much force in disciplining his son.

3. Mr. Jahnke appears to have an explosive temper and a hard time controlling it.

4. Mrs. Jahnke remained quiet throughout the entire inter-view, allowing her husband to communicate for both of them. Appears to be completely dominated by her husband.

5. Debra *[sic]* Jahnke, victim's sister, appeared cheerful, in good health, and stated she had not been struck this date by her father.

They gave the family a few moments alone in a conference room. Richard looked reproachfully at Deborah and Maria—as if to say, "Why didn't you back me up?"—but no words came out. At last Dad broke the silence.

"Look what you're doing to your mother," he said.

Maria studied the floor.

"You're ruining my marriage," Dad continued.

"Hey, don't blame *me*," Richard shot back. "I'm not out to get you. I just want us to be more of a family."

"Is that so?" Dad shook his head. "Look, you little bastard, I don't care what happens to you. You want to go live with that little dwarf—what's her name, that social worker? Go ahead. That would be your family. It'd be like living in a sideshow. You'd fit in perfectly."

Richard turned his back on him and opened the door. Bomar and Sandoval were waiting in the hall.

"I think we're ready to go now," he said.

The Scout was parked outside. Richard got in with the rest of his family. No one said a word. Dad stopped at Saint Mary's and insisted that they all go into the church for a few moments. He emerged in high spirits. On the way home he volunteered to make spaghetti for dinner.

When she was finally alone with her brother, Deborah murmured, "I really admire you for trying. I'm sorry I'm such a wimp."

"That's okay," Richard said. "Maintain."

The next day, in accordance with school policy, Vegvary informed the principal of Central High School, James Godfrey, and the school nurse, Caryl Marion, about the child abuse report. He also briefed several trusted cadets, including Greg Porter, urging them to "keep an eye" on Richard and to report any suspicious injuries to their commander. The semester was almost over, but Vegvary figured that the cadets who joined Richard on Ranger outings and other summer activities would know about any further beatings. In fact, Porter already knew about yesterday's incident. Richard had shown him the bruises.

However, for all practical purposes, the matter was out of the hands of the school authorities and the sheriff's office. As Caryl Marion explained to Richard when she met with him that day, his case was being referred to social services. A worker from Laramie County DPASS would soon be visiting the family; if Richard had further problems with his father, he should contact the worker. He could, of course, call the police in an emergency, but the responsibility for follow-up lay with DPASS.

Richard's complaint was one of 131 cases of suspected child abuse or neglect investigated by Laramie County DPASS in 1982.* It arrived at a time when the agency had only two caseworkers assigned full-time to its child protection intake unit. In the late 1970s the Wyoming legislature had "reallocated" social funding across the state to deal with the increasing "impact problems" of its oil-and-gas boom towns; Cheyenne lost three DPASS social workers to Gillette, Rawlins, and Douglas, respectively. Richard Jahnke's case was assigned to Frank DeLois, a "family/community services specialist" with nearly five years of experience. At the time he received the report on Richard Jahnke, DeLois had been working exclusively on child abuse cases for several months—an average of 40 to 45 ongoing cases a month, almost twice as many as the 25 cases-per-worker standard recommended by the National Association of Social Workers.

A few days after the abuse report was passed on to DPASS, DeLois phoned the Jahnkes to arrange a group interview. He

---

*Ever since a 1961 symposium, "The Battered Child Syndrome," brought the issue to public attention, statistics concerning child abuse have been notoriously difficult to collect, analyze, or extrapolate from. One feels merely half-safe armed with the figures most widely cited by researchers, as the only consensus to emerge is that the research is still grossly inadequate. A 1980 "national incidence study" released by the U.S. Department of Health and Human Services estimated that 1.1 million cases of suspected child abuse and neglect are reported annually. Less than half of the cases are ever substantiated; in any event, the government figure is an unreassuring one, since most cases, perhaps as many as nine out of ten, are never reported at all. Other studies suggest that three-fourths of the perpetrators are the victims' "caretakers" (in most cases, their natural parents), and that the vast majority of abusive parents—again, perhaps nine out of ten—were themselves abused as children.

Almost one-third of the reported cases involve adolescents, but child protection agencies usually assign top priority to those that involve toddlers and infants; presumably, teenagers are in a better position to escape or defend themselves. However, a Colorado study of 200 teenage victims found that only one in three attempted to run away; only one in five attempted to fight back.

finally met with Richard and his parents at their home on Monday, May 24, three weeks after the initial interview at the sheriff's office. From what he saw in the report, DeLois regarded the case as a "one-time substantiated incident," strictly low priority, and nothing he saw that evening at 8736 Cowpoke Road contradicted that opinion. He chatted amiably with the Jahnkes for forty-five minutes and left satisfied that he had offered the necessary, delicate blend of encouragement, advice, and gentle warnings against further violence. However, DeLois did not speak to Richard outside of his father's presence. He didn't meet with Deborah at all; she stayed in her room, listening to records, the entire time he was in the house.

His report sums up his impression at the time:

5-24-82. This worker met with Mr. and Mrs. Jahnke and Richard. They live in a beautiful home on the far north-side of Cheyenne. Mr. Jahnke is employed by the Internal Revenue Service. This family was very pleasant and cooperative. Mr. Jahnke stated that he realized that his means of discipline in this instance was unacceptable. He stated, as did Richard, that their relationship had been good since this incident. Although being very quiet, Mrs. Jahnke agreed with this. This worker advised this family of the counseling services available in Cheyenne. I further stated that further child abuse complaints could possibly bring legal action. . . . This worker told Mr. Jahnke that I had been informed by the school . . . that Mr. Jahnke was welcome to get involved with Richard's school activities. Richard is very involved in ROTC and will participate in a summer program.

Throughout the summer DeLois received no further complaints from the family, school officials, or any other person acquainted with the case. His only other contact with any member of the Jahnke family came five months after the initial interview. On October 28, prior to closing out the case as "inactive," he phoned the Jahnke residence and spoke briefly with Maria. According to DeLois's file, Maria assured him that her husband "is taking the time to listen to his son, and that they are getting along fine."

Twenty days later, Richard and Deborah Jahnke were in jail.

The body of Richard Chester Jahnke lay in a Cheyenne funeral home. A shaken Frank DeLois sat at his desk and stared at his meager notes from a low-priority case, wondering what went wrong.

13

Michael Brinkman didn't know what to do.

Brinkman, a tall, gangly, mop-haired senior, started hanging around with Richard Jahnke in August of 1982. Brinkman wasn't a Ranger, but he was captain of the ROTC ceremonial detachment. He and Richard became close friends. They went to movies together. They called up girls and gave them grief. They talked shop.

Sometimes they hung out at Richard's house. Brinkman met Richard Chester Jahnke, who invited him to go shooting with him and his son. Brinkman told Richard he thought his dad was okay.

"It's all an act," Richard said.

Richard told him about the abuse report. He was extremely angry with the sheriff's office.

"I went to them for help," he said, "and they said they could put me in jail for three days. What kind of help is that?"

Brinkman agreed that wasn't much help.

Richard seemed upset with Vegvary, too—not as upset as he was with the sheriff's office, but a bit miffed. He was under the impression that Major had shot his mouth off to the entire battalion, telling everyone that Jahnke was an abused child and that they should look out for him. Richard felt that other cadets were looking down on him now. Brinkman knew that wasn't true—hell, this was the first he'd heard of any abuse report—but Richard thought Vegvary had betrayed him.

"I went to him for help, not gossip," he said.

Richard's relationship with his commander began to show further signs of strain in the fall. One of the problems, Brinkman realized, was Richard's promotion to command sergeant major, which made him the highest-ranking NCO, in charge of all freshmen. It was a position of great prestige and responsibility, and Richard took it very seriously.

Conflicts arose immediately. One officer complained to Vegvary that a group of freshmen had ignored a direct order, saying they took orders only from Sergeant Jahnke. Other officers claimed to have been ordered out of Jahnke's class when they came to make announcements. Some felt that he was treating the freshmen girls better than the boys, trying to impress them. He was being disrespectful to his superiors. He was on a power trip. He was a real pain in the ass, Major.

Richard told Vegvary that staff officers were bursting into his classroom and trying to "boss my freshmen around." Perplexed, Vegvary tried to explain to him about the proper exercise of the chain of command. The two could not agree on the source of the problem. After several more complaints, Vegvary called a meeting of the staff officers.

"Okay," he said, "I want this understood. They are not *his* freshmen. From here on in, if Jahnke mouths off to an officer, you drop him for ten push-ups. And if I catch you not doing it, I'll drop you."

A few weeks later, on Monday, November 1, Richard got into an argument with the student leader of the Rangers and quit the team. That same day, Vegvary announced an unusual midsemester promotion. Effective immediately, Richard would move up to rank of second lieutenant and the position of battalion adjutant, a desk job. The promotion, which had been in the works for some time, was Vegvary's way of eliminating the friction Richard was causing as command sergeant major. But Richard regarded the move as retaliation for his decision to quit the Rangers. He wasn't playing Vegvary's search-and-rescue game anymore, so Major felt he had a right to take the command of the freshmen away from him. Richard was furious. He started talking about quitting the corps entirely.

Richard told Brinkman that Major was really coming down on him now. Telling him what a good guy his father could be. Telling him they ought to be friends. Major just didn't get it. Dad was still an asshole. Dad was pissed because Richard outranked him now—which sounded pretty flaky, sure, but the truth is old Dad never made it higher than staff sergeant.

Things seemed pretty casual at the Jahnke house whenever Brinkman visited. But from the way Richard acted when his father was around, Brinkman gathered that he was still afraid of him. And sometimes Richard didn't look so good, like maybe he'd been crying or something. Brinkman began to worry. He wondered if he should tell Vegvary that something was wrong. But Richard was a tough nut to crack. If you tried to draw him out on the things he'd said about his dad, he changed the subject. It was like, hey, I don't want to deal with this stuff right now . . . are we out to have a good time or not? And sometimes he said his dad was being pretty cool. He even bought Richard an expensive leather jacket. Brinkman saw it.

So Brinkman could tell Major . . . tell him what? He didn't have any *proof* Richard was still getting hit. He could tell him about his suspicions . . . no, Richard would freak.

Brinkman told Richard, hey, you know you can come stay with me if you need a place to go. Brinkman knew that Greg Porter had made a similar offer (in fact, Greg had jokingly told Rich that if his dad came after him with his mini-14, well, Greg had a 12-gauge that would take care of *that*.) Richard just nodded. He seemed embarrassed.

That fall Deborah was looking forward to her ceramics class at Central. It was terribly important, she told herself, to be doing something creative, and she could think of nothing nobler than shaping clay with her hands. Besides, she knew several students in the class. They were people of some sensitivity and intelligence, like her friends Eric Lee and Chris Lawrence.

Eric was a large, gentle, good-humored senior. Deborah had met him in her psychology class the previous year. He gave her a ride home from school sometimes. She insisted that he drop her off in front of the Hains' house so her parents wouldn't see him bringing her home. When he asked why, she told him about her father. You could tell by his wide eyes that this big, bespectacled teddy bear didn't really believe anyone could be that cruel. Still, he was nice enough to listen to her. He even called her on the phone to talk about everything and nothing. With her other friends, Deborah usually did the calling.

Chris Lawrence was Eric's friend. He was blond, blue-eyed, keenly interested in music, and exasperatingly shy. Deborah had a huge and unrequited crush on him. She wanted to have Chris and Eric over to the house for pizza someday when Mom and Dad weren't home.

But the best reason to take ceramics was the teacher, Eve Whitcomb, a tall, assertive sculptor who had taught art classes in Cheyenne for nine years while raising two boys on her own. A

lot of the more cultured, intellectual people at Central really liked
her. From what she had heard, Deborah figured that Eve Whitcomb
might be the sort of teacher she could talk to.

Whitcomb noticed Deborah from day one. In fact, she soon
came to the conclusion that Deborah Jahnke had to be the most
screwed-up kid she'd ever seen. She was so *childish*, like a
first-grader, really. She couldn't stay with a task for more than
five minutes before something distracted her. And that laugh, so
loud and hysterical, a laugh that wasn't really a laugh; sometimes
she laughed at nothing at all. Whitcomb lost track of the number
of times she had to tell Eric, Chris, and Deborah to quit playing
and get to work. It was clear that the boys were egging Deborah
on, to get a reaction out of her; at the same time, they didn't
know what to make of her. Whitcomb doubted that Deborah had
any real friends. She would come to class in ill-fitting clothes,
hair not quite combed, and haul out a deck of tarot cards, talking
a blue streak the whole time about art and repression and psychic
vampires. Her entire way of carrying herself seemed like a
screaming bid for attention.

Before long Deborah was coming around to work on her
ceramics projects during her study hall. Whitcomb had a planning period that same hour, and she soon realized that Deborah
was dropping in to visit with her more than to work with the
clay. Such an attachment wasn't unusual in Whitcomb's experience; for some reason, kids seemed to follow her around like
baby ducks trailing after their mama. She had practically adopted
students from time to time, letting them stay at her house for
weeks or months when they were having trouble at home. But
Deborah's hyper, off-the-wall behavior was getting on her nerves.
One day, when she was alone with Deborah and the girl was
kneading clay as if she were trying to squeeze juice out of it,
Whitcomb decided to say something.

"You know, Deborah, you seem like an awfully nervous
person," she said.

"Oh? What makes you think that?" Deborah replied.

"Just look at you. I watch you in class. You start working on
something, tear it up, throw it in the slop bucket, and start on
something else. You do that constantly. We must have a dozen
unfinished pieces of yours around here."

Deborah laughed shakily. "I get the impression you don't like
me very much."

"That's not it," Whitcomb said. "I just react to you differently than I do with most kids. There's something about you. I think there's a big conflict between what you show on the outside and what you really feel on the inside."

That was how it started. Within a few weeks Whitcomb knew more than any other outside party about Deborah and her problems: how she hated going home, how her father beat her and kept her cooped up in her room, how her mother was "brainwashed" by Dad, how there was no way out. Whitcomb knew that Deborah had a "dramatic" way of expressing herself, but she tended to believe her. It all rang true. Her own childhood had been very similar.

Whitcomb had grown up in Lincoln, Nebraska, and she, too, had dreaded to go home from school each day. You couldn't really call it a home; it was a place of violence and degradation. She had run away several times, only to be caught and sent back. She had finally escaped after graduating high school. The experience was one of the reasons she had become a teacher. She felt a strong sense of empathy with the misfits, the outcasts, the kids who were just marking time, as she had done. If she could reach just one, she told herself, and keep him going one more day, it would be worth all the extra time she spent with her students.

Deborah gave her some of her journal writings and short stories. Before she could read them, Whitcomb first had to decipher them; Deborah's handwriting was a vertiginous track of loops and swirls. What impressed Whitcomb the most wasn't the degree of physical violence described but the near hysteria of the author. Deborah recounted dreams that were absolutely gruesome: cities full of corpses, virgins fleeing from Nazi fathers who hacked their limbs off. She confessed that she depended on her brother a great deal—and, perhaps, resented him a little, too. Practically everyone else had rejected her, and she was aching for a friend:

I have no home, I have no "family." . . . "Family" is somebody who earnestly loves you and laughs with you rather than at you. "Family" would never throw you out in the gutter and wish you ill just because you have not followed their path in the world nor will they scorn you or beat you or feel disgraced if you ever dared to make a mistake . . .

Half the time I'm on the verge of going emotionally haywire. . . . I meander about wondering why nobody finds me
interesting. I don't understand what it is. I'm warm, intelligent, I love to laugh—it's the ultimate euphoria, and it isn't
even drug-induced (well, maybe sometimes) . . . no one even
looks at me. I was tappeling away on the typewriter and I
typed up my name. I couldn't believe how meaningless it
was—13 bloody letters—it's my life, my being . . .

The more she heard, the more she read, the more Whitcomb
was convinced that Deborah was indeed going haywire. She was
a rubber band stretched in a dozen directions and about to break.
It would take much more than a pat on the back from a sympathetic teacher to lead her out of this angry, fragmented existence;
she needed professional help. But when Whitcomb broached the
subject to her, she discovered she was up against a wall of fear.

"No way," Deborah said.

"Look, I'm an artist, not a psychiatrist. You need some real
counseling."

"My parents would find out. My father would go wild."

"Well, there are steps you can take. There are agencies in
town set up to deal with this sort of thing."

"You don't know my father. He'd come after me. I swear he
would."

Whitcomb went to other faculty members. At least one teacher
who knew Deborah agreed that she needed professional help, but
getting it wasn't that easy. A psychiatric referral for a student
under the age of eighteen was a tricky matter. There were
screening committees, forms in triplicate, and, of course, the
whole process required the permission of the parents. It seemed
as if the best Eve could do, for the present, was to commiserate.

Curiously enough, given her own background, it never occurred
to Eve Whitcomb to report Richard Chester Jahnke for child
abuse. In spite of Deborah's stories about her father's violence,
Whitcomb didn't think of her as an abused child—not physically
abused, anyway. She didn't come to school with obvious injuries: no black eyes, no missing teeth. The possibility of physical
harm didn't seem nearly as serious as her mental and emotional
condition. Whitcomb's primary concern was that Deborah might
try to kill herself.

But as she quickly learned, you can't have a minor removed from her home just because her parents are driving her crazy.

Thanks to hard work, determination, and cost-of-living adjustments in the federal pay scale, Richard Chester Jahnke's salary as an IRS agent had increased to almost $36,000 a year. It was barely enough to get by on. Half of his paycheck was devoured by mortgage payments on the house; the rest went to fuel bills, grocery bills, insurance, taxes, the operating costs of three automobiles, and a dozen other expenses that were a constant source of argument between him and his wife. He told Maria she didn't know how to manage money; she told him he spent too much money on his damn guns. The one point they agreed upon was that they were strapped. When Deborah started talking about the places she'd like to go to college, Dad put her in her place. She would live at home and go to Laramie County Community College, he said, and he wasn't sure they could afford that. She might have to go out and work for a year or two.

Deborah complained bitterly to Richard. It wasn't fair, she said. All her life she had dreamed of the day she would turn eighteen and book on out of here. Now the vampires wanted to send her to LCCC—Last Chance Cowboy College, as the kids at Central called it—and live at home. God forbid! She'd run away first. She'd get her own apartment. But how was she supposed to support herself? She had no skills, no experience. She didn't even know how to drive. What was she going to do, pump gas on Lincolnway?

"They're going to keep me here forever," she moaned.

"We'll work something out," Richard said.

They talked often now, the two of them huddling in Deborah's room with the door closed. As the days grew shorter and the space heaters were brought out again, they talked in private two or three times a week. Most of the time one or the other was angry with their parents, and that was what they talked about.

They kept their voices low. They had to be careful; even when Dad wasn't around to hear them, Mom was. And Mom was getting exceedingly weird. She seemed to think they were conspiring against her. One day she came into Deborah's room while they were talking and demanded that Richard get out. Richard wanted to know why.

"Because I say so, that's why," she said.

"I've got as much right here as you do," he said.

Mom launched into him: how dare he talk back to her, nobody listens to her, they treat her like dirt. She started thowing things at him. He took the first couple of volleys and then left.

At other times, when Dad was out of town, Mom got into ferocious arguments with Deborah. Once, when words failed her, she grabbed her daughter by the arms and started shaking her. Richard had to separate them. When Dad came home, Mom told him the kids weren't showing her any respect.

They did their best talking when neither Mom nor Dad was around to bother them. When they were truly alone together, they talked about how Richard was going to kill Dad. Sometimes Deborah brought it up; sometimes Richard did. But Richard had better ideas than Deborah did. He'd thought the matter through.

One way to do it, he said, would be to leave a note for old Dad. Something like: *Dear Dad: We hate each other, okay? So let's get it over with. I've taken the Scout and one of your assault rifles to such-and-such place in the hills. Meet me there and we'll settle things man to man.*

Christmas would be a good time to do it. The family was supposed to fly to Chicago; Dad's parents were paying their way so they could all be together for the holidays. But Dad didn't want to go. He said he was too busy. So Richard would find an excuse to stay home, too. Then he and Dad would be alone in the house.

Or he might challenge Dad when they were out hunting. They'd already be armed, and that would make things easier. Richard could make it look like a hunting accident.

Or—this was his sister's suggestion—Richard could wait until the next time Dad got pissed at Deborah. It wouldn't take much to get him started. While he was punching her, Richard would come in with a gun. *Adiós,* Dad. Gee, officer, he was attacking my sister, what was I supposed to do?

Deborah found Richard's ideas entertaining. Her own tended to be a little more fanciful, involving the use of improbably big knives or exotic poisons—an indication, perhaps, that she didn't take the discussions all that seriously. It was a lot of talk, like all the rest: Mom talked about leaving him, Deborah talked about killing herself, Richard talked about killing Dad. None of it ever happened. None of it ever would. They were all cowards. Deborah knew that Richard would never be able to ace Dad. It was just another fantasy.

Still, a girl could dream, couldn't she?

That fall Richard spent a lot of time on the phone with a girl he'd met at school. She was the friend of a girl Richard had dated and lost a few months earlier. Richard was trying to figure out what had happened, maybe get back together with his former flame, and her friend was glad to act as a go-between. She called him often, and they talked for hours about "relationships" and the difference between "puppy love" and "the real thing." Richard soon found himself telling her things that he'd never told any of his girlfriends.

A man from the sheriff's office later asked the girl to recall what Richard had said, and she wrote down what she could remember.

"He told me that he was getting fed up with his dad," she wrote. "He told me a lot of times that his dad would hit him and blame him for things that didn't even concern him. He also told me that if it went on much longer that he would either kill himself or his dad or run away. I told him he should move out. . . . He said that he was planning to run away but that he didn't have enough money, so he was going to get a job. . . .

"Recently, he had been telling me that he was getting fed up with everything and had nowhere to turn because of the way Major [Vegvary] was acting towards him, and he felt he couldn't confide in Major anymore the way he used to. . . ."

One time when she called, early in October of 1982, Richard answered the phone in an angry tone of voice. He had been arguing with his father. He told her he was standing in his mother's bedroom with his dad's commando .45 in his hand. He was on his way to the family room, where Dad was watching television, "and he said he was finally going to do it. I told him to unload the gun and put it back because it scared me."

By the time Richard got off the phone, he no longer felt like doing it. He had lost the mood.

14

Over the second weekend of November an arctic cold front descended on Cheyenne, dumping five inches of snow on the city and dropping the temperature with the wind chill factor to twenty degrees below zero. The long, unpredictable Wyoming winter, which had been known to recede for a balmy Christmas, roar back in March, and linger on into April, had arrived in earnest.

On Thursday, as the storm was drawing closer, Richard Chester Jahnke stayed home from work. The attic needed more insulation to keep the chill out, and he had a rifle stock awaiting alterations on the workbench he had built in the basement. He took the next day off, too. Maria had never seen him happier. With the two of them alone in the house and the rest of the world lost in a sea of white flakes, the setting was almost as romantic as their first days of marriage, half a continent away and so many years ago.

But when the kids came home from school, everything changed. Mr. Hyde was back in town. Life was hell, buster.

On Friday, November 12, Richard took time off from school to apply for a part-time job at a Cheyenne supermarket. The store manager told him he'd call that afternoon to let him know if he got the job. Richard went shopping with his mother. When he returned, he asked Dad if anyone had called for him. Dad said he didn't have any idea. He wasn't going to answer the goddam phone on his day off.

On Saturday, November 13, Deborah rose early and went into the kitchen to fix herself some tea. Dad walked in as she was pouring the hot water into a cup. Dad told her to pour it out.

"You're not good enough to use the good china," he said.

"It's not the good china," Deborah said. "It's the old set. There's just a few pieces left, and I use them all the time."

"Don't give me any lip, sister, just do as you're told."

She changed cups and was carrying the tea back to her room when Dad blocked her way in the family room.

148

"Just look at you," he said.

"There's nothing wrong with me," Deborah snapped.

"Your hair looks like shit."

"I just combed it."

"Like hell."

"I did!"

"Hey!" Dad's finger hovered in her face. "Don't you talk back to me, you fucking bitch. I'm sick of you looking like a slut. Now you go comb your hair."

"I won't. I don't deserve for you to call me names—"

The first punch landed on her shoulder. The second caught her in the throat. The hot tea leaped onto her breast. She lost her footing. Dad pulled her up by her hair. She cried out, as much from the scalding as the ripping of strands of hair from their roots. Dad adjusted his grip on her hair and began to slap her face, telling her to shut up.

Then Richard was behind him, telling him to leave her alone. With an unexpected surge of strength, he pulled Dad off her and shoved him up against the wall. Dad wrestled to get free, but Richard had him firmly pinned. Instead of retreating, Deborah turned and started hitting her father in the side with her fist. It was the first time she had ever struck him.

"I hate you!" she shrieked. "You're a monster, and I wish you'd die!"

Everyone started shouting, trying to drown out the others. It was a peculiar stalemate, with Dad and Richard pressing on each other's shoulders and Deborah flailing away ineffectively on the flank. Somehow Maria managed to insert herself into the fray. She stood between her children and her husband and begged them all to calm down. Dad turned his back on them with a familiar air of disgust and stomped off to his room.

Richard brought paper towels from the kitchen. Mom took them and began to sop up the spilled tea. He knelt beside her.

"Mom, wasn't that great?" he asked.

"What are you talking about?"

"We stood up to him. See, if we all stick together, he can't do a damn thing."

Maria looked at him. It was the long, sad, withering look of a scrupulous referee rejecting a bribe from the home team. He thought this was *great,* being disrespectful to his father was just great, something to boast about. The boy had no shame.

Without a word, she stood up and took the cup and saucer into the kitchen.

That afternoon Maria and Deborah braved the storm to go to the Frontier Mall. They saw a matinee at the multiscreen cinema almost every Saturday—good, bad, indifferent, it scarcely mattered, as long as they hadn't seen it before. Movies were the chief excuse to go out in Cheyenne, but there were never enough of them.

On the way Deborah began to talk about the fight that morning.

"I really think Dad's going to lose it one of these days," she said.

"Please, honey, let's not talk about it anymore," Maria said, her eyes on the slick road. "Let's have some peace for a change."

"You know, I see him outside at night sometimes. I see him outside my window. I can't get any sleep."

"Please stop it," Maria said. "All you can talk about is how unhappy you are. Well, I have problems, too. I'm going crazy listening to all of you complain."

"But he's so awful."

"I don't want to hear another word," Maria said.

Eric Lee spotted Deborah standing beside a cookie stand at the mall. She told him she had "lost" her mother. The two had gone window-shopping, separated, and now Deborah wasn't sure what movie her mother was planning to see. This wasn't the first time she'd lost track of Mom, she said. Sometimes Mom drove off without her, and she had to call home for a ride after the movie.

Eric invited her to go downtown with him to a record store. As they were walking to his car in the parking lot, she told him about the fight that morning. She said she wished her father was dead.

"You know," she said, "it's really too bad Richard didn't kill him when he was young enough to get away with it."

Eric wasn't sure if she was joking or not. Nobody else he knew said things like that.

After they went to the record store, Eric offered to drive her home. Deborah became alarmed and insisted that he drive her back to the mall. He pointed out a teacher's house as they drove by it. Deborah asked him to show her where Eve Whitcomb lived. He took a detour to go by it.

"Now show me your house," she said.

"That's too far out of the way," Eric told her.

He took her back to the mall.

On Sunday, November 14, Deborah was sitting in her favorite chair, listening to classical music on her stereo and looking out across the snow-covered plains, her feet propped on the window-sill, when Dad banged on her door.

"What's this shit you're listening to?" he demanded.

"Dad, this isn't shit," she said. "I don't listen to shit. These are Bach cantatas."

"Turn it down."

"If it's any lower I won't be able to hear it. I don't see how you can hear it clear across the house."

He seized the arm of the turntable and dragged it across the record. Then he took the record and whipped it against his knee. He had to bend it with both hands before it would break.

"Someday you'll learn to do what you're told," he said.

Deborah started to cry.

"God," she sobbed, "it's like you want to pretend I'm not here. You don't want to see me, you don't want to hear me, I'm just supposed to disappear."

"Put a lid on it," Dad said. He slammed the door behind him.

For much of the rest of that day Mom and Dad played chess in Dad's room with the door closed. Richard and Deborah stayed in their rooms. That evening Deborah began to write a letter to her creative writing instructor, Ann Garcia:

11/14/82 10:42 p.m.

Ms. Garcia,

I'm not sure if I'm fair in doing this to you, but I'm really lost. It confuses me why it is that most people can't take very much of me. I don't have any close friends, although it's obvious that there are people who like me. Sometimes I sit in my room; and I want ever so badly to shower everybody with affection. I'm somebody who needs to share my thoughts and feelings. I want ever so terribly to be able to love somebody; except there isn't anybody around; and it frightens me . . .

The letter was never finished.

On Tuesday, November 16, Richard got up before dawn. He had a busy day ahead of him: a full schedule of classes beginning at seven o'clock, followed by two funerals of military veterans (he had joined the ceremonial rifle team) and an open house at Central High tonight. Some of his friends would be manning the ROTC display, but Richard had volunteered to help check parents' blood pressure at the health occupations table.

Dad came into the kitchen as he was making breakfast.

"What the hell are you doing up at four-thirty in the morning?" Dad asked.

"It's almost six," Richard said.

During her study hall Deborah dropped by the ceramics studio to see Eve Whitcomb. She began to pace and talk quickly, leaping from subject to subject. When Whitcomb went upstairs to check on the kiln, Deborah followed her, becoming more agitated by the moment. Whitcomb was afraid she was going to break the freshly fired pottery to smithereens. She decided to have her student teacher take over her next class for her. It was time to do something about the walking time bomb in front of her.

"Look, you should be telling all this to a counselor," she said. "Are you ready yet?"

To her surprise, Deborah said that she was. Whitcomb took her to see Lee Everling, guidance counselor for the senior class at Central. Deborah poured out her worries about having no friends, being trapped at home, and having no future. At one point she mentioned that there had been a "fistfight" at home on Saturday. But she didn't dwell on the incident. The discussion revolved around her fears of being unpopular and not being able to afford to go to college. When Everling asked her if a conference with her parents would be a good idea, her answer was an emphatic "No!"

"Deborah, are you feeling suicidal?" Whitcomb asked.

Deborah laughed her familiar nervous laugh. "God, no," she said. "I'm afraid of dying. I'd never do anything that foolish."

"What is it you want to do with your life?" Everling asked.

Deborah looked at Whitcomb. "You're really going to think this is stupid, but I want to be a teacher," she said.

Whitcomb told her she didn't think it was stupid at all. Everling assured her that, if she really wanted to go to college, there were loans and scholarships she could apply for. The notion seemed to cheer her a great deal. He promised to make arrangements for her to talk to the school psychologist about what was bothering her.

Deborah hugged Eve outside Everling's office. Shortly before three o'clock, she walked into her ceramics class and told Eric Lee she was going to find a way to go to college.

Richard Chester Jahnke called his wife three times that afternoon. The first time he called to remind her to be ready at five o'clock for an evening of wine and song, a celebration of the twentieth anniversary of that magical moment in Santurce.

The second time he called to tell her the bank was going to refinance the house; the interest on the mortgage would drop from seventeen percent to twelve percent. Maria agreed that this was wonderful news.

"Now we've really got something to celebrate," he said. "Be sure to be ready at five."

"Okay, I'll fix the kids something quick to eat," Maria said.

"Let them fix their own dinner," he snapped.

"It'll only take a minute," Maria promised. "Richie has to go to open house at school, and I know he'll want to eat early."

"Who cares what he wants? You like waiting on that little prick?"

"I'll be ready at five," she said.

The third time he called to ask what she was doing. She told him she was washing and ironing.

"See you at five," he said.

Maria went into the kitchen to start making dinner. She had so much to do before he came home.

At 4:15 P.M. ROTC battalion commander Eric Needham gave Richard a ride home from school. Despite the fact that he had just attended two funerals on opposite sides of town, firing blanks from an M-16 to honor the departed veterans of combat, Richard seemed to be in a good mood. He and Needham discussed Needham's recent birthday party, which Richard had missed. Needham let him off in the driveway, and he vanished into the garage.

At half-past four Eric Lee called Deborah. They were on the phone only a few moments when Lee heard loud voices in the background. A woman was screaming; another voice chimed in from time to time, lower, more muffled. He couldn't make out the words.

"What's going on?" he asked.

"Oh, my mom and my brother are arguing again," Deborah said.

The noise stopped a couple of minutes later. Then someone was calling Deborah's name.

"I've got to go eat," she said.

Lee said he'd call back later.

Shortly after seven o'clock, Robert Vegvary left the ROTC display table at Central's open house to take an urgent phone call from the Laramie County Sheriff's Office. The dispatcher was trying to locate Richard John Jahnke. There had been a shooting at the Jahnke residence, he explained. Vegvary sought out Donald Morris, the instructor of Richard's health occupations class, and asked him if he'd seen Richard. Morris told him he hadn't.

"I can't understand it," Morris said. "He said he'd be here."

Vegvary returned to the phone and gave the dispatcher the address of another of his cadets, Richard's current girlfriend Donna Haese.

"He might turn up there," he said.

Janet Booth was watching television in her basement with a friend when a news flash came on. A man had been shot at his home in north Cheyenne, the announcer said. Details at ten.

Booth and her friend looked at each other. A shooting! It was hard to believe. People in Cheyenne didn't get shot.

Booth had worked in Cheyenne for many years. For two years, from early 1979 until the spring of 1981, she had been a secretary in the Cheyenne office of the Internal Revenue Service. At first she'd liked the job a great deal. Then the new criminal investigator had arrived from Phoenix, a short, pushy, disagreeable man who seemed to hate everybody. He went off on his own at break times and never socialized with anyone. Other agents said the man belonged in a much bigger office, where he could be among his own kind—New York, maybe. Booth and the other secretary assigned to the criminal division called the new man Little Napoleon.

When he was first transferred, Little Napoleon called Phoenix often to talk to his wife. Booth heard him swearing at her over the phone, treating her like an imbecile. Booth told the other secretary that if her husband ever talked to her like that, she'd go right through the wire and wring his neck.

One day Booth got into an argument with Little Napoleon about the type of travel voucher he was using. He acted like he knew everything. Booth, not known for her temper, became so angry that she wadded up the voucher and threw it at him. The two hardly spoke to each other after that. She was glad to leave the office.

The report of the shooting didn't give any names. It did, however, mention Cowpoke Road. Booth remembered that Little Napoleon lived on Cowpoke Road.

"Gee," she said, "I wonder who got ticked off at Jahnke."

Some of the cadets were drinking beer at one student's house when a man on the radio said something about a shooting.

"Cowpoke Road," one of the cadets said. "Isn't that where Jahnke lives?"

"Richard finally shot his dad," said another.

Everyone laughed.

PART FOUR

JUSTICE

WIZARD: The gods are pleased with you. They
are going to watch the battle.
CONAN: Are they going to help?
WIZARD: No.
CONAN: Then tell them to stay out of the way.

—from *Conan the Barbarian*
(screenplay by John
Milius and Oliver Stone)

15

On the morning after her husband died, Maria Jahnke made the first of many trips downtown to the Colonial East, a one-story building that, with its pale red brick and white trim, bears a striking resemblance to the Jahnke house on Cowpoke Road. The building was home to a Baskin-Robbins ice cream parlor, Ace Investigations, and the law firm of Trierweiler, Bayless, Barrett, and McCartney. Maria wasn't looking for ice cream.

At the county jail that morning a deputy had told her that her children were being questioned and couldn't have visitors. When she returned home and told her newfound friends, the Hains, what had happened, George Hain had urged her to get a lawyer. That advice was soon seconded by James Martin, chief of the IRS's criminal investigation division for Colorado and Wyoming, who had driven up from Denver to offer his condolences and collect Special Agent Jahnke's effects. Martin had known Jahnke only slightly and had few details about the shooting. Still, everything he'd heard suggested that the Jahnke children were going to need the best legal assistance they could find.

But Maria didn't know any lawyers. Lawyers belonged to a strange world she knew little about, the world outside her family and her housekeeping, her trips to the grocery store and the shopping mall. She did know that lawyers were expensive, and she wasn't at all sure she could afford one. Richard hadn't left a will. She knew she had some equity in the house and about a hundred dollars in the bank, no more. Richard had told her that she was the beneficiary of his life insurance policy—God knows, the man was always a good provider—but she had no idea what the policy was worth. Martin promised to expedite the insurance claim and get the money to her as soon as possible.

Hain suggested that Maria talk to his lawyer, Dick Trierweiler, about the estate; Trierweiler would surely be able to recommend a top-notch criminal lawyer for the kids. Maria was then escorted to Trierweiler's office by the Hains and Carolyn Wheeler, the woman who had sold the Jahnkes their house. Wheeler had called the Hains that morning to offer moral support; she figured she was one of the few people in Cheyenne who had actually met Maria prior to the shooting. She was right.

The entire entourage—Maria, George and Sandy Hain, and Carolyn Wheeler—wound up in a meeting with an equal number of attorneys: Dick Trierweiler, James Mitchell, Louis Epps, and James Barrett, the chief criminal lawyer of the firm. The subject of money came up immediately, and there was no hedging on the figures. To prepare a homicide defense for Richard and Deborah, the firm would require a retainer of $15,000 up front. Trial expenses would raise the total cost to at least $25,000, and even at that price, the attorneys would probably be taking a loss. Maria said she didn't know if she could raise that kind of money. The possibility of a public defender was discussed. Maria wavered. By the time the meeting broke up, she thought that she had retained counsel for her children. As far as the attorneys were concerned, though, they still hadn't been hired; Epps and Mitchell had merely agreed to visit the jail and make sure the kids were all right. Barrett wouldn't be able to talk to his prospective clients for a couple of days; he had a grand larceny case going to trial in Rawlins in the morning.

Some confusion over the Jahnkes' legal representation persisted for several days. Mitchell and Epps visited the jail twice that day and cautioned Richard and Deborah not to talk to anyone; Deborah told them she'd already given a statement. Maria was kept informed of the attorneys' visits and was under the impression that her children were holding up well. (Actually, after a phone call from a friend of Deborah who was concerned about her ''high-strung behavior,'' one of the jailers had ordered a twenty-four-hour suicide watch on both teenagers. The jail had also brought in a psychologist from the Southeast Wyoming Mental Health Center to evaluate them.)

The following morning Richard and Deborah were led through a gauntlet of reporters and television cameras to their initial court appearance before Laramie County Judge Robert Allen. Mitchell and Epps waved from the back of the courtroom; since they weren't officially representing the pair, they could do little else. Maria was conspicuously absent—for no other reason, apparently, than that no one had informed her of the proceeding. Standing alone before the judge in their prison uniforms, the two teenagers puzzled over the affidavits they were required to fill out in order to obtain a court-appointed attorney. In response to questions about his net worth, Richard stated that he didn't own a home and had no money at the time of his arrest.

"You don't have anything at all, do you," sighed Judge Allen.

"No, sir," Richard murmured.

"Do you know if your mother can come up with some money?"

"No, sir."

Allen declined to set bond until an attorney could be appointed or hired to represent the teenagers. He sent them back to their cells with the now-familiar warning that anything they said could be used against them.

It would be another four days before Maria signed the papers officially retaining James Hays Barrett to represent her children on charges of conspiracy and first-degree murder. By that time Barrett had arranged bond for Richard and Deborah—two $50,000 recognizance bonds that required Maria's signature but no posting of assets—and Maria had discovered that her husband had been insured at five times his annual rate of pay. He had left an estate of more than a quarter of a million dollars.

Much of the money would be spent defending the son who took his life.

The name Barrett is one to conjure with in Western legal and political circles. Jim Barrett's grandfather Frank served one term as governor of Wyoming, two terms in the U.S. House of Representatives, and one term in the U.S. Senate, where he was one of Senator Joseph McCarthy's staunchest supporters. His uncle and namesake, the Honorable James E. Barrett, is currently a member of the U.S. Tenth Circuit Court of Appeals. James B. Hays, a maternal great-uncle, was the first chief justice of the Supreme Court of the Territory of Idaho.

Frank Barrett, Jr., Jim's father, broke ranks and became a prominent surgeon in Cheyenne. Jim Barrett had also been attracted to medicine at one time, but eventually abandoned his studies after six years of college in three different states, an education frequently interrupted by the chance to work on a railroad or behind a bar. In 1970, with a wife and three children to support, he entered law school at Creighton University in Nebraska. To his surprise, he liked it. He returned to Cheyenne and worked in the state attorney general's office before going into private practice in 1976.

Tall, lanky, and hollow-cheeked, always puffing on a Marlboro, fidgeting with his glasses, or brushing his hair back from his forehead, Barrett has reminded more than one client of a wayward graduate student rather than an attorney. His aw-shucks way of talking—he is fond of exclamations such as "heck" and "by golly" and seems to delight in reminding people that lawyers are just folks—adds to the impression of a certain vestigial youthfulness. Yet his easy drawl acquires a gracious, almost courtly tone before the bench, a tone of courtesy and restraint, of eminent reasonableness, which can be far more effective than the impassioned pleading of a crusader. He is older and more experienced than he seems. At the time the Jahnke case dropped into his lap, he was two weeks shy of his thirty-eighth birthday, practically the same age as Richard Chester Jahnke.

Barrett was curiously suited to defend what would become the most famous criminal case Cheyenne had ever seen. His very first murder case had involved representing a man charged with fatally beating his two-year-old stepson; the man was found guilty of involuntary manslaughter. He subsequently defended another man who killed his eight-month-old son (second-degree murder) and one who shot and killed his wife in a domestic dispute (involuntary manslaughter). At the time the Jahnke shooting occurred, he was in the process of preparing a defense for an eighteen-year-old Arapaho Indian boy who stabbed to death his abusive father on the Wind River Indian Reservation, a case that, due to the differences between federal and state jurisdictions, would be heard in juvenile court and receive scarcely any publicity. The cases had provided Barrett with some background on family violence issues and, most important, a few insights into the nature of the so-called abusive personality.

Of course, he didn't have any evidence yet that the Jahnke parricide was abuse-related. In the initial interview, Maria Jahnke had said nothing along those lines; in fact, she seemed to find it hard to believe that Richie had killed his father. Yet Barrett had a hunch. The newspapers had been content to quote the district attorney's official complaint, characterizing the crime as an "ambush," an "execution," an act of "revenge" by bloodthirsty teens. The language of the complaint left little doubt as to who had done it or how. The only mystery was why. Revenge for what? On Friday, November 19, Barrett returned from his case in Rawlins and found the confirmation he was waiting for, in a front-page headline in the *Wyoming Eagle:*

CHILD ABUSE CALL ANSWERED
AT HOME OF SLAIN IRS AGENT

Someone in the sheriff's office had leaked news of the abuse report filed last May. Sheriff Dennis Flynn was quoted as confirming that an investigation had taken place, but he declined to provide further details.

Barrett picked up Lou Epps and headed for the jail. A tall, soft-spoken, thirty-two-year-old black man from Milwaukee, Epps had met Barrett while serving as a base attorney at Warren Air Force Base three years earlier. He had just left the service and was in the process of joining Barrett's firm when the Jahnke case came along. Like Barrett, Epps had some experience with family violence cases from both sides of the fence. He had prosecuted and defended servicemen accused of beating their children. He had also won acquittal for a woman who had shot her estranged husband when he returned to assault her.

Epps briefed Barrett on the way to the jail. Deborah and Richard Jahnke each had a cell to themselves, he said. They weren't your typical teenagers; in fact, he'd never seen a brother and sister who were so different from each other.

"Are you going to take the case?" Epps asked.

"I think so," Barrett said. "Let me talk to them first."

Deborah began pacing the moment the attorneys walked into her cell. She twirled strands of hair between her fingers and talked nonstop. Barrett had difficulty understanding her. Almost every statement was punctuated with the word "Buddha," her substitute for the word "God"—as in, "I mean, Buddha, you know, I don't understand why they're keeping us, you know, locked up like this, Buddha!" Barrett put his arm around her and hugged her.

"Relax," he said. "It's going to be okay."

Richard scarcely looked up when they arrived. He said little; when he did open his mouth, his teeth chattered and his hands shook. He was like a dog backed into a corner, sullen and resigned, waiting for the whip. Barrett asked him a few questions, but the answers were as brief as Richard could make them. He wasn't volunteering a thing.

"Richard, tell me about your dad," Barrett coaxed. "What kind of guy was he?"

Richard shrugged. "Sometimes he was pretty good. Sometimes he was pretty bad," he said.

"Did your dad beat you?"

"Yeah."

"Did he beat your sister?"

"Yeah."

Following his hunch, Barrett went on, "Did he molest your sister?"

"Yeah."

Barrett decided not to press for details, not yet. He had seen clients behave like this before. Most of them were terribly worried about what was going to happen to them; but a few, the true martyrs, tried to hold everything in. They acted as if they were beyond rescue: I'm finished, no point in talking about it, let's get it over with. You had to get them out of jail and give them something to fight for before they'd cooperate.

In Richard's case, it was probably going to take a lot more than a bond hearing and a hot meal to get some answers. As he left the jail, Barrett wondered how difficult it was going to be to break through Richard's defenses. Everything he had read on the subject suggested that abuse victims have strong resistance to talking about their experiences because the memories are so painful. But he would have to try, whether it hurt or not. Because if Richard Jahnke didn't stop hiding the pain—if he didn't face it, feel it, let it pour out of him like blood oozing from his veins—then he'd never be able to tell a jury about it. And if he didn't do that, he might spend the rest of his life in prison.

The following morning, a sunny Saturday, several dozen mourners gathered at the Church of the Holy Trinity for the funeral mass of Richard Chester Jahnke. The casket, draped with an American flag, stood on a platform at the front of the church. It was one of the most expensive caskets available in Cheyenne; Maria had gone to the funeral parlor with Sandy Hain and picked it out herself. She told Sandy she wanted her husband to go first class.

Maria sat in the front pew with the deceased's mother, Theresa

Jahnke, and his brother Robert. There were flowers from IRS colleagues in Phoenix, and a handful of men in dark suits and sunglasses who had come to pay their respects in person. Central High students, teachers, and neighbors sat behind them; Maria knew hardly any of them. The press kept their distance, particularly after Robert Jahnke ordered a photographer from the *Denver Post* out of the church. At the last moment Deborah entered from a side door, escorted by Sheriff Flynn and one of his deputies. She sat apart from her mother and didn't speak to her. The mass began.

"We have done easier things than what we are about to do here today," said the Reverend Carl Beavers. "It is important to express our sense of sorrow, of emptiness at the tragedy that has happened."

A smaller crowd gathered for the burial at Olivet Cemetery. The ROTC ceremonial detachment from Central High School fired a twenty-one-gun salute to honor the deceased. (The salute, generally reserved for the burial of combat veterans, was the result of a mixup: Captain Michael Brinkman was under the mistaken impression that Rich's father had served in the Korean War.) The flag was folded and given to Maria, and the casket was lowered into the earth.

Afterward Maria went to the jail with Robert and Theresa Jahnke. It was the first time Maria had seen or spoken to her children since the night of the shooting. Robert and Theresa hadn't seen the children since their last visit to Cheyenne more than a year ago. No one was eager to talk about the shooting; Maria's in-laws had refrained from talking to her about it even when they were alone. The visit with Richard deteriorated into an exchange of strained pleasantries, punctuated by long silences. The visit with Deborah was even more awkward.

"We've joined the Holy Trinity church," Maria announced.

"Mom, you know I'm not a Catholic anymore," Deborah said. "When I get out of here I'm going to convert to Zen Buddhism."

"You're going to church," Maria snapped.

"Oh, it's all so phony," Deborah murmured. "When I die, I don't want a big church service like that. I don't want some priest who didn't even know me telling everybody what a good person I was. I want my friends to say something."

"It was a beautiful service," Maria said. "It's what he would have wanted." She turned to Theresa. "Did you see all the flowers from the people he worked with? So many flowers."

Robert and Theresa flew back to Chicago the next day. Deborah didn't tell them what she would later tell others about the funeral: that she had gone, not out of love or even from some nagging sense of obligation, but because she was having trouble accepting one incontrovertible fact. She went to Dad's funeral, she said, because she didn't believe that he was dead. She thought that seeing the casket might persuade her that he was.

Richard and Deborah Jahnke were finally released on bond after a week in the county jail. One reason for the delay was the difficulty of locating foster homes for the pair. Even before he knew much about the case, Barrett had assumed that it wouldn't be a good idea to send Richard and Deborah back to the house on Cowpoke Road. Judge Allen agreed.

Deborah went home with Eve Whitcomb, a logical, if somewhat reluctant, candidate. Whitcomb had been involved in the case from the beginning, ever since she had received a phone call from Eric Lee on the night of the shooting. Lee had told her that Chris Lawrence had just called him and said he'd met up with Deborah while bicycling in north Cheyenne. Deborah had told Chris this wild story about her brother killing her father, and Chris wasn't sure if he believed her or not. She was looking for a warm place to stay for the night, so Chris took her to a stairwell in the Westgate Apartments and left her there.

Whitcomb, Eric, and Lee Everling, the counselor who had met Deborah only hours earlier, spent half the night searching the halls of the Westgate complex for Deborah. They didn't find her. The trio went to the sheriff's office, where Whitcomb extracted a promise from a deputy to call her as soon as they located the girl. The first news she had, however, was a phone call from Deborah herself the next morning, a crying, half-coherent plea for help after she had been questioned and arrested. As Maria had done before her, Eve went to the jail to try to see Deborah and was turned away at the front desk. She returned that evening with a lawyer and held hands with the girl through the bars of her cell.

Yet when Barrett and Epps approached her about becoming Deborah's temporary guardian, Whitcomb hesitated. Recently remarried, she had a new husband and two teenage boys of her own at home. She wasn't sure how her family would react or if she could handle the responsibility of "supervising" someone like Deborah. *You don't understand,* she wanted to tell them, *this is the most screwed-up kid I've ever seen.* But Deborah didn't have anywhere else to go, and the authorities were as eager as the attorneys to find a place for her; having a seventeen-year-old female as one of its most famous inmates wasn't exactly great publicity for the county jail. Whitcomb finally agreed to give it a try.

Richard was harder to place. After making a few inquiries, Barrett decided to take Richard home with him; the youth would have to shuttle back and forth between the Barretts and the Eppses until they could find someone else brave enough to take a mad-dog teen killer into their home. It would be Barrett's responsibility to see that his client not only received the best possible legal representation on charges of first-degree murder and conspiracy, but did his American history assignments while he was on "temporary leave" from school.

The next few weeks were the busiest of Barrett's career. He had to try to get to know the Jahnke family as well as he knew his own. He had to assemble the cast of characters for the defense, including witnesses, doctors, and private investigators. And he had to prepare several motions on behalf of Richard and Deborah, starting with a motion to transfer the case to juvenile court.

The proposed move to juvenile court would be a crucial battle, for several reasons. In an adult court, Richard and Deborah could expect to face an adult jury and adult penalties, including the possibility of a life sentence in an adult penitentiary. Juvenile court was another world, one governed by the philosophy that the court was acting not only in the best interests of society but as the juvenile's "protector" or substitute parent. Juvenile court offered the same constitutional guarantees to a defendant as adult court, but the juvenile proceedings were closed to the public and the press. And the juvenile court's powers of punishment were severely limited; the court's jurisdiction ended when the defendant turned twenty-one. A juvenile court judge couldn't possibly sentence Richard Jahnke to more than five years in a juvenile facility.

The motion to transfer the case would lead to a hearing, at which time Barrett could challenge the notion that a minor accused of homicide should invariably be tried as an adult. In making such an argument, Barrett fully expected to meet with strong opposition from the district attorney-elect.

The office of Laramie County District Attorney had just been created in the November election. Officially, it wouldn't exist until January, but the man who occupied the post was no stranger. Tom Carroll had spent most of his life in Cheyenne; for the past twelve years he had been the county attorney. He was a fifty-eight-year-old Democrat who had served eight years in the state legislature and now had no political ambitions beyond the scope of his new job, which would allow him to concentrate full-time on criminal prosecution for the first time in his career. Barrett had first met him twenty years ago, when Carroll, then in private practice, had defended an eighteen-year-old hell-raiser on a "driving under the influence" charge (eventually reduced to a fine for speeding). The defendant's name was James H. Barrett.

Barrett had come up against Carroll rarely since that case, but he regarded Cheyenne's first professional prosecutor as a formidable adversary. A short, dapper man with a graying mustache, Carroll bore a slight resemblance to William Faulkner. He was a sharp, polite, prowling interrogator who could be lethal on cross-examination. He had a reputation for trying his case on rebuttal, after the defense had rested. And he had a devoted staff, notably Deputy District Attorney Jon Forwood, a tall, bearded 1976 graduate of the University of Wyoming Law School. Forwood's enthusiasm for prosecuting quite possibly exceeded Carroll's own zeal. Barrett suspected that the sensational rhetoric of the official complaint, which suggested that both Richard and Deborah had planned the "execution" of their father like professional assassins, was Forwood's work.

Barrett's first move was to waive a preliminary hearing to determine if there was sufficient evidence to have Richard and Deborah bound over for trial. Barrett knew there was plenty of evidence, including the autopsy and ballistics reports, Richard's fingerprints on the shotgun, and Deborah's interview with detectives Greene and Fresquez. Nothing would be gained by giving Carroll a chance to present it before a defense could be prepared.

The next hurdle was the arraignment. Barrett made discreet inquiries about the possibility of a voluntary transfer to juvenile court, to be followed by a plea of guilty to a reduced charge, an arrangement that would probably land Richard in a juvenile facility for a few months or years. The response from Carroll's office was a flat refusal. Any plea-bargain agreement would be made in adult court, with adult consequences. And even if Richard Jahnke agreed to plead guilty to a lesser charge, Carroll would refuse to make any recommendations regarding sentencing; he didn't feel he had any right to tell a judge what to do. The district attorney's stance left Barrett with no choice but to appear with his clients before the Honorable Joseph Maier on December 3, Barrett's birthday, at which time both Richard and Deborah pleaded innocent to all charges.

Judge Maier, a white-haired, sixtyish juror with an aloof, owlish demeanor, presided over the First District Court of Wyoming. At the time of the arraignment, he was scheduled to hear all motions in the Jahnke case; he would also be the trial judge if the case ended up in adult court. Barrett promptly asked Judge Maier to excuse himself from Richard's case. (At the time, a sitting judge could be "challenged" in Wyoming without showing cause, and disqualification was usually automatic.) The request was a bid to ensure separate trials for Richard and Deborah. Having one trial instead of two would save the county some money, but Barrett saw it as a distinct disadvantage. The evidence against Richard and that against Deborah would be inextricably linked, and one might be dragged down by the case against the other—guilt by association, as it were. With two judges involved, there would have to be two trials, and Carroll would have to prove his case twice.

In compliance with Barrett's request, Maier appointed Judge Paul Liamos of Newcastle to hear Richard's case. Liamos, a crew-cut, bullet-headed, no-nonsense ex-Marine, was known for his brisk courtroom manner. He often made lightninglike rulings on pending motions and heard testimony at nights and on weekends in order to wrap up cases on schedule. Maier would continue to be the sitting judge in Deborah's case.

Separating the cases had other consequences as well. It would be unethical for Barrett to continue to represent both Richard and Deborah. A clear conflict of interest would arise if, say, a plea bargain was offered Deborah, contingent upon her testifying against Richard, or vice versa. To avoid even the appearance of impropriety, another attorney had to be found to represent Deborah—the easier case, in Barrett's mind, to give up. Barrett figured he knew just the right man for the job.

Terrence Wayne Mackey practiced law out of the seventh floor of a bank building in downtown Cheyenne. His office was across the street from the sheriff's offce, an institution Mackey once sued on behalf of a visitor who had been raped by a trustee in the county jail. When the jury awarded the rape victim a sizable cash judgment, Mackey found himself buttonholed by the livid sheriff of Laramie County.

"When I die, I hope they bury me face down," the man seethed, "so you can kiss my ass."

Such sentiments were not uncommon among those caught in Terry Mackey's courtroom machinations. He and Jim Barrett were both family men, both roughly the same age, but there the resemblance ended. Barrett's family was steeped in the law; Mackey was the son of a sheepherder, the first of his family to go to college. Barrett was tall, quiet, and lean to the point of gauntness; Mackey was short, broad-chested, and downright cantankerous. And while Barrett reasoned with jurors as one decent fella to another, Mackey upbraided them, inspired them, begged them, filled them with his own indignation at the vile misdeeds, the gross betrayals of sacred trust and holy law, perpetrated by his opponent. He was a fighter who had mixed it up with Tom Carroll for years; he wasn't always successful, but he had managed to outfox Carroll on appeal several times. He wasn't the sort of man who could be intimidated by the dour Judge Maier or the sort of press the case was starting to attract. Barrett thought he was perfect.

Terry Mackey joined the defense team two weeks after the arraignment. The same day, Richard and Deborah began ten days of psychiatric evaluation at the Denver Children's Home, a short-term residential treatment facility. Barrett hoped to present sufficient testimony about the teenagers' mental and emotional condition to persuade both judges that their cases belonged in juvenile court.

Of course, the evaluations had a second purpose as well. Depending on the results, Barrett or Mackey might plead his client not guilty by reason of insanity. But neither attorney held much stock in an insanity defense, for several reasons. First, the legal definition of insanity in Wyoming was very narrow; it demanded a readily identifiable mental defect or deficiency. Even if a Denver psychiatrist found that one or both of the teenagers had been insane at the time of the crime, the opinion would probably be challenged by the notoriously skeptical doctors at the state hospital in Evanston.

Second, the insanity defense was increasingly unpopular with the average citizen. The national furor over the recently successful insanity plea of John W. Hinckley, Jr., would-be assassin of President Reagan, had made it almost impossible to find prospective jurors who weren't openly hostile to the insanity defense. Any lawyer who attempted it had better have a drooling, babbling maniac for a client, preferably one with fifty distinct personalities in his pocket.

Third, and most obvious, neither Richard nor Deborah seemed to be insane. Despite Deborah's history of eccentric behavior, both of the Jahnkes struck Barrett as decent, responsible teenagers who had been through a shock and were pulling out of it. Troubled, yes. Disturbed, maybe. Deranged, no. Indeed, the more Barrett learned about the case, the more he came to regard Richard's actions as entirely logical—that is, according to the logic of an abused adolescent. It was a truism, he was finding out, among psychiatrists who had studied parricide cases: *most of the kids who kill their parents don't do it because they're crazy; they do it because their parents are killing them.*

The idea that the "execution" of Richard Chester Jahnke could be considered an act of self-defense had occurred to Barrett from the very beginning. The notion became more and more attractive as other options were examined and rejected; in Barrett's opinion, it was certainly more viable than the insanity defense. Yet to argue that Richard shot his father in self-defense would entail showing that the boy believed he was "in imminent danger of death or serious bodily harm," presumably as a result of years of physical and mental abuse, and that argument had its own risks.

Such a defense would be without precedent in the state of Wyoming. Courts in other states had recognized that child abuse and wife-beating can be mitigating factors in domestic homicides. A few had even recognized the "battered woman's syndrome," a term coined by Dr. Lenore Walker, a clinical psychologist, to describe abused women's low self-image, "learned helplessness," and common perception that their abusers were "beyond the grasp of the law." The syndrome had been cited to help explain why some women stay with their abusers and ultimately kill them when they can no longer endure further punishment. However, in Wyoming's one previous brush with the battered woman's syndrome, the trial judge had refused to accept Dr. Walker as an expert witness, while leaving open the possibility that expert testimony such as hers might be admissible in other cases.

Furthermore, most of the battered women who had won acquittal in other states didn't plead self-defense. They pleaded temporary insanity under a "diminished capacity" statute. Wyoming had no such statute; the state didn't even have a justifiable homicide law.

Pleading self-defense posed other problems as well. Barrett would have to give a jury plenty of hard evidence to support Richard's and Deborah's claims of years of physical, mental, and possibly sexual abuse. Yet no crime was more private, or more elusive, than the one Richard Chester Jahnke had inflicted on his family. The abuse report filed with the sheriff's office was a mighty weapon for the defense, but it was practically the only documentation that Richard's father had ever beat him. Barrett had obtained copies of Deborah's journals, the ones the police had seized, and read them with increasing sadness. It was obvious that the author had grown up in a violent home; but given the angry tone of the journals, Barrett wondered if they might prove to be of more use to the prosecution than the defense. What the defense needed were witnesses to the abuse, and witnesses were scarce.

Barrett started with his client's mother. Maria clearly wanted to help her children, but as Barrett quickly discovered, she felt an eerie loyalty to her dead husband as well. It pained her to speak ill of him; her recollections were vague, confused, and quite different from those of Richard and Deborah. In her first interview with the private investigators Barrett had hired, Maria had said that, prior to moving to Cheyenne, her husband had beat her perhaps once a year. The children insisted that it was more like once a week. Other details shifted with each succeeding interview. Barrett wasn't sure if she would be an asset in the murder trial of her son. Like her children, Maria was a victim of family violence, but she was also the grieving widow of Richard Chester Jahnke.

Other relatives had little, if any, helpful information. Anticipating the defense's efforts to put the late Richard Chester Jahnke on trial for child abuse, Detective Tim Greene had interviewed the

deceased's parents, brother, and sister. All of them insisted that
they had never seen any evidence of abuse during their infrequent
visits with Richard's family. Theresa Jahnke had acknowledged
that her son seemed to get "upset" easily after his return from
Korea, but she'd never seen him raise a hand to his children.
When Greene raised the ticklish question of whether Richard
Chester Jahnke had been raised in an abusive environment, both
parents firmly denied it; Richard John Jahnke, the victim's
father, could recall only one instance in which he had struck his
son. Subsequent digging by Barrett's own operatives revealed
little of interest.

As for Maria's mother, Virginia Rodriguez, Barrett didn't see
any point in putting her on the stand. The woman didn't even
know how her son-in-law had died. Maria had told her mother
that Richard was killed by someone he was investigating. Safely
tucked away in Puerto Rico, Virginia would remain ignorant of
the true circumstances of the crime throughout the trials and the
national publicity that followed.

But what about the Jahnkes' teachers, neighbors, and classmates? In the past few months, Robert Vegvary and Eve Whitcomb
had learned of the Jahnkes' plight, but what about all the years
before that? Private investigators and sheriff's deputies took turns
questioning possible witnesses in Cheyenne and Phoenix. Barrett
himself confronted one of Richard's former gym teachers on a
Scottsdale playground because he was convinced the man knew
more about the case than he was telling. In almost every
instance, the information gleaned was hearsay or idle speculation
about the father's "bad temper"; no one seemed to have much
firsthand knowledge of child abuse in the Jahnke family. If they
did, they weren't about to admit it. After all, every question
carried with it an implicit reproach: if people knew that the man
was abusing his family, then why didn't they do something?

In the end, Barrett's case hinged on what the Jahnkes themselves would say. Most of all, it hinged on Richard. He was the
only one who knew what he was thinking and feeling when he
went into the garage that night; he was the only one who could
show the jury the kind of fear that stalked his home. But Richard
wasn't talking. He was still being incredibly tight-lipped, even
with his own attorneys.

For long, dreary December afternoons, Barrett and Epps ganged
up on him in the firm's law library. One of the attorneys would

gently prod him with questions; the other would rip into each answer, challenging him, calling him out. It was a variation of the good cop/bad cop routine used by police officers everywhere.

"What did your father call you?" Barrett asked.

"Leather Lips," Richard murmured.

"What was that?"

"Leather Lips," he said, a little louder.

"How'd you feel about that?" Epps asked. He crouched over Richard, their noses almost touching. "Did it make you feel good?"

"No."

"Did it make you feel mad?"

"Sometimes."

"If I called you Leather Lips, would you get mad at me?"

"You're not my dad," Richard said.

When they were successful, Richard would become upset and blurt out something useful, some shame-ridden detail they had never heard before. He would end his tale sobbing, and Barrett would pat him on the back. That's okay, Richard, he would say, it's okay to cry, we know you're not a sissy.

Then they would press on. They didn't have much time; this wasn't a one-year therapeutic program. Christmas had already come and gone, a dismal Christmas wrapped in one of the worst blizzards in years. The hearings to transfer the case to juvenile court were only days away.

It was strange to wake up at the Barretts' house and find everyone going about their business. Barrett and his lovely wife Robyn and their twelve-year-old son and the two gorgeous teenage daughters acted like he belonged there. Nobody bothered him or hollered at him to do something. Barrett had promised there would be no legal stuff at home, and that was the way things went.

It was strange to be surrounded by so much noise and commotion—cheerful, everyday noise. He was used to outbursts of maniac noise, followed by those terrible silences that were as bad as any of the fighting.

It was strange to unfold the morning newspaper and see some dorky yearbook picture of himself plastered all over the front page. It wasn't just embarrassing, it was frightening. The person in the newspaper was . . . well, such a *kid* . . . that wasn't him. Was it?

He spent his days at the firm. That was what Barrett called the law offices: *let's go to the firm and talk it over*. Sure thing, Jimmy boy.

He liked Barrett. The first time he saw him, Richard thought, awww no, he's just out of law school! But Barrett was the same age as Dad. Bizarre.

Barrett was nothing like Dad. The first day at the firm, he ran out of cigarettes. He fished a buck out of his wallet. "I think we can trust you for half a block," he said. And his infamous client left the firm totally unsupervised, walked right past a cop car, and bought a pack of Marlboros at the Coffee Cup Cafe, thereby violating the terms of his bail as well as every law known to man and God forbidding the purchase of tobacco by minors. Damn!

Epps was okay, too. A little cagey, a little tough to figure out, but basically okay. Epps drove him home sometimes. The first day Richard was out of jail, Epps started talking about the case in the car.

"Let me tell you what Jim and I think might have happened," Epps said. "We think you may have gone into the garage to confront your father, to tell him he had to stop behaving that way. But when you saw him coming, you got scared and opened fire."

Richard knew Epps was waiting for him to say what did happen, but he didn't say much. Confront him, sure, I was just going to confront him, sounds plausible enough. . . . Richard stored the suggestion away for future use.

He spent much of his time with Jim Billis, a young private investigator who was doing much of the legwork for the defense. The son of a federal marshal, Billis impressed Richard as someone he could trust when the chips were down. At lunch Billis would tell jokes, tease the waitress, sabotage the salt shaker— he'd do just about anything he could think of to get Richard to relax. Richard did his best to answer Billis's questions about former schoolmates and so on, but in some areas he was coming up against a blank wall. It was the same lapse of memory he had experienced when he went to the sheriff's office to report his father for child abuse; specific incidents of violence were difficult to recall.

Billis readily shared the results of his research. Every affidavit, every progress report went first to the attorneys, then to Richard and Deborah. One item Richard found particularly galling was

the police report of Deputy Tim Olsen, the first officer on the
scene of the shooting. Olsen claimed that, shortly after his
arrival, Maria blurted out, "My son did it." Maria would always
deny that she said any such thing—she certainly didn't repeat the
charge to anyone else that night—but Richard figured Olsen
didn't have any reason to lie. As far as he was concerned, the
report showed where his mother's first loyalties lay.

Equally disconcerting was the thirty-page transcript of Deborah's interview with detectives Greene and Fresquez. Richard
read through it with increasing alarm. She told them *everything*,
including some things that were just plain nuts. She even took
credit for arranging the lights, when that was his idea.

"Jesus Christ, Deborah," he said, "did you have to tell them
a book's worth of stuff?"

"You told me to tell the truth," Deborah said.

"I didn't tell you to get us both hanged," he said.

She started crying. She had only wanted to put in a good word
for him, she sobbed. She wanted them to know he didn't just go
crazy and start shooting. She was sorry, she couldn't help being
so stupid, but somebody had to tell them what was going on.

He let it drop. Deborah was not in good shape. Ever since the
shooting—before that, probably—they had fallen into this weird
oh-Richard-save-me routine. He was the white knight, she was
the damsel in distress, and he was supposed to rescue her from
all the dragons of life. But when he tried to talk to her about what
he wanted to do—here's the deal, he said, when I went into the
garage I was planning to *confront* Dad; and another thing, you're
going to have to tell them all about him feeling you up—she
started crying. He knew they were giving her some powerful
tranquilizers; once in a while he'd go looking for her at the firm
and find her crashed out on the floor of an empty office. Or she
would be all wired up and ready to go partying with her jerky
friends, and he'd have to explain to her that it wasn't smart to
leave the firm, that trying to play hooky on a $50,000 bond
wasn't quite the same as trying to ditch school.

Richard saw his old friends from ROTC less and less. Vegvary
had visited him at the jail the morning after the shooting. ("Don't
tell me what happened," Vegvary said. "Don't tell anyone until
you have a lawyer. And then, for God's sake, tell him everything. Don't hold back.") Mike Brinkman, Greg Porter, and a
few others came over to the firm a few times with pizza or ice

cream, but there didn't seem to be much to say. The shooting had put the entire department on the defensive. Everybody at school was talking about it, freaking out about it, man. Other students were coming up to cadets and asking, "What do they teach you down there—twenty-one ways to shoot your father?" Detective Greene, a former Central cadet, had asked Vegvary what kind of grade he gave Richard in raids and ambushes. Vegvary had coldly replied that the program no longer taught courses of a tactical nature.

Listening to the cadets talk about the reaction at school—and then go right on talking about Ranger outings and drill team and all this other gung-ho stuff—Richard felt as if he were surrounded by ghosts. Or maybe he was the ghost. Very strange, troops, mondo bizarro.

But dealing with Mom was the strangest experience of all. Richard saw her at the firm sometimes, but he put off visiting her. His sister said Mom was losing it. Deborah had gone back to the house to pick up some clothes. She'd turned on her stereo so she could have some music while she was packing, and Mom had come in all dressed in black and turned it off. "There's not to be any music in this house," she said.

Richard went back to the house for the first time early in December. The bloodstains were still on the driveway. Mom was going from room to room, a housecleaning dynamo. She wanted Richard to help her clean the garage.

He told her he wasn't going to do that. He couldn't handle it. She didn't understand. She kept saying Dad's death was "a terrible tragedy"—a terrible tragedy, a terrible tragedy, as if Dad had been run over by a truck or something.

"Mom, I did it for you," he said.

She stared at him, her eyes widening, her lips twisted into an ugly grimace. "Don't say that," she gasped.

"It's true."

"I never wanted that. Never." She started to cry. "God, I wish I was dead."

When Epps came to pick him up, Richard was waiting outside.

16

Deborah met her new attorney for the first time on December 13, 1982, over lunch at a Denver restaurant. She nodded sympathetically as Jim Barrett explained why he could no longer represent her. She smiled at Terry Mackey and shook his hand when it was offered to her. Then she went back to her room at the Denver Children's Home and cried.

It was all so terribly unfair. All her life she'd been told she wasn't old enough to do this or that, she had no rights, she belonged to her parents. Now, for the purpose of prosecution, the state of Wyoming had decided that she was an adult, but she still didn't have the power of an adult. She had no control, no money, no say in where she was going to live or who was going to defend her in court. All these decisions were being made for her, as if she were still a child. But she could go to prison like an adult. She was trapped in a twilight zone between childhood and adulthood, and she was getting the worst of both worlds.

She wanted Jim Barrett to represent her. She liked Barrett; he was so refined and soft-spoken, a real gentleman. Terry Mackey was another story. His nose was broad and flat, and he was given to wearing loud shirts half unbuttoned, presumably so he could show off the gold chain around his neck and his smooth, tanned chest. He told coarse jokes in a booming voice and called her "kiddo" and "little girl." He didn't look like he read books or listened to classical music or anything like that. He looked like a shyster.

"I want you to know something," he told her. "I can't afford to get personally involved in this case. I have to be very careful about that, because getting involved could impair my judgment, and I have to be objective if I'm going to do a good job."

She was appalled. Buddha, she thought, Barrett would never say something like that. This creep doesn't even want to care about what happens to me.

Yet over the next few weeks Deborah found herself relying

177

more and more on Terry Mackey. She didn't quite understand
why she trusted him. Perhaps it was because no one else had ever
taken such an aggressive interest in her affairs without being
cruel or violent. And, despite his habit of addressing her as
"little girl," he generally treated her as a fellow adult—that is,
he didn't baby her. When she complained about the unfairness of
her situation, Mackey was more likely to mock her self-pity than
to offer consolation. When she lapsed into what he took to be an
affected English accent, he told her to knock it off. At first his
teasing and his gruffness intimidated her, but she soon learned to
respond in a similar vein. A playful, sometimes heated banter
developed between them, a sign of growing affection and respect.

The relationship became even more important to her as her
friendship with Eve Whitcomb began to collapse under the strain
of Eve's new role as foster parent. Eve had several complaints:
Deborah's "personality conflicts" with other members of the
Whitcomb family, her general distractedness and inability to do
her share of the household chores, her insomnia and moodiness,
her unauthorized use of the telephone to call her friends—
particularly Chris Lawrence, with whom she was developing a
budding romance—and more. It was obvious to Eve that Deborah
had never dealt with the usual obligations of a domestic situation
before; she had survived by ducking authority and being devious.
With the right kind of supervision she could probably adjust to a
more "normal" environment, but Eve's patience was soon
exhausted.

In January Deborah moved into the home of Byron Barry,
superintendent of the Cheyenne public schools. Barry had agreed
to let Deborah stay with his family, provided that the arrangement could be kept anonymous; given Barry's position in the
community, he didn't want to appear to be taking sides in
the Jahnke case. Once again Deborah found herself among
strangers. She responded by drawing closer to Mackey. The pair
spent entire days together at Mackey's office or his home,
preparing for the transfer hearings.

Despite his speech about being objective, Mackey was becoming as "personally involved" in the case as anyone. From the
very first he had seen his client as a highly vulnerable, emotionally stunted little girl. Her sophisticated airs and quick mind
couldn't hide her basic terror of the adult world, a world that
events had thrust upon her before she was prepared to deal with

it. The first time he brought her to his house, Mackey noticed that Deborah seemed to be far more comfortable playing with his five-year-old daughter than with his thirteen-year-old. Emotionally, the two were on the same wavelength.

Yet Mackey also sensed a certain resiliency in Deborah. Clearly, she wasn't as fragile as people thought, or she would have been lost long ago. The more he learned about the ordeal she had been through, the more he admired her instinct for survival. She was going to need it, he told her, for the ordeals that still lay ahead.

As Mackey saw it, the case against Deborah was largely circumstantial, a matter of being in the wrong place at the wrong time. The police had inked her small, sweaty fingers several times before they obtained a decent set of fingerprints—and then they had been unable find her prints on any of the guns seized from the Jahnke house. The only real evidence against her was the statement she gave to the detectives the morning after the shooting, in which she admitted that she had handled one gun and would have fired in self-defense if her father had come after her with a weapon.

Mackey read the transcript of the interview over and over, with mounting indignation. The questions were leading, the language deceptive. Deborah's answers were ambiguous and often contradictory—indicative, perhaps, of her exhaustion and emotional turmoil at the time.

Mackey believed that the way the statement had been obtained raised several possible constitutional issues. True, Deborah had been informed of her rights and had waived her right to an attorney before she was questioned. But the law was supposed to make certain allowances when questioning minors without their parents present. Would Deborah have talked to Detective Greene if her mother or Eve Whitcomb had been allowed to see her first? Would it have made any difference if Greene had informed her she was under arrest before the interview, instead of afterward? If a lawyer had been present to advise her that "tacit agreement" were code words for the crime of conspiracy, would she have been so eager to agree with Greene's suggestion that she and Richard had "kind of a tacit agreement" to do something about Dad? And what had occurred during the earlier, unrecorded interview, an hour of questioning for which Mackey had received no transcript?

The statement was the key to the state's case, Mackey decided.

Without it, Carroll's argument of a conspiracy involving Deborah Jahnke was mere innuendo.

The statement—"the confession," as the state had referred to it—was everything. Mackey couldn't wait to get into the courtroom and tear it apart.

Omnibus hearings in the case of Deborah Ann Jahnke versus the state of Wyoming began January 10, 1983, a few days before similar hearings in Richard's case. That morning Mackey met with Judge Maier, District Attorney Tom Carroll, and Deputy District Attorney Jon Forwood in Maier's chambers to request that the proceedings be closed to the public. Reporters were already gathering in the courtroom, he said, and he didn't want them there.

Media interest in the case had been building steadily since the night of the shooting. The Cheyenne papers had given prominent play to each minor development in the story, but what was surprising was the degree of regional and even national attention it was attracting. In December *Time* magazine had run a short, lurid piece with a kicker that implied that Deborah had participated in the shooting ("A father is shot dead with his own gun—by his own children"). Even more disturbing, in Mackey's view, was a four-thousand-word article by *Denver Post* reporter Dana Parsons, which had appeared in the Sunday *Post* only days before. Parsons had interviewed neighbors, teachers, and acquaintances of the Jahnkes in Scottsdale and Cheyenne. Their information wasn't entirely accurate, but the resulting story was laced with the sort of tantalizing details—anecdotes about Richard's ROTC exploits and Deborah's accent and "dramatic flair"—bound to bring more reporters to the hearings.

The tone of the coverage was generally sympathetic to the Jahnke children, but Mackey knew from past experience that pretrial publicity could backfire at any moment. He planned to present testimony in support of several defense motions, including the motion to transfer the case to juvenile court, another to suppress Deborah's statement, and one that would require the state to return Deborah's journals and other personal materials seized from the house. Some of the testimony would be of a highly personal, perhaps scandalous nature. He didn't want the contents of Deborah's statement made public when the statement itself might not be admissible in court. He didn't want Deborah's

right to a fair trial imperiled by premature disclosures before
Judge Maier had the chance to transfer her case to the sanctuary
of juvenile court. The only way to protect his client's rights, he
said, was to close the hearings.

Tom Carroll opposed Mackey's request. "The state doesn't
like the glare of publicity, and I am sure the court doesn't like it.
It is still something that we have to suffer with," he said. "There
is nothing that I've heard that would indicate, at least to me, that
there is a clear and present danger that this defendant cannot have
a fair trial."

Judge Maier offered a compromise. He would not close the
hearings, but he would inform the press that "certain material
might be brought forth that would be inadmissible" at trial, and
he'd ask them to cooperate in not publishing such material.

"What results it will have, I don't know," he said. "I will say
that on one other occasion I did this, and the media people, rather
than objecting or doing anything else, simply got up and left the
courtroom at that time."

Despite Maier's hopes of media cooperation, not one news
organization voluntarily excused itself from any portion of the
Jahnke hearings. In fact, at least one newspaper openly defied the
judge's request not to publish potentially inadmissible material.
When Tom Carroll read aloud an excerpt from Deborah's statement, Ray Flack, the *Denver Post*'s veteran trial reporter, quoted
one line—"I would have killed him if I had to because he was
not a real person"—in his article, published the next day.

Flack then added, "Maier warned against public use of quota-
tions from Miss Jahnke's statement because of the possibility it
will not be admissible during trial and might prejudice her right
to a fair trial."

Mackey's first witness was Raymond Muhr, the clinical psychologist who had been summoned to Deborah's cell during the
"suicide watch" after her arrest. Muhr, the director of the Southeast Wyoming Mental Health Center, testified that he had found
Deborah to be "emotionally unstable" and "very immature for
seventeen," but not imminently suicidal. In his opinion, Deborah
probably was not capable of intelligently waiving her rights when
the detectives questioned her. He believed her case belonged in
juvenile court.

On cross-examination, Tom Carroll promptly established that

Muhr had spent only two hours with Deborah and that his diagnosis was based solely on his impressions of her during that time.

Mackey was unperturbed by Carroll's counterattack. Dr. Muhr was merely a warm-up. The defense had much higher hopes for its next witness, a short, gray-haired man who looked like a miniature version of Edward Everett Horton and spoke with a heavy accent, one that sounded British or Scottish to Wyomingites but that any Londoner would recognize as coming from Down Under. The man was Dr. John M. Macdonald, the psychiatrist who had evaluated Richard and Deborah at the Denver Children's Home for ten days in December.

Macdonald's credentials were exceptional, even by the standards of an expert witness. A New Zealander by birth, he had trained in psychiatry in London and Edinburgh and was a Fellow of the Royal College of Physicians. For the past thirty years he had been associated with the University of Colorado Health Sciences Center in Denver, where he was currently the director of forensic psychiatry. He was the author of eight books and numerous articles on criminal behavior, including studies of murder, rape, arson, burglary, and indecent exposure. He had testified in court more than two hundred times. Including the Jahnke case, he had been consulted in nine cases of patricide and eleven of matricide (including three adolescents who killed both parents); in roughly half of the cases, child abuse had been a strong factor.

Ironically, Macdonald had a reputation for being prosecution-oriented. In previous courtroom appearances, he had testified more often for the prosecution than the defense. Jim Barrett had met him when one of his clients underwent a court-ordered psychiatric evaluation; Barrett had been surprised to discover that he and the doctor saw eye to eye on the case. Barrett had subsequently called on Macdonald in the case of the Arapaho Indian boy who killed his father, to buttress his argument that the case should be heard in juvenile court. Now Mackey was hoping that Macdonald would be able to do the same for Deborah Jahnke.

Mackey led Macdonald through a brisk rendition of Deborah's history of emotional instability, tying it to the violence and fear in the Jahnke household. He then asked the doctor to describe the sexual abuse Deborah had told him about.

"This occurred between the ages of seven and twelve," Mac-donald said. "She thinks it occurred at least once a week . . . her father would fondle her breasts or buttocks and genitals . . . he would slip his hand underneath the clothing—there was no penetration or anything of that nature. This stopped at the age of twelve, after the brother witnessed the father fondling her buttocks. On one occasion, the father lay on top of her. He'd also kiss her on the mouth, in a way she did not feel was appropriate for a father-daughter relationship."

"Did you find any evidence of suicidal behavior in Deborah?" Mackey asked.

"She told me she first had suicidal thoughts at the age of eleven, when her parents threatened to send her to a juvenile home," Macdonald replied. "Since that time, she has thought about it a lot. . . . One time, when she was dusting, she opened a drawer and there was a firearm. She picked it out and put it to her temple, stood in front of a mirror—she said she wished 'something bad would happen to me,' so that the act would be justifiable. She didn't do anything.

"She did try slashing her wrist three times, and at the time that I examined her I could see three scars on her wrist. Two were about a quarter of an inch long; one was half an inch long. . . . She says that it hurt too much. This [attempt] was in August of 1982."

In Macdonald's opinion, Deborah was suffering from a "mixed personality disorder"—that is, she displayed features of more than one mental disorder, but not of any single disorder in sufficient degree to meet the requirements of the *Diagnostic and Statistical Manual of Mental Disorders*, third edition, also known as *DSM-III*, the standard diagnostic manual.

"I don't pay too much attention to that manual," Macdonald said. "She did have features of a histrionic personality disorder, in terms of her immaturity; her very great dramatization of situations; her emotional instability; her flights into romantic fantasy; her tendency not always to be strictly truthful. . . ."

"Is Deborah aggressive?" Mackey asked.

"It depends on how you use the term. She was a little impudent at times during the interviews . . . when she picked something up off of my desk and I would tell her to put it down, a few minutes later I'd find that she was looking at it again. . . . But I would suspect that she is really not aggressive. It's just a facade.

The outrageous behavior might make it seem as though she is a pushy little girl. But I think underneath she's just the opposite.''

The direct examination concluded with Macdonald seconding Muhr: in his opinion, Deborah wasn't capable of intelligently waiving her rights prior to being questioned by the detectives, and her case belonged in juvenile court.

Once again, the cross-examination was conducted by Tom Carroll. ''Dr. Macdonald,'' he said, ''did I hear you say that you don't pay much attention to the manual, the *DSM,* put out by the American Psychiatric Association?''

For several minutes Carroll sparred with Macdonald about the clinical value of the section on personality disorders in *DSM-III.* Carroll had brought a copy of the manual with him, along with Macdonald's reports on Richard and Deborah Jahnke. If Deborah Jahnke was suffering from a mental deficiency, he wanted someone to show it to him in the book, or else leave off all this talk of ''emotional instability'' as a result of child abuse. Macdonald quietly enumerated his objections to *DSM-III,* using the opportunity to elaborate on his diagnosis.

Deborah sat silently in her seat, following the proceedings with growing frustration and embarrassment. Anticipating that his client would find it difficult to sit still while her personal life and mental condition were being openly discussed, Mackey had urged her to write down her comments on a yellow legal pad. As soon as he returned to the defense table, she began scribbling notes to him.

I'm not an emotional cripple, Terry, she wrote.

Mackey replied on the same sheet. *O.K. But we have got to provide an explanation for how you got in that chair,* referring to her vigil with the carbine in the family room on the night of the shooting.

''Now, what was her relationship with her mother, if you know?'' Carroll asked.

''I would say it was unfriendly,'' Macdonald said.

''Would you say, at least, to the point of hatred?''

''Yes, I think so. It was a complex relationship in that I think she saw her mother as a victim also. I think she hated her mother because her mother did not protect her from her father. Or if she did protect her, which I'm sure she did at times, it was inadequate protection. . . . And she felt in some ways that her mother was a child; that she was the parent. I think she was referring to both her parents. She said, 'We were the adults; they were the children.' Meaning that at times she had to tell her parents what to do, in an adult kind of way."

I don't hate my mum, Deborah protested.

We know that but what else can Carroll do? Mackey replied.

My father always led her to believe that 'the world was out to get her'—she would never believe me when I told her otherwise. I think she understands that now.

She is becoming much more open, Mackey agreed.

Macdonald added that, in his opinion, Maria Jahnke had tended to minimize the degree of violence in the family when he interviewed her.

"At the first interview," he said, "I thought that the mother was concealing so much information that I sort of gave up the effort . . . although I never really confronted her as much as I could. I saw it—quite frankly, I saw the mother as a victim of her husband's abuse. . . . I thought she was very phlegmatic. She just sat there. There was very little spontaneous conversation. She struck me as being very depressed herself. In fact, she talked about going into years of mourning and not having any parties, not going out. . . . She was really turning a deaf ear and a blind eye to what had gone on in her life."

Carroll asked, "Would the fact that her husband had been shot to death and her two children were charged with having committed a crime in that regard, wouldn't that have some effect on her?"

"I'm sure it would."

"Would it be fair to say that the defendant tended to *exaggerate* and fantasize or maximize what went on?"

"No, I think her response to me was very much like that of battered children I have examined. I would ask her to make a list of everything that went wrong in her home, and she wouldn't do it. . . . Often examples of things came out incidentally . . . just as simple a thing as the fact that mother was present during the beating the night of the tragedy. The boy never told me about that, but the girl—it just came out after many, many hours of evaluation."

"Did they love their father?" Carroll asked.

"It is very difficult for children not to have some feelings of love for their father," Macdonald said.

We didn't know about our father, Deborah wrote. *We never knew who he was.*

But did you love him?

No. I was afraid of him.

"Is this defendant the typical child abuse victim?" Carroll asked.

"I don't know if there is a typical child abuse victim," Macdonald said. "But I think the situation is typical in the sense that the children really do not document in full detail what they've gone through. I just managed to get it out of them. I'm sure that there's a lot more that went on that these children haven't told me."

Carroll returned to Deborah's alleged suicide attempt in August. "Did she tell you what method was used in this attempted suicide?"

"Yes, she cut her wrist," Macdonald replied.

"Did she tell you that it was with a paper clip?"

Razor blade, Deborah insisted.

"I don't know what she used. I never asked her. I didn't get the feeling it was a deep cut. It was clearly more of a suicide gesture than a suicide attempt."

I didn't want to kill myself. I needed to feel *something, that's why I cut myself.*

Just relax for a while, Mackey urged. *Tom is trying to get to you.*

"Now, the defendant was given to extensive fantasizing, was she not?"

"Yes, sir."

"And she complained of a sexual assault by her father upon her person?"

"Yes."

"And could she be fantasizing that?"

How deranged of Carroll, Jesus! That I would want my father—yuck!

"Well, she'd have to fantasize that her brother saw it as well," Macdonald replied. "The brother saw him feeling her buttocks and reported that to the mother. . . . The mother did not witness this herself, so it's Deborah's word that we have to rely on, plus the brother's word."

"Could it be that Deborah is so preoccupied with sex or sexual fantasies that she misinterpreted her father's touching of her?"

"If, in fact, her father touched her genitals, touched her breasts, touched her buttocks, then I think that Deborah's 'fantasies' are fully justifed," Macdonald replied.

"You conclude sexual advances rather than teasing or rudeness or just fatherly affection?"

"Fatherly affection doesn't consist of lying on top of a daughter, presumably with an erection, because she told me she could feel his sex. . . . I still don't think it's normal behavior to feel a daughter's genitals, a daughter's breasts, and a daughter's buttocks. Nothing will ever convince me that it's normal to do that, not just once, not twice, but at least once a week over a period of five years."

While Deborah was fuming over Carroll's seeming obtuseness, Mackey was elated. Instead of skirting Deborah's claim of sexual abuse, the prosecutor was attempting to confront the issue head-on—which put him in the awkward position of defending the alleged fondling of a seven-year-old child as "fatherly affection." Mackey felt enough confidence in the progress of his case to confine his "redirect" examination of the witness to a few brisk questions aimed at discrediting Deborah's statement.

In reading over the transcript of the statement, Macdonald said, he had found some of the detectives' questions "very difficult to understand." He believed that the detectives sometimes took Deborah's remarks out of context to formulate even more confusing questions. He cited one convoluted query by Detective Fresquez that stretched to 280 words and contained no less than eight questions. In his opinion, the interview conducted by Greene and Fresquez amounted to a "heavy interrogation," one that was, at times, incoherent as well.

Mackey's next witness was Dr. Brandt Steele, a Denver psychiatrist and one of the authors of the original medical article on the "battered child syndrome." Steele had been summoned to support the contention that Deborah's case belonged in juvenile court. He had not examined Deborah himself, but he had studied Macdonald's report and police reports in order to testify that the Jahnke home appeared to be a "fairly typical" abusive environment.

Rather than challenge Steele's assertion, Carroll decided to take the discussion of "typical" abuse situations in a novel direction.

"Would it be typical that the child develops a fear of the parent who is abusing [him], and thus becomes withdrawn and nonconfrontational towards that parent?" he asked.

"That is a common manifestation," Steele agreed. "It isn't universal."

"And would it be typical for a child in that situation, after he became, let's say, a teenager, to be vengeful towards that parent, wanting to get even or punish?"

"I would not say that's typical, no. It is more typical to try to forget it and not do anything about it."

"He wouldn't feel hatred, an abiding hatred?"

"That's much more likely to happen in the child who has been more severely abused. The more severely abused, the more likely the child is to retaliate."

"Are you familiar with any cases where there's a tendency to stay in the family unit, with the intent to create problems and gain revenge against that abusive parent?"

"I wouldn't say with that intent, no," Steele replied. "They stay in the family because they don't have the maturity and independence to figure out ways of leaving. They can run away. The majority of runaway kids, adolescent or otherwise, are running away from physical abuse or other forms of abuse. I've worked with the juvenile pickup, and about ninety percent of runaways are running away from physical abuse. About fifty percent of the runaway girls are running away from incest or other types of abuse, too."

"Would that be the more typical reaction?"

"A healthier reaction, probably."

The second day of hearings commenced with the testimony of Maria Jahnke. Wearing a dress for the first time in fifteen years and obviously terrified at the prospect of having to speak in public, Maria gave her first answers in such a small, timid voice that even Judge Maier, seated an arm's length from the witness box, had difficulty hearing her. With Mackey gently urging her to speak up, she embarked on a long, largely unemotional account of her life with Richard Chester Jahnke.

As the children grew older, she said, her husband's violence had been chiefly directed toward his son. Richie's attempt to report his father to the authorities had only increased his wrath, to the point where Richie "would get hit practically every day."

Deborah was struck only "a couple of times" after the family moved to Cheyenne. As for Maria herself, she had been physically abused "once every six months" before they came to Cheyenne, and never afterward.

Deborah scarcely looked at her mother as she testified. As Carroll began his cross-examination, Deborah scrawled a note across the top of a fresh page and handed it to Mackey.

Her testimony seemed pretty weak, she wrote.

Her testimony has been very helpful, Mackey replied.

Her English isn't exactly impeccable.

I hope you can learn to love your mom as much as she loves you.

Carroll asked Maria if she was "sorry" her husband was dead. She said she was. Carroll asked her if she missed him. Maria said she hadn't "stopped to think" if she did.

"You are feeling protective of your children, and you want to protect them in any way that you can?" the prosecutor asked.

"Well, I want to help them as much as I can," Maria said.

"You don't want them to go to jail?"

"Of course not."

Carroll moved on to Richard Chester Jahnke's tendency to "nitpick" and "quarrel" with his family. Wasn't it true, the prosecutor asked, that the father wasn't the only one who got mad? Didn't Maria become angry when the children didn't behave?

"Yes, I did," Maria said, "very angry."

"Very angry. Would you describe that as a rage?"

"Sometimes I would get into rages because I felt I was in between," Maria said. "I was trying to make everybody understand and keep peace in the home, and nobody seemed to understand what I was trying to do."

"And when you would get into these rages, as you call them, you would throw things at the children, wouldn't you?"

"Just one time, that night, I had a box of"—Maria faltered—"I can't think—I did get angry, and I picked it up and threw it at my son."

More often than that, Deborah wrote. *She's thrown a heavy ceramic mug one time.*

"You also threw a candle at him that night, didn't you?"

"I guess I did," Maria said.

"And when your husband came home, you proceeded to tell him about your son being disobedient, didn't you?"

"I was very angry, and he noticed that I was angry. He said, 'Are they giving you any problems?' I was trying not to say anything because I didn't want any more violence. I just wanted to get out of there as fast as I could. But he knew, and I said, 'Richard and I, we just had words.' "

"And you knew at that time that your husband would do something to Richard, that he would hit him or beat him or discipline him, didn't you?"

"I knew he was going to discipline him," Maria said.

hmmmm. "Discipline" usually meant beatings.

"If your daughter says—and I have reason to believe she will—that you even lied to your husband, telling him things that Richard did that he didn't do, would that be true?"

"That is untrue," Maria said. "It would be the opposite. I would cover up for them."

Liar! Deborah wrote.

She can't "lie" about this, Mackey replied.

"During your marriage and during the disciplining of your children, you never, ever felt that it was necessary to give either one of them medical attention for any disciplining that your husband inflicted upon them, did you?"

"No."

Liar! Ask her about the time when she knocked me down & I required stitches.

No way, Mackey replied. It was all very well for Carroll to attempt to shift some of the blame from the late Richard Chester Jahnke to his widow, but Mackey wasn't about to impeach the credibility of his own witness. Yet Deborah continued to vent her anger at her mother's testimony, her handwriting becoming wilder with each succeeding note. Meanwhile, Carroll was pressing Maria for her reasons for not cooperating with the abuse investigation her son had initiated.

"Wasn't one of the problems the fact that you had two teenagers who were becoming difficult—I suppose as all teenagers sometimes do—becoming difficult to handle?" Carroll said. "Isn't that kind of what went on?"

Difficult! Jesus Christ. She threw me up against a wall choking me because it was 9:30 & I hadn't yet taken my shower.

"Yes," Maria said, "but it is also hard to get a person to go to counseling. He was dead set against going to counseling. He refused. He thought there was nothing wrong with these rages.

He couldn't remember what he'd said or done an hour before that.''

"Why didn't you seek counseling yourself?" Carroll asked.

"I was afraid to."

Maria's testimony was followed by that of Eve Whitcomb. The teacher described her efforts to help Deborah, including her unsuccessful attempts to see Deborah at the jail on the morning of November 17, during and after her interrogation by the detectives. Despite their recent differences, Whitcomb's appearance had a calming effect on Deborah. For Mackey the testimony served to lay a foundation for the assault on his next and last witness, Detective Tim Greene.

Challenging police officers on matters of procedure and conduct is one of the routine duties of criminal trial lawyers; Mackey excelled at it. Greene proved to be an experienced, unflappable witness, one who sidestepped many of the traps Mackey laid for him by qualifying each response. Yet Mackey extracted several helpful admissions from the detective: that Greene had made up his mind to arrest Deborah before the taped interview took place; that the sheriff's department had seized Deborah's writings from the house without a search warrant (but with, Greene insisted, Maria Jahnke's explicit permission to search for materials that might help them locate Deborah); and that Greene and Fresquez had strayed from department policy by "detaining" Deborah for hours before notifying the county attorney's office. The last may have been a moot point: policy required the detectives to notify the district judge, a parent, or the county attorney whenever a juvenile was placed under arrest, and Deborah wasn't officially under arrest until after the interview. But Mackey made the officers' conduct sound grave indeed.

The most interesting revelation came when Mackey asked Greene what he did with his notes from the first, unrecorded interview with Deborah.

"I don't know," Greene said. "I believe they were shredded. I had other documents that I was keeping . . . and I was sorting them out and making piles of what to throw away and what to keep, and in trying to keep myself organized they might have got shredded."

Mackey stared at the witness with a grand show of incredulity. Greene's admission was either very good news or very bad news for the defense. Although the detective would insist that there was nothing said in the first interview that wasn't covered again in the second, Mackey had other information. According to Deborah, she had dwelt at greater length on past incidents of abuse in the first interview. Detective Fresquez's recollections of the first interview, when he was questioned by Barrett and Epps two days after Christmas, had also indicated some discrepancies. Without a clear record of the first interview, it was impossible to determine whether key words such as "execution" had been volunteered by Deborah (as Greene claimed) or planted by the officers (as Deborah claimed). As Mackey saw it, Greene's inability to produce his notes strengthened the argument to exclude Deborah's statement entirely. He rested his case.

The prosecution responded by recalling Greene to the stand as a witness for the state. Deputy District Attorney Forwood handed the detective State's Exhibit # 1 and asked him to identify it.

"This is a report of mine that I submitted," Greene said, "an interview with a Timothy James McNally."

Oh, oh, Deborah wrote. McNally had graduated from Central High last spring and was now attending the California Institute of Technology in Pasadena. Deborah had already read Greene's report and had been mortified by its contents.

At Forwood's request, Greene began to summarize the report.

"Mr. McNally stated that during the spring of 1982, while he and Miss Jahnke were walking at the high school, that Miss Jahnke stated that she wished her father dead. Mr. McNally stated that he suggested using a poisonous mushroom and cyanide, and further that he and Miss Jahnke openly discussed methods of death. McNally stated on this occasion he did not believe that Miss Jahnke was serious . . . on another occasion in the spring of 1982 he and Miss Jahnke discussed inducing a 'psychic heart attack' on Miss Jahnke's father by having a group of individuals picture the heart and then stop the heart through thought."

Can this hurt? Deborah asked.

Don't worry about that, Mackey replied.

Why not?

Because McNally said a lot of other things, too.

Such as?

Just watch!

I'm scared . . .

Don't be.

"Did he tell you," Forwood prompted, "what opportunity, if any, he had to observe any evidence of bruises or other physical abuse?"

"Yes, sir," Greene replied, "he did state that he had an occasion to observe Miss Jahnke in the nude in the summer of 1982, and at that time he observed no marks on her body . . ."

ooooh no . . .

". . . McNally stated that Jahnke spoke in 'derogatory' terms of her mother . . ."

I cared about Mum lots, but was angry with her because she was so submissive.

". . . McNally stated that Miss Jahnke had a hard time making friends and seemed not to very often feel guilt, in addition to being self-centered. . . . On one occasion, two weeks prior to the summer break of 1982, Miss Jahnke cut her wrist with a paper clip, however the cuts were not deep . . ."

Razor blade, Deborah again maintained.

Forwood asked Greene if his interviews with McNally and the defendant had convinced him that the slaying of Richard Chester Jahnke was "aggressive, violent, premeditated, or committed in a willful manner?" Greene affirmed that they had.

On cross-examination, Mackey pointed out that Greene had not presented the full contents of his report, including McNally's description of Deborah as "troubled, sometimes very silent, rarely laughed, and seemed like she was in inner turmoil." But when it was Carroll's turn to redirect the witness, he echoed Mackey's line of questioning, introducing even more embarrassing charges into the record.

"What else is in the report that you have not referred to in your testimony?" Carroll asked.

Greene considered. "Mr. McNally's statement to me that Miss Jahnke indicated to him on one occasion that she was bisexual, having one sexual experience with another female in Phoenix, Arizona. She also indicated [to McNally] that she attempted to have a sexual relationship with another female here in Cheyenne, but that was refused."

Now they're going to say I'm gay, Deborah wrote.

I hope so, Mackey replied.

Why, it isn't true.

Trust me.

But Mackey's attempt to recross-examine Detective Greene
was rejected by Judge Maier. With the defense unable to refute
the charge, or at least dismiss it as irrelevant, Deborah's alleged
"tendency toward bisexuality" was reported on the front page of
the *Wyoming Eagle* the next morning, under the headline TESTI-
MONY REVEALS SLAYING PLOT.

The second day of hearings concluded with the testimony of
several sheriff's deputies who had been involved in the collection
of evidence at the Jahnke house. A third day was devoted to
formal arguments on the pending defense motions. The most
spirited debate revolved around the question of whether Deborah's case belonged in juvenile or adult court.

"This offender is not a child of tender years," Carroll insisted.
"By some standards she is a woman. . . . I think the Virgin
Mary was thirteen at the time of the birth of Christ, and we didn't
call her a child bride."

"Without meaning to sound flip, Your Honor, I would argue
that the Virgin Mary ought to also be transferred to juvenile court
under these circumstances," Mackey replied. "Children of eleven
and ten are biologically capable of producing other children. For
that are they adults? I think not, Your Honor . . . yes, [Deborah]
is seventeen years old. She is biologically functional as a woman.
But why should we play around with all those words? . . . Who
is she really? She is a child who can have children, that's who
she is."

Judge Maier promised a speedy decision on all motions pending before him. Not as speedy, however, as the actions of Judge
Paul Liamos. Liamos lived up to his reputation for swift justice
by holding omnibus hearings in Richard's case on Friday, January 21, wrapping up closing arguments on Saturday morning, and
delivering his ruling the same day.

The testimony in support of the motion to transfer Richard's
case was similar to that presented on Deborah's behalf—with a
few significant differences. While Mackey had relied strongly on
medical testimony, Barrett and Epps began with Deputy Robert
Bomar, DPASS worker Pat Sandoval, and the abuse report filed
last May—a clear attempt to establish a history of child abuse
through the state's own records.

Once again Maria Jahnke took the stand to denounce her
husband and defend her children. More composed the second

time around (she had, in fact, taken a mild tranquilizer before her appearance), she presented a fuller, more detailed picture of the violence in her home, from the viewpoint of a benumbed bystander and occasional victim.

But if Maria was better prepared, so was her adversary. Tom Carroll had studied Macdonald's confidential report on Deborah, in which Deborah claimed that both her parents had abused her; Macdonald described two alleged incidents involving Maria Jahnke. On cross-examination, Carroll steered Maria back to her earlier admission that at times she had been "very angry" with her children. Barrett's objection on grounds of relevancy was quickly overruled by Judge Liamos.

"Mrs. Jahnke," Carroll continued, "did you, when your daughter was six or seven years old, did you strike her several times, knocking her down, at which time her head hit the towel rack, [so] that she had to have the wound sutured, and . . . you told her to say that when you came in the bathroom you suddenly scared her, so that she fell down accidentally and hurt herself?"

"No, that's not the way it happened," Maria said firmly. "She was getting ready for school. She was washing up, and she did fall and hit her head . . . I took her right away to the doctor."

"Are you saying you did hit her?"

"I didn't."

"So if your daughter says that, that's a lie?"

"One of us must be lying, then," Maria said. "I never hurt my kids in a violent way."

"Do you recall at the age of fourteen [sic], that you had an argument with your daughter in a swimming pool, and that you grabbed her by the hair, pulled her down under the water, and she nearly drowned? Do you remember that?"

"No, I don't."

"If your daughter said that did happen, are you going to say here under oath that it did not happen?"

"It did not happen."

"If your daughter says [that] from time to time you've called her a bastard, a bitch, a swine, an asshole—is that untrue?"

"Her father was the one that would call her that," Maria said.

"I asked you, did you call her that?"

"No. I might have said something to her."

"Did you say that to her?"

"Not a bastard."

"Well, a bitch, did you call her a bitch?"

"I don't remember calling her that."

Carroll pressed on. If Maria was so concerned about her children, why didn't she tell her story to Deputy Bomar, to the social worker from DPASS, or any of the others who tried to help her family?

"How did you think this would finally end up?" he asked, a note of exasperation rising in his voice.

"You always have hope," Maria said softly, "especially when you love three people the way I loved them. You always have hope that eventually things will get better. And then violence becomes a way of life."

"You all got swept up in this atmosphere of violence and fighting and bickering and nagging and hatred, didn't you? Every one of you?"

"Yes, I guess so," Maria said, her voice flat and dreamlike.

"And that culminated in this terrible tragedy, didn't it?"

"I guess you're right."

Sitting stiffly at the defense table, Richard felt a brief flush of admiration for Tom Carroll. He was being awfully hard on Mom, but at least the man wasn't blaming everything on him or Deborah. Maybe Tom Carroll wasn't such a bad guy after all.

After Carroll's withering interrogation of Maria, John Macdonald's testimony in support of the motion of transfer seemed anticlimactic. Louis Epps conducted the doctor through an assessment of Richard's mental condition that seemed quite mild in comparison with his previous description of Deborah's "mixed" disorders. Richard simply didn't have the emotional problems, Macdonald explained, that his sister did.

"The end effect on Richard, surprisingly enough, has not been as bad as you might expect after all these years of abuse," he said. "He is way above average intelligence, and in many ways he's a very responsible, law-abiding sort of citizen. This was noticed at the Denver Children's Home, where he sort of took over the responsibility of teaching other children to do various things; he almost played the role of supervisor.

"But the appearance you get, I think, is deceptive. There's a pseudo-maturity about the boy—the youth, I should say. . . . I think there is a brittle quality to him. . . . I don't think he has the capacity of other children of his age to handle a great deal of stress effectively. . . . He's not really an adult, he's not really even a juvenile at the age he appears to be.''

When it was time to cross-examine, Carroll asked Macdonald if he was saying that he hadn't found Richard to be suffering from any definable mental illness or personality disorder.

"I don't think it would be fair to say that," Macdonald replied. "This youth has a mental problem—a mental disorder, but you wouldn't find it listed in *DSM-III*. I know that's the book you have so much respect for, sir. But they really don't have any category for battered youths, and I think he is a battered youth.''

As before, Carroll and Macdonald squared off on whether the doctor's diagnosis had to fit the list of personality disorders found in *DSM-III*. Carroll quickly moved on, however, to Richard's "state of mind" on the night of the homicide.

"On the night in question, was he angry with his father—did he tell you about that?"

"I'm sure he was," Macdonald said.

"Did he tell you how he arranged the guns and so on, in preparation for his father's return?"

"I'm going to object, Your Honor," Epps said. "I believe this goes beyond the scope of this hearing."

"The objection will be overruled," Liamos said. "You may continue."

"His plans were to defend himself against his father," Macdonald said. "He said he didn't really know what he was doing when he went through the house putting the guns in various places. But then he had this fantasy. He was reminded of—I think it was *Conan the Barbarian* or something. He'd seen a film of this man protecting his home, where, I take it, he had weapons in every room. And so he, in a sense, was thinking that if something went wrong there'd be a weapon to protect that particular room—"

"What did he think might go wrong?"

"If his father fired at him, I take it."

"Did he tell you his father made any aggressive acts toward him upon his return to the family home that evening?"

"No, he didn't make any aggressive acts other than the way he walked. So far as Richard was concerned, this was the way he walked when a beating was about to take place. He stomped. It reminded him of his father's behavior before beatings.''

"Did he tell you that's what provoked him into shooting his father through that closed garage door?"

"I think that was the factor that provoked the shooting."

Now it was Barrett's turn to object. A lengthy huddle at the bench followed. The state was on a "fishing expedition," Barrett argued, trying to convict his client of first-degree murder even before the trial began. Carroll responded that he was conducting a proper cross-examination. Judge Liamos agreed. Despite Barrett's protests, Liamos declined to restrain Carroll, close the hearing to the press, or caution the press about "inadmissible testimony" as Judge Maier had done. Carroll resumed his cross-examination.

"Did he tell you what, if anything, he intended to do after the shooting?" Carroll asked.

"He hadn't really made any plans," Macdonald said. "His intention was to have a confrontation with his father . . . not to shoot his father, but simply to tell his father that he wasn't going to be beaten any more."

Carroll asked the doctor to elaborate on what he meant by a "confrontation."

"His intention was to go up to his father and say, let's forget all this nonsense. I'm not quoting his exact words, I'm giving the general trend of his conversation. He was going to hug his father and say, you know, let's not have these arguments. . . . I think he had this sort of fleeting, magical belief that it could all be resolved by saying, Father, let's be friends. . . . But then he remembered that he tried that approach before and it didn't work, he just got a further beating."

"He didn't say that to his father when his father approached the garage door, did he?" Carroll asked.

"No, he didn't," Macdonald said.

"Just shot him?"

"That's right."

Macdonald's testimony was followed by a fifteen-minute recess. For the defense team, it was time to regroup. Carroll's unexpected foray into the defendant's state of mind at the time of the shooting had exposed more of Barrett's hand than he would have liked. The state now had plenty to work with in shaping its argument against a transfer to juvenile court, as well as some indication of the direction the anticipated self-defense plea would take. Barrett knew he would have to salvage what he could by putting the state's own witnesses through the wringer. Little could be done with Detective Greene, who took the stand simply to deliver a transcript of Deborah's statement to Judge Liamos; or with Major Vegvary, who testifed that he had no knowledge of further abuse in the Jahnke home after the abuse report of May 2. But Frank DeLois was fair game.

DeLois, the social worker who had visited the Jahnkes three weeks after the abuse report was filed, said that he had considered Richard's problems with his father to be a "low priority" case. On cross-examination, Barrett ripped into DeLois for the way he conducted his interview with the family.

"Now, on May 24," Barrett said, "did you say, 'Has he ever done this to you before, Richie?' "

"No, I didn't," DeLois admitted.

"Did you say, 'Richie, let's go and talk alone for a minute'?"

"No."

"Did Richard Chester Jahnke know you were going to visit?"

"Yes, he did."

"Has it been your experience that some parents might set things up—things will go good for a little while, so when you show up things are fine?"

"Yes."

"How do you find out if that's happened?"

"Like I've said earlier, I learned that this boy had a strong advocate through the school, someone whom he would talk to a lot more freely and openly than he would probably with me."

"Let somebody else do it, then?"

"Let someone else, yes," DeLois said. "I trust the system enough to know that schools will contact us."

Barrett asked the witness if he had left his card with any members of the family.

"Probably the father," DeLois said. "I think I was sitting closer to him than the boy."

"And this case was low priority?"

"That was my opinion."

"What's a high-priority case?"

"A high-priority case for me would be small children who aren't able to verbalize exactly what's going on or understand what is acceptable and what isn't acceptable as far as parental behavior."

Barrett frowned. "So adolescents in general just aren't high priority with you?"

"Not necessarily. I have some adolescents currently on my caseload that I had back then, that I have weekly contact with."

"How many of these high-priority adolescents do you have that call you at home—any time, any place?"

"I probably get a call at home once a month—which isn't a tremendous amount, I know," DeLois said.

Barrett's expression turned into an icy glare. "People just aren't inclined to report to you, huh?"

"Not directly," DeLois said.

Formal arguments commenced at nine o'clock the next morning. Louis Epps's characterization of Richard Jahnke as a youth who "got lost between the cracks of the system" was hotly disputed by Tom Carroll.

"I'm sure this court is aware that fifteen-year-olds have been sentenced directly into the penitentiary in this state for homicide," Carroll said. "We've got a young man here of seventeen [sic] years of age! He's intelligent, he's—was well-adjusted in his social life. He had friends, he was successful, he was in a command position with ROTC. For counsel to say to this court that the system completely failed him is at best an exaggeration and is, in fact, not true. . . .

"His actions in this instance certainly don't smack of the actions of a child. . . . This, according to the evidence, was premeditated. Carefully planned. Children, I submit, do not carefully plan homicides, Your Honor. . . .

"I don't hate this boy. I feel sorry for this boy. I'm sorry that he killed his father. I think he's probably sorry that he killed his father, too. But we have the responsibility . . . [to] let youngsters in the community know that if they have some intent, some thought about killing somebody, they're not going to be slapped on the wrists. They are going to face the criminal justice system and be accountable for their actions."

Judge Liamos declared a recess. He returned twenty-five minutes later with his ruling. Richard Jahnke, he noted, was intelligent, and his "emotional attitude" appeared to be "good"; he didn't come from "a home wherein he was deprived of proper sustenance." Despite Dr. Macdonald's finding of a "pseudo-maturity," Liamos believed that Richard was "certainly as sophisticated and mature as others of his age, and probably more so than the majority.''

The motion to transfer the case to juvenile court was denied.

Judge Maier's ruling in Deborah's case arrived two days later. In a letter to the attorneys in the case, Maier noted several factors, including Deborah's age and intelligence, that supported the argument for a trial in adult court. Only one factor—the defendant's lack of a previous record—appeared to him to favor a move to juvenile court. He denied the motion to transfer the case. Furthermore, he found that Deborah's statement had been obtained voluntarily, with full regard for her constitutional rights, and that the police had taken Deborah's writings from her room with the consent of her parent and legal guardian, Maria Jahnke. Mackey had struck out on all three counts.

Both teenagers would stand trial as adults. Richard would go first. Jury selection in his case would begin on Valentine's Day, February 14, 1983—two years to the day after he and his father drove past the HOWDY! sign at the state line and became subject to the laws of Wyoming.

17

By midmorning on Monday, February 14, 1983, the Laramie County courthouse was swarming with people, more people than could be found at the Cheyenne bus depot at any hour of the day. The clerk of the First District Court had summoned 119 prospective jurors for the trial of Richard Jahnke. Two aged bailiffs steered the throng into the recesses of Courtroom B for *voir dire*, the tedious process of interview and peremptory challenge by which a dozen jurors and two alternates would be selected. An assortment of reporters, onlookers, and potential witnesses—the state had subpoenaed thirty-seven witnesses, the defense less than a dozen—lined the hallway outside the courtroom, waiting for the trial to begin.

Kirk Knox, the garrulous, white-haired, veteran reporter and columnist for the *Wyoming State Tribune*, surveyed the scene with astonishment. Judging by the number of journalists already on the scene, the trial of young Jahnke was going to be the biggest story to hit Cheyenne in Knox's thirty-year tenure on the *Tribune*. By the end of the week, the press corps would include not only representatives of the Cheyenne and Casper dailies, the wire services, local radio and television stations, and the expected "northern bureau" reporters from Denver's television and print media, but also correspondents for the *Chicago Tribune*, *Rolling Stone*, *People*, the national television networks—even a free-lance writer who, Knox learned, hoped to sell a piece on the trial to *Hustler* magazine. Knox couldn't recall a local crime story kicking up so much fuss since nineteen-year-old joy-killer Charlie Starkweather was captured outside of Douglas in '58.

The media presence was one of the consequences of Judge Liamos's refusal to transfer the case to juvenile court. The crime of parricide is uncommon in America but not totally unknown; a large city might have several in the course of a year. But a parricide case that leads to a public trial . . . a parricide case in which the victim was an IRS special agent, the accused a former

Boy Scout, ROTC officer, and all-American lad . . . a case seasoned with allegations of child abuse, mental torture, and a hint of incest . . . the whole family trapped on the edge of the prairie, the edge of the American dream, with their guns and bad blood and twisted loyalties to each other . . . at a time when the whole blessed country was going bananas about child abuse, drowning in it, the waves of hysteria rippling from exposé to exposé, first Joan Crawford's daughter and now this—well! Why not?

People were worked up about the case, no doubt about it. Knox's paper had received letters from readers throughout Wyoming, most of them critical of Tom Carroll's insistence on trying the teenagers as adults. Professional child advocates were getting into the act, too. The sharpest attack had come from Dr. Richard Krugman, director of the Henry Kempe National Center for the Prevention and Treatment of Child Abuse and Neglect in Denver, in a letter to the *Denver Post*.

"I do not condone what these adolescents did to their father," Krugman wrote, "but I could understand Carroll's position more easily if I knew . . . that adults who face the criminal justice system for the abuse and murder of children were prosecuted with the same zeal the district attorney is exhibiting in the Jahnke case. The usual indictment for child murderers is felony child abuse; the usual sentence is two to four years. This double standard is appalling.

"The real tragedy, though, is that all this could have been prevented. Both Jahnke children had asked many adults for help all along. . . . Perhaps the Jahnke children should use their newly acquired 'adult' status to put on trial all these adults for failing their responsibility to them and to children everywhere."

The object of all this outcry arrived early, flanked by his attorneys and private investigator Jim Billis. Knox caught a glimpse of him before he vanished into the courtroom. Dressed in an ill-fitting navy blue suit, with a small gold cross on one lapel and a white carnation on the other, white shirt, red sweater, red tie, his hair neatly trimmed, Richard Jahnke didn't look like someone about to put the adult world on trial; he looked like a good Catholic boy on his way to choir practice.

During recesses Richard emerged from the courtroom to loiter nervously in the hallway, with Barrett, Epps, or Billis always hovering over him. Knox and the other reporters kept their distance, but a number of people walked up to the youth to hug him or try to boost his spirits. Maria Jahnke was there, and her own support group—Carolyn Wheeler and George and Sandy Hain. Also present were Dan Munn, the school psychologist at Central High, and his wife, Corrine; the Munns had volunteered to become Richard's foster parents shortly before the transfer hearings. He was now living at their house and visiting a local psychiatrist once a week. Several others weren't so easily identifiable: teenagers from Central, a pretty, long-haired blonde who flirted with the boy, a few adults who wanted to wish him good luck.

Richard accepted the greetings with a nod and a whisper of thanks. He seemed to have difficulty smiling, perhaps because his attorneys had warned him against letting the press catch him smiling, perhaps because he scarcely knew some of his well-wishers. He appeared to be as amazed by all the attention as anyone else in the courthouse.

Seating a jury proved to be less difficult than both sides had anticipated. Virtually every prospective juror had heard or read something about the case, but only a handful had formed strong opinions about it. The selection process was streamlined by Judge Liamos's denial of Barrett's request to examine the candidates in detail regarding their attitudes about physical and mental abuse. Some of the questions Barrett proposed were rather outrageous—for example, he wanted to ask the candidates if they thought it was acceptable for a father to put his hand inside his daughter's pants—but he had hoped for a compromise. At the very least, he hoped to be allowed to ask panelists if they believed there was any situation that justified the taking of a human life. Judge Liamos told him it sounded as if he wanted to try his case on *voir dire*. The defense would confine itself, Liamos said, to asking jurors how they disciplined their own children.

Yet the subject of child abuse came up repeatedly during *voir dire* without Barrett's help. A panel of thirty-two finalists had scarcely been selected when one woman asked to speak to Judge Liamos in private. Once in his chambers, she explained that her daughter had attended school with Richard Jahnke. After the shooting, she'd heard about "the condition the kid comes to school in, the bruises, the state of utter defeat."

"I could not," the woman continued, "I could not sit on that jury because I—you really want to know my opinion?"

"Yes, go ahead," Liamos said.

"I think the young man ought to sue the state of Wyoming."

"Why is that, ma'am?"

"He asked for help and he didn't get it. And to me, Wyoming contributed to this catastrophe. Can you imagine the utter hell that those kids—I just can't sit on this jury. No way."

"All right, ma'am, the court will excuse you," Liamos said.

One member of the panel was excused because she'd had previous contact with child abuse cases; another because her father had abused her and, as she explained to Judge Liamos, "I know what it's like to want to do something like that very strongly." Others knew someone who had been abused, or else they had "strong feelings" that the case didn't belong in adult court.

Such admissions struck Barrett as highly ironic. In his view, the people who would be most likely to comprehend his client's situation were voluntarily disqualifying themselves, while he was unable to ask the type of questions that might weed out any hard-nosed advocates of "old-fashioned discipline." His own notion of the ideal juror was a middle-aged, middle-class housewife with grown children and fond memories of child-rearing. A telephone survey commissioned by his firm had indicated that the parents of younger children tended to be more in favor of corporal punishment, while working mothers and upper-class parents usually had less time for their kids.

Yet Barrett had few qualms about the panel of five men and seven women that was eventually selected. They included a developer, a nurse's assistant, a teacher, a lab technician, several secretaries and office workers, and one bona fide housewife. All but one of the jurors had children. Nine had children under the age of twenty-one. Five had teenagers at home. Under the circumstances, it was impossible for Richard Jahnke to be tried by a true jury of his peers; but perhaps the eleven parents sitting in judgment would have occasion to ponder what their own children might have done if their father had been Richard Chester Jahnke.

Opening statements commenced on Tuesday morning. Tom Carroll gave a step-by-step account of the events of November 16, beginning with the senior Jahnkes' departure for their anniversary dinner. He spoke of a "plot" being hatched against Richard Chester Jahnke, of a "military-type operation" under way at the house on Cowpoke Road. He described the victim's return home, the shots that were fired at him from behind the garage door, and his death from "this tremendously destructive three-quarters-of-an-inch-in-diameter slug that just literally threw him down."

"Medically, he died from what we call exsanguination," Carroll explained. "He strangled, suffocated in his own blood."

He concluded by promising a stream of witnesses who would establish that Richard John Jahnke had conspired to kill his father and had fired the fatal shots.

Jim Barrett adjusted his glasses and walked to the lectern to address the jury.

"Mr. Carroll has outlined to you one day—in fact, less than one day—in the life of the defendant," he began. "We intend to do more than that for you."

Barrett proceeded to describe "a period of some twelve years" during which his client "was physically and emotionally abused and brutalized by his father, and to some extent even by his mother." (Later, the time frame would be corrected to fourteen years.) To those in the courtroom who had followed the transfer hearings, the charges were familiar ones. But as Barrett reached the final argument and beating of November 16, he began to raise the curtain on his planned defense. Richard went into the garage that night, he declared, to "confront" his father.

"But Dad was always armed," he said. "So Richard, quite frankly, thinking about everything that had happened to him in the last twelve years, laid a weapon here and a weapon there. And he loaded the shotgun, and he went to the garage with the shotgun, with the pistol, with a knife and two speed-loaders, intending just to confront his father. . . . His father was five feet, eight inches tall, 210 pounds, a big man . . . and when he was on his way to beat Mom, or when he lost his temper, he stomped. And when his father approached the garage door that night, it was the same thing.

"And when you hear the evidence, you're going to conclude that at that point there were six shots fired. Richard Jahnke fired the first shot through the window . . . he fired once, backed up, twice, backed up, and still backing away, fired four more shots that he doesn't even really remember, through a lower panel . . .

the shots that struck, and, unfortunately, killed Richard Jahnke, Sr., were not the shots fired through the window, not the shots fired from closest up, but were, in fact, fired while Richard Jahnke, my client, was retreating. . . .

"The evidence will show that Richard Jahnke had a reasonable apprehension of harm both to himself and to others, that he acted out of that and out of fear. And the evidence, it's going to be the evidence of a lifetime and not one day."

Carroll immediately lodged an objection to Barrett's opening statement. The child abuse claim was irrelevant, he said, and Barrett's version of the shooting would appear to rule out a claim of self-defense. "If all the facts were to be true as expressed by counsel, then this definitely would not be a self-defense case," he said.

Liamos replied that he saw nothing "improper" in either opening statement. Then he declared a recess.

For the next two days Carroll and Forwood laid out their case like coolies laying track for a railroad. There were no tricks, no surprises, only a steady, monotonous accumulation of facts, one linked to the next, iron rails for the engine of justice to chug along to its fixed purpose.

Deputy Timothy Olsen described his arrival at 8736 Cowpoke Road, his search of the premises, and the loaded weapons he found in the garage, basement, family room, and bedrooms. A paramedic told of his unsuccessful efforts to revive the victim in the driveway. Clarence Ketcham and Officer Charlie Hidalgo testified about their conversations with the defendant, during which Richard admitted that he shot his father "for revenge," "for past things." A lab technician introduced dozens of exhibits: guns and ammunition, photographs of the house, and the results of trace metal tests and fingerprinting. The latter indicated 69 points of comparison between the prints on the shotgun found in the garage and the left and right hands of Richard Jahnke. A pathologist presented autopsy photos that plainly depicted the damage four lead slugs had wreaked on the body of the victim. A ballistics expert confirmed that the slugs were fired from the shotgun found in the garage. Detective Greene testified that the victim couldn't have seen his assailant as he walked toward the garage, while someone standing in the darkened garage could perceive, through the plastic blinds, an approaching silhouette.

As the arduous display of police science dragged into its second day, boredom began to spread across the faces of the jury like a plague. No one doubted that Richard Jahnke had shot his father through the garage door; Barrett had admitted as much at the very beginning. A few of the jurors clearly felt that the prosecution was overdoing it. The gruesome autopsy photos were passed from hand to hand so rapidly that Judge Liamos had to remind one woman that she had an obligation to view the evidence.

Reporters drifted out of the courtroom frequently for cigarette breaks. Occasionally one of them would try to strike up a casual conversation with Maria Jahnke, who sat nervously in the hallway with her friends; as a possible witness, she was barred from the courtroom. Her daughter was nowhere to be seen: against his client's wishes, Mackey had instructed the Barrys to keep Deborah at home. Richard appeared during recesses to hug his mother and visit with the pretty blonde girl. The rest of the time he sat stoically at the defense table with Louis Epps. They were both suffering from potent head colds.

Barrett had few objections to the state's case. There was very little to argue about, only a few minor physical details to underscore. His cross-examination of the ballistics expert and the pathologist suggested that the shots through the lower panel of the garage door were indeed fired in retreat, that the victim may have ducked rather than fallen to the ground, and that two of the slugs had "probably" ricocheted off the pavement. It was also possible, though, that Richard Chester Jahnke had been killed by the very first shot through the glass pane above the door handle.

Curiously, Carroll did not attempt to introduce any portion of Deborah's statement to support the conspiracy charge. Instead, he called Michael Brinkman to the stand.

The lean, long-legged ROTC captain walked quickly into the courtroom with his head down. He was appearing under subpoena, the result of a casual conversation he'd had with Richard at Barrett's office a week or so after the shooting. The conversation had pricked his conscience; he had gone to Vegvary, and ultimately to the district attorney. In the past several days Brinkman had been interrogated by both sides about the exact wording of the discussion, to no one's satisfaction—least of all his own. Richard glared at him as he took the oath.

Carroll asked the witness to relate what Richard had told him regarding the night of the shooting.

"He said when his parents left that he had the feeling that, if he was in the house when his father was to come back, that he would not be alive," Brinkman said, the words tumbling out in one breath.

"What did he say to you then?" Carroll asked.

"He said that they put weapons and ammunition at every window and door in the house."

"Who did he mean by 'they'?"

"Himself and Deborah."

Reporters exchanged puzzled glances. Judging from previous testimony, "weapons and ammunition at every window and door" was an exaggeration, but whose? At the transfer hearings, Macdonald had said that Richard had put weapons in fallback positions, just as the hero had done in *Conan the Barbarian*. (In the movie, which Richard had seen at a drive-in in the summer of 1982, the warrior Conan prepares for an assault by enemy troops by laying traps and concealing spears and axes around the battleground.) Brinkman's version sounded more like the movie *Billy Jack*.

"Then he had Deborah wait in the living room," Brinkman continued, "armed with a .30 caliber something, and he waited in the garage. . . . He said he put the dogs and cats and everything downstairs so that they wouldn't get hurt. . . . He said he was scared he might freeze up and that's why he had Deborah wait in the living room, and then he said he saw a shadow and he wasn't sure, you know—it wasn't really clear—but he said he saw a shadow, and he started to fire. He said he didn't hear any noise, and he doesn't remember the gun moving or anything. . . ."

"Was there any conversation as to why Deborah was armed with whatever gun it was?" Carroll asked.

"Because of his philosophy of whatever can go wrong, will go wrong. In case he was afraid, in case he was to freeze, then she could follow through."

On cross-examination Barrett asked Brinkman what else Richard had said. Before the witness could reply, Carroll called for a conference at the bench.

"Mr. Barrett wants to try to get into the child abuse case," Carroll complained. "I carefully brought out only the testimony in relation to the incident itself."

Barrett replied that the state's witness had "opened the door" by saying that Richard felt he wouldn't be alive when his father got home. The defense had a right to follow up on that point, he insisted. Judge Liamos agreed.

Barrett returned to the lectern and asked Brinkman if it was true Richard had told him that he feared for his life.

"I can't remember the exact words," Brinkman said.

"But words to that effect?" Barrett asked.

"Words to that effect," Brinkman echoed. "He said that his mom was very jittery and nervous that night, and he thinks it's because of their anniversary. And when his father came home he asked her why she was so uppity. I don't think she really gave him a reason. And he said, 'It's those kids.' "

" 'Those'—you hesitated there. Was there some other word used?"

"Is it okay to say it?" Brinkman asked.

"Sure," Barrett said.

" 'Those goddamned kids.' "

Brinkman said that Richard's father attempted to strike Deborah. Richard tried to hold him back, "and his father threw him down and said, 'You two had better not be in this house when I return'. . . . [Richard] felt his life to be threatened."

Barrett sat down. As he saw it, he may not have entirely defused the conspiracy charge, but he had done something much more important. Using the state's witness, he had laid the groundwork for a plea of self-defense, based on the defendant's "reasonable" fear for his own life and that of his sister.

The state rested its case shortly after the noon recess on Wednesday. Barrett promptly moved for a judgment of acquittal on both charges. The prosecution had failed to establish the elements of premeditation and malice essential to a charge of first-degree murder, he argued; nor had it demonstrated that Richard Jahnke had conspired with anyone.

The motion was expected, and Jon Forwood rose up to quash it.

"Premeditation can be instantaneous," he said. "In this case we have evidence of planning and willful acts in preparation of, and lying in wait in anticipation of, the return of Richard Chester Jahnke."

Arguing in turn that Barrett had failed to establish grounds of self-defense, Forwood gasped, in mock horror, "If the law were

as Mr. Barrett is arguing to this court, that scares me to death.
. . . Mr. Barrett wants us to believe the issue is, if you are
afraid, you can hide behind a door and kill somebody, and that's
self-defense. And if, in that person's mind, [the fear] was reasonable, that's all you have to prove. . . . Fear is only the first
hurdle to be overcome, Your Honor. There must be proof of an
aggressive act [on the part of the victim]."

Liamos denied the motion for acquittal. "The jury is the fact
finder in this case," he sniffed. "The jury will decide as to
whom and what to believe."

The defense called its first witness, Dr. John Macdonald.
Within minutes Barrett saw his case collapse.

Louis Epps had no sooner asked Macdonald to recount what
Richard had told him about "his growing-up experiences," prim-
ing the witness for a full-scale diagnosis of the defendant's
mental and emotional condition, than Carroll was on his feet,
requesting another conference at the bench.

"The state objects to the question as being irrelevant," Carroll
said. "We do not have an insanity plea before the court."

The prosecutor cited a crucial bit of Wyoming case law, *State
v. Smith,* a 1977 ruling that held that "the state of mind of the
accused is the proper subject for expert testimony when the
defense is based on insanity, but not when not based on such a
plea."

Barrett contended that Macdonald had a right to give an opinion, if not about Richard's state of mind at the time of the
shooting, then about his condition at the time he was evaluated in
December. "I think we have a right to have that opinion before
the court, before the triers of fact," he said.

"He's trying to clutter up the trial, to bring in some sympathy
factors," Carroll retorted.

Liamos frowned. "I think it is hearsay in regard to this matter," he said. "I think what you are trying to present is some sort
of mental deficiency."

"Your Honor," Epps protested, "we have made no claim of
mental deficiency."

"You are doing it indirectly," Liamos said. "I've just given
my ruling. Now, I think you are clearly out of bounds in that
regard, and I'm not going to listen to this."

Barrett requested a hearing to discuss the issue. Liamos announced a recess and sent the jury away for the rest of the day.

Barrett, Epps, and Macdonald huddled at the defense table for five minutes while reporters in the first two rows of spectators tried to figure out what was going on. Then both sides presented their arguments regarding the admissibility of Macdonald's testimony, an exchange that grew increasingly heated.

"Dr. Macdonald would testify that he believes the defendant is emotionally impaired and is a battered child," Carroll said. "Now what does that mean? If the court please, it would be based on hearsay, pure and simple hearsay. . . ."

"Your Honor," Barrett said, "Mr. Carroll seeks, by way of tirade, I suppose, to mislead the court with regard to what we intend—"

"Your Honor, I object to the use of the word 'tirade,' " Carroll snapped.

"Your Honor, we did not, and do not now, and never intended to plead or to indicate that Richard Jahnke is insane," Barrett said. "It wasn't Richard Jahnke who had the severe problem. . . ."

Liamos waited for tempers to subside and then delivered his ruling without pause.

"I haven't been presented any evidence of any court's acceptance of the science of the battered child, what can be predicted from the battered child," he said. "I believe that the testimony, the opinions, and the conclusions of Dr. Macdonald would invade the province of the jury. The jury, I believe, is to determine the reasonableness of any fears, and they should determine that by evidence of a person who testifies as to the facts, and draw their conclusions. The court is sustaining the objections of the state to this testimony."

Barrett couldn't believe what he was hearing. He had been counting on Macdonald to provide the jury with the psychological perspective it needed to acquit his client. The psychiatrist would have testified that Richard Jahnke was a textbook example of the battered child. He was "old beyond his years," yet immature and unable to cope with stress. He was stoic, protective, quick to deny his fear and helplessness, yet afflicted by a fantastic sense of the invincibility of his abuser. But he was not insane by any means. If his mental condition at the time of the shooting resembled anything found in the diagnostic manual, Macdonald believed it would be that recently diagnosed legacy of the Vietnam War, post-traumatic stress disorder—a reliving of a severe trauma outside the realm of "normal" human experience. In other words,

Richard Jahnke had felt an overwhelming need to defend himself from his father at a moment when, to outside eyes, his father clearly posed no threat to him.

Barrett could have contested Liamos's ruling by presenting evidence that a science of the battered child did exist, but he wasn't optimistic about his chances of persuading the judge to change his mind. As matters stood, the exclusion of the expert witness left a gaping hole in his defense. If Barrett had entertained any hopes of keeping his client off the stand, he now dispensed with them. He returned to the defense table and put his hand on Richard's shoulder.

"I guess it's up to you now," he said.

With court in recess until the following morning, the defense team retreated to the Little America motel complex to ponder their next move. Joining them there for dinner were Macdonald, Terry Mackey, and several witnesses Barrett had summoned from Arizona. The latter included Richard's former neighbors, Roger and Jacqueline Carrel and their children. Years ago, Richard had considered the younger Carrels to be his enemies; now they were prepared to testify that his father had threatened their father and appeared to dominate his family.

The mood was far from relaxed. Richard, in particular, seemed edgy. Jim Billis studied him with increasing uneasiness. The young private investigator had grown remarkably close to Richard in the past few weeks, almost like an older brother coming to the rescue of a sibling besieged by bullies. At lunch today they had reviewed the facts of the shooting one more time, and Billis had asked him, "Were you really afraid that your dad would kill you?"

"Yeah," Richard had said.

"You wouldn't lie to me, would you?" Billis had asked.

Richard had said he wouldn't. But now Richard could scarcely bear to look at him.

After dinner, as the coffee was being served, Richard leaned over and whispered in Billis's ear. "I've got to talk to you. Now."

The pair excused themselves and headed for the men's room. In the lobby Richard paused to make sure no one could hear them. He then turned to Billis with a face drained of blood.

"You're right, I can't lie to you," he said. "See, that night—

all along I've been telling you and Jim and Dr. Macdonald, everybody, that I was going to get Deborah out of there and then come back and confront Dad."

"But you couldn't find the car keys," Billis said.

"Right, I couldn't find the keys," he said. "But the thing is—I lied. I wanted to kill Dad. I wasn't sure I could do it, but I knew I had to. I knew it as soon as he left the house."

Billis returned to the table and motioned to Barrett.

"We've got a problem," he said.

The lights burned late into the night at the law firm of Trier-weiler, Bayless, Barrett, and McCartney. Richard Jahnke sat in the smoke-filled law library, addressing a hushed audience of five: Barrett, Epps, Billis, Mackey, and Macdonald. It was not a speech, not a monologue, but a torrent of words, spilling in all directions, as if a dam had burst and the dark waters it held could no longer be guided or tamed but must rush wildly to the empty places.

"A smile," he said softly. "Mom said he had a smile on his face when the first shot hit him."

Macdonald began to take notes, in his small, crabbed physician's hand.

"I came to care for you guys," Richard said. "I knew once I got on the stand I wouldn't be able to pull it off. If I got torn apart by the prosecution and broke down, I'd make you guys look like assholes. . . . Mom said he was smiling." He began to sob. "Can you believe that? Maybe he wanted me to do it."

"Easy, Richard," Barrett said. "It's okay."

"I didn't tell anyone what really happened. I didn't even tell my therapist, and she's subpoena-proof. All my life I've been lying, covering up. Pretending things didn't happen the way they did. But I'm telling you now. I don't think Dad would have killed me. Not physically. But I felt I was dying anyway. Mental death for me if I didn't do it. I was scared to death. There was nothing else to do."

"I wish you'd leveled with us when we had manslaughter," Barrett said, referring to the state's offer of an unconditional plea bargain.

"I know," Richard said, gulping back the tears. "But I was scared. It's like Mom said, he was like Jekyll and Hyde. I loved him and I hated him. And I always felt like I was the one who was wrong. Whenever I tried to tell people what it was really like, they didn't believe me.''

''Let's hear it now,'' Barrett said, ''starting with the fight on the weekend before the shooting.''

''Okay. Saturday morning. Dad told Deborah she looked like hell,'' Richard began. ''He started to hit her. I told him, 'Leave my sister alone, you bastard!' I had so much hate in me, I slammed him up against the wall. First time I'd ever done that. After she was safe I let him go . . . then he hit her again. Then Mom and I got between Deborah and him. He stomped off to his room. I told Mom, hey, we stood up to him. But she just went, 'What?' You know, pretending it didn't happen. The next day we were arguing and she was on his side again. . . .''

Two hours later Richard sat numb and exhausted, his story told at last. A damp-eyed Terry Mackey was smoking his first cigarette in six years. Jim Barrett put in a call to Tom Carroll. He told the prosecutor that Richard wanted to change his plea from innocent to guilty of voluntary manslaughter.

18

The following morning the attorneys for the prosecution and the defense met in chambers to present the plea-bargain arrangement to Judge Liamos. Since the matter would have an impact on Deborah's case, Terry Mackey was also present. The agreement called for Richard to repeat his confession to the prosecution and the judge, who listened without interruption. Then a court reporter was summoned to take down the other conditions of the plea bargain: the state would accept the manslaughter plea but would make no recommendation regarding sentencing, leaving it to Liamos to impose a sentence of up to twenty years in the state penitentiary; the charge of conspiracy would be dropped; and Richard would agree to testify at his sister's trial.

"Your Honor, I think that justice will be served by the plea," Carroll said. "I don't mean to invade the court's province, but philosophically, I do not feel that it would take anything in excess of twenty years to rehabilitate this defendant."

"Do you think that the facts of this case show manslaughter?" Liamos asked.

"Well, the court has heard the facts pretty much as they were, as much as I have," Carroll said. "This is a crime of passion, in a sense."

Liamos turned to Barrett. "Why does your client want to enter a plea of guilty to manslaughter instead of leaving it to the jury?"

"Quite frankly," Barrett said, "we had been advised by our client that the chief motivating factor as he stood in the garage was fear. . . . But we later determined that, although there was fear involved in what he did, the motivating factor was anger, that explosion of anger. . . .

"I believe this is Richard's way of telling the truth—getting it off his chest, if you will—clearing his soul and facing the consequences."

"Mr. Jahnke, do you understand all of this?" Liamos asked.

Richard nodded that he did.

"Anything that you would like to add here in this room?"

Richard paused. "It hurt too much to keep in the truth," he said.

"I wouldn't think of accepting this arrangement without it being done in open court," Liamos said. "And I would want Mr. Jahnke to know that he should think about it before he agrees to this—that in all probability he will receive a penitentiary sentence."

Barrett looked at his client, who was staring at the floor. "Does that change your mind, Rich?"

"No."

Forwood promised to have the necessary papers drawn up within an hour. Liamos said that he would dismiss the jury until one-thirty that afternoon, at which time the plea bargain would be disclosed and accepted, the jury discharged. Sentencing would take place tomorrow morning.

Barrett and Epps escorted Richard into the courtroom, past reporters who had been impatiently cooling their heels for the better part of the morning. Barrett tried to read his client's face, but Richard was as withdrawn as when the attorneys had first visited him in jail. It was the old "my life's over, what's the use" routine. He was the good son, marching sullenly to his doom with his father's laughter ringing in his ears.

The trio stood before the defense table as the jury entered. For a moment Richard's eyes locked with those of a middle-aged woman on the panel, who gave him—what?—a look of encouragement, hope, a go-ahead nod? We're with you, boy.

Don't give up, you fucking jerk.

Barrett was staring at him. "Richard, are you sure you want to do this?"

"No, I'm not," Richard whispered.

Liamos was about to address the jury. Barrett asked to approach the bench.

Once there, he tugged at his glasses and began in a low voice, "Your Honor, just this moment, in talking with Mr. Jahnke . . . ah, he has only just this moment, in spite of what he indicated in chambers, now indicated that he would rather have the matter placed before the jury. If that is, in fact, his wish, I don't know what alternative we have but to put him on the stand."

Liamos declared a recess.

*   *   *

They stopped at a Burger King restaurant for burgers and fries and had a picnic in Holliday Park, a public park not far from the law firm. Then the attorneys sent Richard off on his own to make up his mind once and for all. He walked around the lake and lay on the grass with the sun in his face.

A dozen possible fates raced through his mind. He saw himself gambling on the jury and watching helplessly as they declared him guilty of first-degree murder. He heard a voice sentencing him to life imprisonment. But hey, Tom Carroll would stand up for him. He'd say, This poor boy doesn't deserve more than, oh, twenty years.

He saw himself accepting the plea bargain and being led off to prison, where he would be raped and stabbed by big, ugly dudes time and again. If he didn't get killed he would be out in a few years, as big and ugly as the rest of them. Every day for the rest of his life he would wonder if things could have been different.

He saw the juror who had looked at him arguing passionately for acquittal. He saw himself emerging from the courtroom to the cheers of the crowd, reporters rushing to interview him. Ha! No way, José.

After lunch they took him to Terry Mackey's office, across the street from the courthouse. He sat in a chair surrounded by attorneys, with his foster parents, Dan and Corrine Munn, crouched on either side of him. He wanted someone to tell him what to do, but no one would.

"This has to be your decision," Barrett insisted.

Richard began to feel angry. What good were lawyers if they couldn't tell you what to do? He turned to Billis.

"What do you think I'd get if I plead guilty to manslaughter?" he asked.

"With that judge?" Billis shook his head. "Seven to fourteen years. That's just my opinion, of course."

Richard thought about the newspapers—all the stories about a "slaying plot," an "execution," the boy who killed his father for revenge. He thought about the jokes going around ROTC about staying away from Richard's garage. He thought about Deborah and what he would have to say under oath, if he went ahead and testified—what Carroll and the judge had already heard but the rest of the world didn't know.

When he couldn't think anymore, he announced that he wanted to tell his story one more time.

*   *   *

The battle was on again.

With Macdonald out of the picture, the defense's first witness was Luke Massengill, records supervisor for the Laramie County Department of Public Assistance and Social Services. Massengill was called to identify Defense Exhibit A—the DPASS child abuse report on Richard Chester Jahnke. As anticipated, Carroll rose to object that the abuse report was "immaterial, irrelevant, and incompetent."

"Thank you, counsel," Liamos said, after Carroll had finished. "Exhibit A will be received."

Deputy Robert Bomar was summoned to describe his interviews with the Jahnkes and to identify Defense Exhibits B and C, the photographs of Richard's bruised back taken on May 2. Once again a frustrated Tom Carroll objected, and once again the exhibits were received.

The next witness was DPASS caseworker Frank DeLois, who described his two brief and uneventful contacts with the Jahnkes.

DeLois was followed by Maria Jahnke. As she was sworn in, Maria scarcely glanced at her son, looking instead for support and encouragement from Carolyn Wheeler, who was sitting in the front row of spectators.

Barrett steered Maria back in time to her husband's return from Korea and the years of violence that followed. Carroll popped up and down with objections like a dapper jack-in-the-box. When the subject of Richard Chester Jahnke's alleged fondling of his daughter surfaced, an act Maria claimed not to have witnessed but merely heard about from her children, the furious prosecutor made a beeline for the bench.

"This is turning into a fiasco," he complained. "The defendant is being allowed to ask hearsay questions that are irrelevant . . . apparently there's no limit to what can be brought in. . . . the defense that is being asserted here is one of sympathy, pure sympathy."

Barrett insisted that the testimony was highly relevant. Liamos sighed.

"I'm not telling the state how to conduct their case," he said, "[but] I think that if the state just sat down, let the defendant put on [his] case, and then they can put on their rebuttal and argue it, I think they would be a lot better off."

Barrett wrapped up his examination quickly by having Maria

describe the trip to the sheriff's office on May 2 and the subsequent violence in the house.

"Did there come a time when your husband commented to you about his son having reported him?" Barrett asked.

Maria nodded. "He was very angry," she said. "He said he would never forgive his son for reporting him."

"Are those the words he used?"

"Yes. And he said that he hated him for doing that."

"Did he explain to you why he felt that way?"

"Yes, because he had an important job, and what if someone checked up on him and found out what type of person he was really like?"

On cross-examination Carroll lit into the witness with even more vigor than he had displayed at the transfer hearings. He read aloud from Maria's interviews with the police the night of the homicide, in which she claimed that her son had been "nasty" to her lately, and that her husband had been threatening to throw him out of the house. Maria said she didn't remember saying such things. The prosecutor then challenged her assertion that her husband's punishment of Richard that night had upset her; if that was so, he asked, why did she hug her husband after the beating?

"I didn't do that," Maria said. "I was trying to get out of there as soon as possible, and I was trying to rush him out."

"Bearing in mind you are under oath," Carroll said, "you are saying absolutely you did not walk up to your husband . . . just after he'd, as you described, beat up your son, and say, 'Richard, I love you'—put your arm around him and say, 'You are so good to me'?"

"I don't remember saying that," Maria said. "I'm sorry."

Barrett made no attempt to halt Carroll's attack. Maria Jahnke was not on trial. Maria Jahnke was not even his client. If the state wanted to make her look like a demon—well, perhaps the jury would commiserate with Richard all the more.

On redirect Barrett had Maria enumerate her husband's virtues: he was a good provider, a hard worker, a conscientious gardener. Then he casually dropped a bomb.

"Do you think your husband was an honest man?" he asked.

"He tried to be as honest as he possibly could," Maria said.

"Did your husband ever tell you that he did a year's probation for auto tampering?"

Before the witness could reply, Carroll was on his feet again.

This time his frantic objection was sustained. Barrett had plucked the misdemeanor charge from Richard Chester Jahnke's military records, which indicated that he had been arrested in 1960, at the age of sixteen. The trial was held in family court in Chicago, a supposedly confidential proceeding. The conviction had received mention in his file because the youthful offender had required a morals waiver for military enlistment. The fact that Richard's father had himself been adjudicated a juvenile delinquent was, perhaps, too fine an irony for Barrett to pass up, but Judge Liamos admonished him for straying far afield of his case in an effort to "try the deceased." He instructed the jury to disregard the question.

Barrett decided to quit while he was still ahead. The witness stepped down, and court was in recess for the day. A dozen television and newspaper reporters headed for their offices or the nearest phone. To the press, ignorant of Richard's flirtation with a plea bargain earlier in the day, Maria's testimony had been the first taste of genuine courtroom drama in the trial. Carroll's persistent attempts to fend off the "child abuse defense" had only whetted their appetites for more. The account in the *Denver Post* was headlined, MRS. JAHNKE SAYS INSIDE THE HOUSE 'WAS PURE HELL.'

The moment the crowd had been waiting for arrived shortly after nine in the morning on Friday, the fifth day of the trial. Wearing the familiar blue suit, his face pale, the circles under his eyes darker than ever from lack of sleep, Richard Jahnke took the stand in his own defense.

Barrett handed Richard Defense Exhibit B and asked him to identify it.

"It's a picture of my back, bruises all over it," he said.

"Do you know how those bruises got there, Richard?"

"Yes, I do."

"Richard," Barrett coaxed, "tell us what happened to you on May 2, 1982."

And so he told his story again, the story of the beating he received May 2, of the years of beatings and humiliation before that, of the final months of private warfare after the sheriff's office sent him home. It was, for the most part, the same story he had poured out in a sobbing fit two nights before in the law library, and again, more calmly, in Liamos's chambers the previ-

ous day. It had not paled with repetition. Scarcely a word was
uttered that did not contain its measure of jagged emotion. Richard gazed past Barrett at a spot on the far wall and struggled to
control the pitch of his voice, but the voice shook. It seethed with
long-simmering rancor, receded to a barely audible murmur of
shame, cracked with exquisite pain. At times he seemed to be in
a trance, numbly recounting the scenes of battles past that flashed
before his watery eyes; at times he seemed possessed by the spirit
of his father, which leaped from his throat in angry, guttural
threats and execration. Depending on one's capacity for belief in
such things, it was either the most affecting display of raw truth
or the most magnificent act of fraud the people of Cheyenne had
ever witnessed.

"What was he yelling at you, Richard? What was he saying?"
Barrett asked.

"Saying, 'You *bastard*!' " Richard snarled. " 'What the hell
are you goddam doing—playing around? I told you to sweep the
floor.' " He began to sob. "As he started walking toward me I
knew he was going to hit me. I was really scared. . . .' "

Barrett asked him to recall the day he stopped his father from
beating his mother.

"What did you see?"

"I saw my dad grabbing Mom and throwing her up against
furniture. Putting her down on the ground and pounding on her,"
he whispered.

The crowd leaned forward in their seats, straining to hear.

"How was he pounding on her, Richard?"

"Like *this!*" he screamed, and slammed his fist on the podium
with all his might. The crowd jumped back in alarm.

"Hard as he could," he went on. "Loved doing that. . . . I
would turn off the lights and hide in the closet or under my bed.
. . . Later on I finally got disgusted with myself, I guess."

"Why, Richard?"

"I thought I should protect my mom," he mumbled.

"How old were you?"

"I was ten or eleven."

He told the jury that, after he finally made Dad leave Mom
alone and go after him instead, he tried to do something about the
"games" Dad played with Deborah.

"I remember one time he came home from work and Mom
was cooking in the kitchen. Deborah and I were setting the table.

Deborah stopped, and Dad was talking. Dad looked up and stuck his hands down her pants. He was feeling her up. . . . She looked so scared. She was stiff. She was shaking. And Mom was pretending like it wasn't even anything.''

Later, he added, "I talked to my mother about it."

"And did it stop?" Barrett asked.

"My mother got angry with my sister. Told her that it was her fault for wearing all those shorts. . . . And she told my sister, 'Just tell Dad no, tell him not to touch you.' And my sister did."

Barrett brought him back to the beating of May 2. Richard Chester Jahnke had told Deputy Bomar that his son had threatened to kill him, but the defendant now claimed he had feared for his own life.

"When he got tired of beating me, he started stomping off. I got mad. We were supposed to go on this hunting trip. I think I stood up and said, 'I'm not going on a hunting trip with you. You're such a crazy lunatic you'd probably kill me.' ''

"Did your father ever discuss your report to the sheriff's [office] with you?"

"A couple of times he'd yell at me about it. . . . Say, 'You son of a bitch . . . the next time I'm really going to give you something to report to the sheriff, if you can speak.' ''

He recited several other threats his father had made in the final months of his life, leading up to the final outburst on the night of the shooting.

"November 16th, my mom was uptight," he said. "I told her that night I had to go to school for an open house. . . . She said, 'I'm not going to be your damn chauffeur. Sick of being your damn chauffeur.'

"And then she just started screaming. She was telling me I was a bastard . . . that it was my fault about her marriage . . . she even started screaming about this vest that I had loaned out to one of my friends the week before. . . . the reason my dad and I didn't get along, she kept saying, 'It takes two to tango. It takes two to tango. Right away, oh, yeah, I'm the enemy.' She kept saying that: 'Right away, I'm the enemy. Well, Richard, you're not a perfect angel. You're a bastard. It takes two to tango.' She kept going on and on and on. . . .

"And I hit the table. Got to me. Hit the table hard, and I said,

'Shut up,' as loud as I could. . . . Then she really got angry. . . . she threw a big can of dog food at me, which hit me . . . she threw a candle at me. . . . she kept on exploding. So I just went to my room.

"My father got home. Right away she said, 'I can't take it anymore, Richard. They're such bastards. I'm sick of it. He told me that I'm a horrible mother.' She started crying. She kept telling him all these things, that I was really nasty to her, that it's all my fault. . . .

"Then Dad came stomping down. He banged on my door, told me to open up. I opened up the door. Right away he started hitting me. He said, 'Being disrespectful to my wife? You asshole. If you don't like it here, get the hell out.' Said, 'I don't care what I have to do. I'm going to get rid of you. I don't know how, but I'm going to get rid of you, you bastard.'

"That's when my sister came to my room, and she said, 'Where he's going, I'm going, too.' And he went and screamed at her. . . . Then he came back in a little while, pounded on my door. . . . He started hitting me again. I wasn't going to be hit. So I was pushing him away, grabbing his fists, I was dodging. He was able to hit me a couple times. And my mother came into the room when it looked like Dad was ready to stop hitting me. She said, 'Oh, and he called me a martyr, too.' She was taking pleasure in watching me being hit."

His voice dropped low. His father, he said, ordered him into the kitchen to clean up the grape juice he'd spilled in the earlier argument with his mother.

"He stood in the doorway so I would have to go through him, so he could hit me a couple more times. I gathered my courage. I got hit a couple of times. I went to the kitchen, started cleaning up the mess. . . . My mother was there . . . smelling the flowers that he got her. It was their twentieth anniversary since they first met. She looked so pleased and so peaceful. When he came back, she hugged my father. She goes, 'Oh, you're so good to me. I love you.' And he said, 'Let's go to dinner. I can't stand the sight of these bastards.'

"Just before he was going to leave, he came back and shoved me up against the wall. He told me, 'I'm disgusted with the shit you turned out to be. I don't want you to be here when I get back.'

"He told me to get the garbage cans [out of the driveway].

And when he left I went and got the garbage cans, put them away. I felt horrible.''

Judge Liamos declared a half-hour recess.

During the recess members of the jury and the press complained that they were having difficulty hearing the witness. When court resumed, Liamos made a brief speech about the necessity of silence in the courtroom. Richard picked up where he left off, his voice more subdued than ever. The standing-room-only crowd hung on every word; a hush prevailed, so profound that those in the front rows could hear the asthmatic wheeze of the defendant's breathing.

"When your parents left that night, Richard, what did you do?" Barrett asked.

"At first I went and obeyed. I went and got the garbage cans and brought them in. And I felt disgusted with myself. Because I just—whatever he does, I still just kiss his ass.''

"Did you see your sister after your parents left?"

"Yes. She was crying and shaking . . . she was going crazy. She was losing it. She was being hurt so much. She needed to be free. I had to free her. I had to free her, my mother, and myself.''

"Be free from what, Richard?"

"The pain my father had given us. Misery.''

"You could have left, couldn't you?"

"There was no place to go.''

"Couldn't you have gone to the sheriff's office?"

"They didn't believe me the first time. My dad is so smart, he can talk his way out of it and make it look like it was my fault.''

"What about your friend, Major Vegvary, couldn't you go to him again?"

"He was no longer a friend. After that case in May he told everybody what had happened to me, and he was very pompous towards me. . . . I couldn't trust him.''

"Couldn't you have just run away, Richard?"

"No. I would have probably starved to death someplace. I didn't have any place to go. There was no one out there. Not even my grandparents would have helped me. No one.''

"So what did you do, Richard?"

"Changed my clothes to darker clothes. Dark blue. . . . grabbed all the weapons. Most of them were already loaded. . . . looked for the keys to the car, but there were none there. . . . So I told Deborah she was going to have to stay in the house.''

Barrett asked what weapons he selected for himself.

"A .38, a Marine knife, and a 12-gauge shotgun," Richard replied. "Dad referred to it as a riot gun. Always loved that riot gun. He would teach me how to shoot it—combat shoot it, firing it rapidly. It was loaded with what Dad called a candy cane mix—birdshot, buckshot, slugs. I changed the ammunition to all slugs. If I was going to shoot at something, I wanted to hit what I was shooting at, nothing else."

He said that he showed Deborah how to fire the carbine "in case I got killed." Then he put the pets in the basement and lowered the garage door to the ground so his father wouldn't see his feet. He figured that his father might not "kill me physically," but in time "he would have killed me mentally." He went into the garage, he said, thinking, "My father's son is going to be a man for the first time in his life."

"I was thinking of all that happened to me, and I saw the Volkswagen drive up. . . . I said, 'Oh, my God. Am I really going to do it? I can't.' I said, 'I can't do it. No, I can't do it.' But as my dad walked toward the garage door I thought—well, first I thought, 'I'll just drop the guns, and when he opens the garage door, I'll hug him. I'll tell him, Dad, we need help.' "

"Why didn't you do that, Richard?"

"I remembered [one time] I hugged him when he was beating me. I told him I loved him, that we've got to stop that. He just kept hitting me and beating me for it. And I thought, 'He's going to see me with all these guns'—he used to get really mad if anyone would touch his guns—'here I've got them laid out all over the house. He'll beat us for sure.'

"Then I said, 'No. He's never going to touch any of us again.'

"I had this whistle. My command sergeant major's whistle. Used it for courage. At the last second I became a battalion command sergeant major—this tough person who doesn't take shit from anybody. I learned that from ROTC.

"I blew that whistle. I opened fire. Every shot that I fired hurt me so much. Almost as if I was getting shot also. I tried to get the shotgun away from me. I felt like it was stuck to me. My ears started to ring from the noise. I heard this ringing—only it wasn't a ringing. It was my mom screaming. I couldn't handle that. I couldn't handle what I just did. I threw down the shotgun and ran."

Barrett sat down. The spectators released a collective sigh and dared to relax, cough, breathe deeply, shift in their seats—in some cases, wipe away tears and mutter under their breath—before settling into silence again.

Tom Carroll came out swinging. Much of his cross-examination was devoted to challenging Richard's claim that no one could have rescued him from his predicament. What about Major Vegvary, Michael Brinkman, Deputy Bomar, Frank DeLois, Nurse Marion, all of whom had offered to help? What made it so difficult for a bright sixteen-year-old to turn to any one of them?

What did Richard think Major Vegvary would have done, Carroll asked, "if you would have told him that you were being hit again by your father?"

Richard shrugged. "He probably would have told everybody else," he said.

"Don't you think he would have taken you back down to the sheriff's office?"

"That would have been very dangerous for me, if he did that."

"You thought the sheriff's officers were afraid of your father?"

"Yes, because he was a criminal investigator for the Internal Revenue Service. There was also one thing—Dad was very mad at me for reporting him, because they were going to indict Sheriff Flynn for tax evasion and running a hooker ring and drug rings."

A ripple of confusion ran up and down the press bench. What the hell—what did the kid just say about—come again? The charge was outrageous; it was also unverifiable. The IRS cannot comment on or even confirm the existence of an investigation where no indictment has been made; Dennis Flynn, who had left office in January after losing the November election, was never charged with any offense. No allegation of the sort Richard had made had ever appeared in the local newspapers, either. In any case, it was hard to see how an alleged IRS investigation of the sheriff's office had any bearing on the death of Richard Chester Jahnke at the hands of his son—except, of course, to momentarily distract the prosecutor in the midst of his suffocating cross-examination.

But Carroll refused to be sidetracked. After pressing on with several more questions about Richard's failure to report his father to the authorities a second time, he turned to the defendant's relationship with his mother. Wasn't it true, as Maria claimed, that Richard was getting "sassy" in the weeks preceding the homicide, prompting much of the fighting in the home? Richard denied it.

"You are saying you never sassed her?" Carroll asked.

"I didn't *sass* her," Richard said. "I wasn't cruel to her. What she was doing on the stand, she was protecting herself the best way she could."

"Are you saying she was lying?"

"She was protecting herself and making it seem like she was never part of any of the abuse. What you saw was this sweet old lady."

"You're saying she was a part of the abuse?"

"Oh, yes, especially with my sister."

"Was that physical or mental?"

"She would get physical with my sister."

"Were you afraid that your mother was going to harm your sister?"

"Every once in a while she would. I was more worried about my father harming them."

Carroll produced a photograph, taken after Richard's arrest, that depicted the "injuries" incurred by his father's beating that night—a small bruise on his right arm.

"Were there any other marks?" he asked.

"Nothing visible," Richard said. He sighed. "You wouldn't be able to see my heart."

Barrett felt like hugging his client. *You wouldn't be able to see my heart.* It was not a planned remark—damn, it was the first time he'd heard Richard put it that way—but it hit the mark. He heard gasps behind him and the press boys scribbling it down for the evening broadcast and the morning edition. Richard was doing better than anyone had expected. But Carroll wasn't finished yet.

"After you shot your father, how did you feel?"

"I felt hurt," Richard said. "I regretted it."

"Did you feel like your troubles were over?"

"I felt my life was over."

"Did you think he was dead?"

"I really didn't know if he was dead."

"Did you hope that he was?"

"I just hoped he didn't suffer."

Carroll paused to confer with Forwood. He had one last card to play. It had to do with something Richard had said when he was making a clean breast of it yesterday morning in Liamos's chambers; something he had better admit now, or face possible perjury charges.

"Did your sister ever come into the garage?"

"She did once," Richard said. "I just told her to go back in the living room."

"And did she say anything to you at that time?"

"She said, 'I can't believe this is all happening.' "

Carroll scowled. "Did she mention your mother at that time?"

"I remember—"

"Speak up so I can hear you," Carroll snapped.

"She asked me if I was going to kill Mom, too."

"What did you say?"

"I said no."

"What did she say?"

"She was upset. She asked me to kill Mom."

"She asked you to kill your mother?"

Richard nodded sadly. "Yes," he said.

Carroll turned to the bench. "I believe that's all the questions I have, Your Honor."

Barrett's redirect was brief.

"When you fired the first shot from the garage, did you aim directly at your father?"

"No," Richard said.

"After the first shot was fired, what did you see your father do?"

"Saw him duck."

"Did you see your father at all after that?"

"No, I didn't."

"Mr. Carroll asked you whether or not you had the other guns around the house so you could use them while you were retreating. I believe your answer was yes. What did you expect to be retreating from, Richard?"

"My father with a gun, firing at me."

"You honestly believe that was a possibility?"

"To me it was a possibility."

Barrett drew himself up to his full height and tugged solemnly at his glasses.

"Did you love your father, Richard?"

"Yes."

"Did he love you back?"

"I believe the only way he knew how to love was through pain," Richard said.

After two and a half hours of testimony, the witness stepped down, and the defense rested its case.

The afternoon session was taken up with the testimony of rebuttal witnesses offered by the state. In building their case, Carroll and Forwood had presented less than a third of their original pool of witnesses, keeping the rest in reserve until they could see what Barrett was going to do. They now decided to call seven more (including Michael Brinkman on his second time around), one more witness in rebuttal than the defense had used to present its entire case.

Major Vegvary, Greg Porter, and Michael Brinkman—Richard's closest associates in ROTC—took the stand to affirm that Lieutenant Jahnke had a bit of a temper himself; that he was at times insubordinate; that he had, in effect, rejected numerous offers of help that were made after his father's abusiveness was first reported in May. Caryl Marion, the school nurse, described her own efforts to counsel the witness, which included telling him to call 911 if he had any more problems at home. Dale Allen Dannaman, a former federal prosecutor from Arizona, remembered Richard Chester Jahnke as "the most outstanding IRS agent that I had ever had any experience with," a man who "wanted a better life for his children" and did not seem at all violent.

The jury sat impassively throughout the rebuttal testimony, like weary passersby obliged, by good manners or civic duty, to watch a parade of street sweepers. Their curiosity was stirred only briefly, when Robert Jahnke and Donna Jahnke Zimny, younger brother and sister of the deceased, were called to the stand.

Donna Zimny turned out to be a short, perky blonde in her mid-twenties, blessed with a sunny smile that seemed utterly out of place in the gloomy atmosphere of the courtroom. She had been nine years old when Richard Chester Jahnke first brought his family to Chicago; she had visited them in Arizona twice, most recently three years ago. Despite the infrequent contact, she felt that she had been getting closer to her oldest brother in recent years, through letters and phone calls. The brother she knew bore little resemblance to the vicious tyrant she had been reading about in the papers. She didn't know anything about any fights, child abuse investigations, or the like. The brother she knew was a hardworking family man, an outdoorsman, and a solicitous host who always showed her and other relatives a good time. Someone had to stick up for that man. She did. And as she left the witness stand, she smiled at her nephew Richie, who sat grimly at the defense table.

Robert Jahnke did not smile. Physically, he was a leaner, younger version of the deceased, with closely cropped dark hair and a muscular build. He sat tensely in the witness box and rattled off his impressions of his brother ("a normal family man"), his nephew Richard ("just a normal kid"), and his brother's household ("just normal family atmosphere") in a tone of thinly veiled resentment, as if he were outraged that anyone should try to defile his brother's memory.

"I never questioned myself as to what kind of guy Richard was," he told the jury, his Chicago accent ringing harsh on Western ears. "He was my brother, you know. He was nothing different than anybody else."

"What kind of a temperament did he have?" Carroll asked.

"Just normal temperament," the witness said.

"Did he have a temper?"

"The only temper I saw my brother had is when driving. He was a driver that didn't like being cut off. Like me—I'm the same. I don't know if you are."

Barrett had waived cross-examination of the first rebuttal witnesses. With Robert Jahnke, however, he made an exception.

"Mr. Jahnke," he began, "this has all been pretty difficult for you, hasn't it?"

"It sure has," Robert Jahnke agreed.

"And your brother's temper—would you compare it to yours?"

"Yeah, definitely."

"How did your brother react to pressure?"

"I don't know. He was like a normal person . . . what do you mean by pressure?"

"Well, during your brother's funeral—you were there?"

"Sure."

"And did you say anything to a photographer outside the funeral [service] that day?"

"Yeah. 'Don't take pictures in the church.' "

"Or what?"

"Or what—what do you mean, 'or what'?"

"Do you remember threatening the photographer?"

Robert Jahnke shook his head. "I just told him 'don't take any pictures in the church.' "

"You didn't tell him, 'or I'll smash that camera in your face'?"

The witness's face darkened, as if Barrett had struck him. "No," he said.

Barrett sat down. He could have called rebuttal witnesses of his own—Roger and Jacqueline Carrel, for instance, who had a rather different account of the Jahnkes' life in Arizona than Dale Dannaman, who had never visited Special Agent Jahnke at home. He could have summoned the *Denver Post* photographer Robert Jahnke had allegedly threatened to give his side of the incident. But it was better, he decided, not to dilute his case. Better to leave the jury with the image of Robert Jahnke glaring at him, and let them wonder what his older brother's temper must have been like.

Each day Maria arrived early, found a parking place behind the courthouse, and sat in the car until the last possible moment. Then she climbed the stairs to the second floor hallway, where Carolyn Wheeler and sometimes the Hains would be waiting for her. On Saturday she arrived even earlier than usual. She bought a *Denver Post* at the corner box and returned to the car to read the account of Richard's testimony yesterday. She made it through the first three paragraphs, and then the words began to dance before her eyes:

> Jahnke also testified that his sister had asked him that day to kill their mother, too, but that he told her he would not do that. His 17-year-old sister, Deborah Jahnke, faces trial in March . . .

She put the paper down. It wasn't right, she told herself, putting Richie on the stand. A kid who wasn't right in the head, they shouldn't be putting him through this, making him say all these terrible things. She hadn't wanted him to testify, but the lawyers didn't care. They never consulted her. Who was she, anyway, she was just the one paying the bills; she was just the one they were trying to crucify so Richard could go free, and she was happy to do it, but getting Richie to say these things wasn't right. Richie was so mixed up. Look at what he said—the poor boy just hung himself and his sister, too. And the idea that Deborah could have wanted to kill her . . . it was all too painful. Where was it going to end?

She got out of the car and walked slowly toward the court-house. She was going to have to be strong today, stronger than ever. Everybody felt sorry for Richard and Deborah, oh yes, but nobody cared about her. Nobody was going to give her the benefit of the doubt. Nobody saw her as a victim, too, oh no, she was just the mother that got away. She was the bad guy. And she would have to sit there and endure the dirty looks and the muttered remarks of strangers and be strong about it, because today the trial was over, they were going to let her into the courtroom to hear the verdict. And she had to be there, with Richie, oh yes, she was going to be there no matter what.

Judge Liamos met briefly with the opposing attorneys in chambers that morning.

"Gentlemen, during your summations and argument, I'll ask you to stand behind the lectern that is close to the witness box," he began. "The court will allow you wide latitude in arguing, but you shouldn't enlarge the issue, so as to say, Mr. Barrett, 'If you convict Richard of this crime you'll be giving carte blanche to every father in the United States to abuse his child'—or the state to say, 'If you do not convict this man no father in America is safe.' Because that doesn't belong in the case at all. . . .

"There are quite a few instructions. It will take a while to read them. . . ."

Judge Liamos gave a total of twenty-one pattern instructions to the jury, on everything from the criteria for finding someone guilty of first-degree murder and conspiracy to a very detailed definition of self-defense. The latter concluded:

If the person so confronted [by an assailant] acts in self-defense upon such appearances of danger from honest belief, his right of self-defense is the same whether the danger is real or merely apparent. On the other hand, a bare fear of death or

serious bodily harm is not sufficient to justify the killing of
another person.

Cradling the shotgun found in the garage, Jon Forwood gave
the jury a short course in premeditation. Consider, he said, the
defendant's actions in reloading the murder weapon with slugs,
in placing weapons throughout the house, in changing his clothes,
hiding the pets, adjusting the lights; and finally, consider the
shooting itself.

"He sees the head and shoulders." Forwood pumped the
unloaded 12-gauge. "One shot. But to fire you have to eject and
do it again." Pump. "Shot him again." Pump. "We're not
through. We've got four more times."

Richard Jahnke, he continued, "gets a fair trial, a fairer trial
than he gave his father. He gave his father no trial. He was the
judge. He was the jury. Then he was the executioner. . . .

"He testified he was afraid that his dad would mentally hurt
him. He put up with this for years—mental abuse. Well, that's
not the [self-defense] statute. It's serious *bodily* harm or imminent danger of death.

"The self-defense argument is a sham.

"He wants you to believe it was an abusive environment. Let's
pretend everything he said was true—because we'll never know
the truth. You put his testimony against his mother's, they're
calling each other liars. One refutes the other. His friends never
saw any abuse. He never told anybody about this abuse. Did it
ever happen? We obviously can't ask the victim.

"But let's pretend that it did. Was it that bad, that it required
the murder, the execution, the ambush slaying of his father?"

"Let's not pretend," Jim Barrett said. "These things did
happen. And we can't ignore it.

"So what's a little abuse? That's the attitude we're supposed
to take toward Richard Jahnke or any of his children. A little
abuse is all right. If it doesn't hurt as much as having your bones
broken, your head scalped, and your fingers burned, that's
okay. . . .

"I would submit to you that for a period of fourteen years
Richard Chester Jahnke was the aggressor against his son, his
daughter, and his wife. For fourteen years he beat his son, for
fourteen years he mentally tortured and abused his son . . . for

fourteen years this man murdered his son by inches, took bits and pieces of him away, tried day after day, week after week, to destroy Richie. To strike him verbally; to mentally pick him up and throw him down and crash him against every obstacle he could. That's the crime—that slow torture, that slow, day-to-day, week-by-week punishment. Not because his son did anything wrong, but because his son was there. Simply to do it. Cruel. Heartless. Premeditated. Willful. Malicious.''

Barrett's voice grew warmer, softer, folksier. ''Blame Richie and everything is okay,'' he said. ''We don't have to think about what happened. We don't. Because it's all Richie's fault. Damn kid. Why didn't he do something?

''All of us adults sit around with our thumbs God knows where. We don't do a thing. All we do is wait for something to happen and then blame it on somebody else.

''That's not you in that garage. That's Richie Jahnke . . . but Richie Jahnke was acting in self-defense just as surely as you or I.

''Somebody had to stop it. Nobody would. Nobody could. And right up to the last second, thoughts were going through Richie's mind that he just could not do this, could not kill, but, my God, what if he finds me here?

''For once, ladies and gentlemen, believe him. For once, don't blame him. For once, hear him. For once, listen and understand and believe. Because it's about time somebody did.''

As is customary, the prosecution had the last word. It was delivered by the district attorney in an unaccustomed tone of defensiveness.

''I can't believe that the system let this defendant down,'' Carroll said. ''He was given every opportunity, if it be true that he was undergoing such abuse, to speak out so that the system could help him. He did not speak out.''

The system wasn't on trial, Carroll insisted. Tom Carroll wasn't on trial. The deceased wasn't on trial. The ''only issue'' was whether Richard Jahnke murdered his father.

Carroll noted that the defendant claimed to have been beaten on the Saturday before the shooting and on the day of the shooting. ''How badly was he beaten? You heard it described graphically. His dad was a real mean person, and he beat him badly. As a result of those two beatings within less than a week, the only injury that he had on his body of any kind was a slight scratch on his arm. . . . I submit, ladies and gentlemen, there has to be some exaggeration here. . . .

"There is child abuse. We know it because it crops up time and time again. Seems like every time you pick up the paper, you're reading about some horrible offense, abuse against a child. They are easy victims because before they get to school years they can be secluded in the family home, they can be hidden from public view, and they are pretty much entirely at the mercy of a parent.

"But we're not talking about a situation like that. We're talking about teenaged children. We're talking about a seventeen-year-old girl and a sixteen-year-old boy who were out in society. They were attending school regularly. They were under the observation of adults and other children for many years. . . . But no witnesses were brought forth to show you, to corroborate what this mother and this son are telling you. . . .

"The evidence is not contradicted that he went into that garage with the full intent to kill his father. And he got the job done. And then he tells why he did it. Revenge.

"Well, he's not entitled to revenge."

The bailiffs took the jury to lunch at a nearby motel and then back to the jury room. Deliberations began shortly after two o'clock.

The conpiracy charge was scarcely discussed. No one felt strongly about it, particularly after Michael Brinkman's confusing description of Deborah as a "backup" who would "follow through" if—if what? If Richard got killed? No, the real question, everyone agreed, was whether they were looking at a crime of passion, self-defense, or cold-blooded murder.

Within minutes it became apparent that opinion was divided largely along gender lines. Three of the five men (all fathers) didn't see how an ambush slaying could be anything but murder. Several of the women clung fiercely to the self-defense argument. The rest were caught in the middle. By the end of the first hour, they all knew where they stood: seven leaning toward acquittal (some more strongly than others), three pushing for first-degree murder, two undecided.

They went back over the evidence and the instructions Judge Liamos had given them. The discussion revolved around the legal definitions of first-degree murder, second-degree murder, and voluntary manslaughter. First-degree: purposeful, malicious, deliberate, with premeditation. Second-degree: purposeful and malicious, but without premeditation. Voluntary manslaughter: an intentional killing, but one committed in the heat of passion, without malice aforethought.

Judge Liamos had warned them not to consider the likely penalty in each instance, but it proved impossible not to consider it. The pro-acquittal group on the panel would never allow a verdict of first-degree murder; everyone knew that first-degree meant an automatic life term in the state penitentiary. (With time off for good behavior, "life" usually translated to a minimum of twelve years.) Second-degree was almost as grim: a sentence of twenty years to life. By the same token, the pro-homicide members refused to let the boy off with a warning after he'd plugged his daddy—his unarmed daddy, that is; never mind all this talk about how Dad always carried a gun, nobody found a gun on the body that night. A suitable compromise had to be found, something that might allow Judge Liamos to put the teenager on probation perhaps, or send him to do a little time at the psychiatric hospital or the boys' reform school at Worland—but not a sure prison sentence or a clean slate. No way.

They took a half hour for dinner and returned to read the instructions again. At 8:50 in the evening, after six hours of mulling it over, the jury informed the bailiffs that they had reached a decision.

The crowd reassembled in Courtroom B at half-past nine. Richard clutched his wristwatch and a gold bracelet, a gift from Billis, in one hand. Barrett had told him that if the decision went against him, Liamos would probably revoke his bond pending sentencing; it was best to go into the courtroom stripped down, ready for another session in the county jail.

The jury came in with heads lowered. The woman who had looked at Richard earlier, spurring his decision to testify, wouldn't look at him now. Another woman was crying. Tears, bad news—*you're taking the fall, boy.*

The foreman, a lab technician with four teenage children, handed the verdict forms to the court reporter, who read them aloud.

". . . not guilty of the crime of conspiracy . . ."

". . . guilty of the crime of voluntary manslaughter . . ."

Liamos announced that no one was to move until the jury was out of the courtroom. Speedy to the core, he thanked the jurors with a few well-chosen words and dismissed them. Richard offered Barrett a wan smile and handed him the watch and bracelet. Then he hugged his mother and left, escorted by his attorneys, Billis, and two deputies. Liamos, Carroll, and Forwood departed just as quickly.

For several moments no one spoke. A low, hollow snuffling sound arose from the front of the spectators' gallery, turning into loud sobs and finally an unearthly wail. It was Maria Jahnke.

"He always won, and he won again," she howled. "I hope he's rotting in hell!"

19

Two weeks after Richard Jahnke was found guilty of voluntary manslaughter, in the final, snow-ridden days of February, a crude handbill began to circulate in the streets of Cheyenne. The single sheet was tacked onto telephone poles, posted in supermarkets, and taped to student lockers in the halls of Central High School. It read:

FOR PEOPLE WHO BELIEVE IN PEOPLE

We need your support. Our concern is not only for Richard John Jahnke, but also for other people who have been physically or mentally abused or maltreated. We wish to insure that victims of abuse have visible alternatives to prevent unhappy or tragic outcomes.

Please take a few minutes and write a letter in support of Richard, who is awaiting what could be a 20 year prison sentence. We feel Richard has been punished enough throughout his life and now is the time for our community to offer our help instead of punishment.

Richard is interested in working to prevent child abuse and his input has already been requested by various organizations and agencies . . .

The flyer asked that letters urging leniency be sent to Judge Liamos care of "The Committee to Help Richard John Jahnke, P.O. Box 15720." At the bottom of the page was an excerpt from a front-page story in the *Rocky Mountain News*, headlined JAHNKE URGES ABUSE VICTIMS TO SEEK HELP. According to the article, Richard had told Sharon Tilley, a Denver "child-abuse expert" who had visited him in the county jail the day after the verdict, that "he wants to prevent this from ever happening again." Tilley said that Richard had expressed interest in establishing a telephone hotline in his name for victims of child abuse.

239

The Committee to Help Richard John Jahnke had little to do with Tilley's visit, or, for that matter, with the legal efforts of Jim Barrett and Louis Epps on Richard's behalf. When reporters contacted Barrett about the committee, he described the group as "some local folks" who were concerned about Richard's future; he didn't start it, but heck, he thought they were entitled to let the judge know how they felt.

In fact, the letter-writing campaign represented the first stirrings of an organized community response to the Jahnke case. The ad hoc committee consisted of a dozen neighbors and recent acquaintances of the Jahnkes, including Richard's foster parents, Dan and Corrine Munn, and freckle-faced, seventeen-year-old Troy Schwamb, who had known Richard and Deborah only slightly before the shooting but had since become their most outspoken defender at Central High. The chief organizer was Maria's neighbor and informal adviser, George Hain. Usually a man of strong opinions, Hain had been "on the fence," as he put it, until the day Richard testified. The youth's story had brought tears to his eyes, and he was now determined to use his influence to campaign for probation for Richard. He planned to distribute petitions throughout Cheyenne and to take out ads in newspapers to solicit letters nationwide.

Hain's call for action was quickly taken up by others. Within days of the verdict, the local radio talk shows and letters-to-the-editor columns were filled with pleas for mercy and pious condemnations of the horrors of child abuse. Clearly, a great number of people in Cheyenne felt compelled to "do something" about the Jahnke case, to show the world, perhaps, that their town wasn't as blind or uncaring as the Jahnkes' experience might suggest. An article in *People* magazine, featuring excerpts from Richard's testimony and Maria's first press interview ("My son has freed me," she explained), fanned the flames across the country.

Not everyone in Cheyenne greeted Hain's crusade with enthusiasm. The United States attorney for the state of Wyoming told reporters that the committee was a "very dangerous and very unusual" attempt to put pressure on Judge Liamos, who had a duty to consider the evidence rather than public sentiment in determining Richard's fate. Dan Munn clashed with Central High principal James Godfrey over whether it was "appropriate" for the school psychologist to campaign so visibly for Richard's release. The ROTC program was suffering from a bigger image problem than ever, particularly after Richard testified that he blew his NCO whistle "for courage" when he fired the shotgun, and many of the cadets wished the Jahnke case would just go away.

The case had put the local Department of Public Assistance and Social Services on the defensive, too. In response to mounting public criticism of the way Richard's abuse report was handled, Ralph McConahy, director of Laramie County DPASS, said that it was department policy to interview abuse victims individually. Frank DeLois had evidently violated that policy by failing to interview Richard outside the presence of his father. Stan Torvik, director of Wyoming's Department of Health and Social Services, conceded that the county DPASS lacked "people who are truly qualified to handle these delicate situations." The problem, he explained, was inadequate salaries, not understaffing or current abuse investigation policies. Torvik also claimed that if Richard and Deborah had run away from home, "the system would have accommodated them."

"This is an ironic situation," he told one reporter. "It's inexcusable—but nonetheless, had they done anything to get them into trouble with the law, they would have been protected."

Amid all the breast beating, finger pointing, and bubbling controversy, one voice was strangely silent. Deborah Jahnke signed one of Hain's petitions, but she declined to make any public statements in support of her brother. She kept her peace under the strict orders of Terry Mackey, who viewed the well-intentioned bandwagon forming around Richard with increasing alarm. Mackey had no quarrel with people expressing their opinion, but he didn't want Deborah mixed up in it. Petitions, talk shows, a three-page spread in *People* magazine—Mackey didn't know what effect all the publicity would have on Judge Liamos, but he was certain that Judge Maier wouldn't appreciate it. And Maier was already proving to be much less favorably disposed toward his client than Mackey would have liked.

On Thursday, February 24, Mackey had returned to court to move for the dismissal of the charges against Deborah. Richard had been acquitted of the charge of conspiracy to commit murder, he noted; and "it would be difficult" for Deborah "to conspire with herself." He also opposed the charge of aiding and abetting first-degree murder when the principal in the case had already been found guilty of the lesser offense of voluntary manslaughter.

But Forwood and Carroll were still eager to prosecute the case, and Judge Maier ruled that Wyoming law was on their side. "Our statute is clear in saying that one who is charged as an accessory with aiding and abetting in the commission of a felony may be indicted, informed against, tried, and convicted in the same manner as a principal," Maier said. "It is immaterial whether the principal was found guilty of a lesser offense or, in fact, acquitted . . . we cannot require that juries be logical from one case to the next."

Mackey accepted the decision with a quiet nod of the head. Regardless of the charges, he didn't expect any jury to find Deborah guilty of a more serious crime than that committed by her brother; after all, Richard was the one who pulled the trigger. And yet, stranger things had happened. He had expected to get the case transferred to juvenile court and to suppress Deborah's statement to the detectives, but Maier had ruled against him there, too. He had also hoped that the debacle of Richard's trial would have made Carroll willing to deal, but the rising tide of support for the Jahnkes had only served to strengthen the prosecutor's resolve. As in Richard's case, the prosecutor refused to discuss any plea bargain that would require him to recommend a light sentence or probation. Given the prevailing mood in the courtroom, Mackey couldn't afford to indulge in optimism.

The trial was scheduled to begin March 7, nine days before Deborah's eighteenth birthday. The defendant and her attorney met practically every day in the intervening weeks; on stormy nights, when the unpaved road to Byron Barry's north-side home was too icy or snowbound for even four-wheel-drive, Deborah spent the night with the Mackeys. Mackey also took her to the jail on several occasions to see her brother. The ostensible purpose of the visits was to "discuss the case," but Richard and Deborah spent much of their time together simply trying to cheer each other up.

On Sunday, March 6, the eve of Deborah's trial, candles flickered in the windows of thousands of homes in Cheyenne. The Committee to Help Richard John Jahnke had called for the candlelight vigil "to send love to the judge," in George Hain's words, so that Liamos would "make the right decision" when Richard was sentenced in mid-March. An uninformed visitor,

seeing house after house so eerily lit, might have concluded that
Christmas had come early to Cheyenne—either that or the town
was in the grip of a bizarre new cult.

Months later, when he was asked what it was like to try to
mount a defense for Deborah in the wake of the outcry surrounding Richard's case, Terry Mackey responded with a derisive snort
and a question of his own.

"Did you ever take off in a Piper Cub behind a Boeing 727?"

Mackey arrived at the courthouse early Monday morning with
a briefcase under one arm and his client tucked under the other.
For a man who had growled about not getting personally involved in the case, he seemed oddly maternal, a mother hen
attempting to shelter its favorite chick under one wing. Wearing a
beige tweed skirt and a pink blouse with a high collar, Deborah
appeared to have just stepped out of a civics class at a New
England prep school. She kept her head down in an effort to
avoid the glare of the television cameras lurking in the corridors;
after pursuing her brother and his attorneys up and down the
courthouse for a solid week, the cameramen had become profi-
cient at lying in wait for their entry-and-exit footage. Mackey's
assistant, a tall, curly-haired paralegal named Jeff Brinkerhoff,
trailed along behind them, virtually ignored.

The jury selection process occupied the better part of the day.
Unlike Barrett, Mackey made no attempt to interrogate the panelists on their attitudes about child abuse. The *voir dire* examination revolved around the standard questions, which revealed, to
no one's surprise, that virtually every candidate had heard or read
something about the case. The panel of nine women and three
men that was eventually seated was a mix of housewives, office
workers, and government employees. Like Richard's jury, Deborah's panel was made up overwhelmingly of young to middle-
aged parents, including one divorcée.

Mackey had a good feeling about them. Deborah was less
confident. She didn't think it was a good idea to have so many
women hearing her case; not counting Dad, it had been her
experience that she got along better with men than with women.
But then, she wasn't sure what Terry had in mind, either. Although he had consulted often with her in the past few weeks, he
had refused to reveal his strategy to her or even let her know if he
wanted to put her on the stand. "Trust me," he kept saying, and

when she raised her objections to certain members of the jury, he said it again.

For his opening statement Carroll once again gave a *Dragnet*-like summary of the events of November 16, lingering on two points: Deborah's admission to the detectives that she had asked for the gun "that kicks the least" and her alleged request that Richard "kill Mom, too." The state would prove, he said, "that this defendant counseled, encouraged, and otherwise procured the killing of her father"—language lifted from the statutory definition of the crime of aiding and abetting first-degree murder.

When it was Mackey's turn to speak, the defense attorney stood up and announced, "At this time, Your Honor, we will reserve our opening statement until the opening of our case."

Judge Maier seemed surprised. Only minutes ago, in a pretrial conference, Mackey had indicated that he'd need a half hour for his opening statement. Now he had evidently decided to hold back.

"Very well," Maier said. "State may call your first witness."

It soon became clear that Mackey's decision to reserve his opening statement was no momentary caprice. It was, in fact, a crucial move in his defense strategy, a strategy quite different from that adopted in Richard's case. While Barrett and Epps had slugged it out with the prosecution from day one, countering argument with argument, testimony with testimony, Mackey planned to proceed from ambush. By not responding to Carroll's overview of the crime with one of his own, he allowed the state's version of events to enter the record unchallenged; but he also gained certain advantages. The state would have to lay out its whole case with little idea of what was waiting for them down the line. Then, if he chose, Mackey could attempt to refute their evidence in his opening statement. It was almost like getting two closing statements for the price of one—almost, but not quite, since the opening statement was supposed to be factual in nature, with the closing reserved for legal argument.

Most important of all, Mackey's silence put the burden of proof squarely where it belonged: on the shoulders of the prosecution. Mackey wasn't going to begin by promising the jury evidence of child abuse and self-defense; better to let such claims emerge on cross-examination, out of the defects of the state's case. Mackey was under no obligation to make any claims at all.

His client was innocent until proved different. And proving the charges against Deborah was no easy matter. The prosecution first had to establish that the shooting was an act of first-degree murder, something they had been unable to prove to the jury's satisfaction at Richard's trial. Then they had to show that Deborah had conspired with her brother to commit that murder and had aided in its commission—two distinct charges requiring separate proofs. Mackey didn't believe they could pull it off.

For the rest of the afternoon and the following morning the prosecution trotted out its squad of deputies, ballistics experts, and medical personnel. Their testimony was virtually identical to that offered at Richard's trial, and Mackey lodged few objections. On cross-examination he pointed out a few interesting details—for example, the fact that the police hadn't found Deborah's fingerprints on any of the guns in the house—but several witnesses escaped with no cross-examination whatsoever. When it came time to bring on the pathologist who had performed the autopsy on Richard Chester Jahnke, the defense even offered to "shorten things up a little bit" by conceding that the victim died of wounds caused by slugs fired from the shotgun found in the garage, thereby sparing the jury the gruesome autopsy photos. Carroll, of course, declined the offer.

Deborah sat with her hands clasped in her lap throughout much of the testimony, a prim figure who bore little resemblance to the defiant, agitated girl who had thrust notes at her attorney throughout the transfer hearings. For weeks Mackey had been lecturing her about the importance of restraint and decorum in the courtroom. At one point she had threatened to wear her favorite "protest button" to the trial, the one that read EAT SHIT AND DIE. Instead she followed the proceedings from the defense table with a stiff-backed, polite, somewhat distant interest. She knew there were only one or two witnesses on Carroll's list who really mattered.

The first was summoned Tuesday afternoon.

"The state would call Richard Jahnke," Carroll said.

Wearing the cheap blue suit that had been his daily costume throughout his own trial, Richard entered the courtroom in the company of a sheriff's deputy and Jim Barrett. He had lost weight and color during his past two weeks in an isolated cell in the county jail. Under the bright lights of Courtroom B, he appeared as pale as a waxworks vampire. Deborah took one look at him and lost her composure. She buried her face in Brinkerhoff's shoulder to stifle her sobs.

At Judge Maier's request, Barrett "qualified" his client for the record.

"You understand that you are appearing here under subpoena by the State of Wyoming?" Barrett asked.

"I do," Richard replied.

"Do you choose to testify in this case or not to testify?"

"I choose to testify."

"Is that decision free and voluntary, Richard?"

"Yes, it is."

Carroll requested and was granted permission to examine Richard as a hostile witness, a procedure that allowed the prosecutor considerable latitude in the type of questions he could ask. He wasted no time. After Richard admitted that he had placed guns around the house in preparation for his father's return, Carroll walked over to a table full of state's exhibits and picked up the M-1 carbine found in the family room.

"Did you hand what is marked State's Exhibit #37 to your sister?" he asked.

"No, I didn't, sir," Richard said. "What I did was place it near her."

"I'm talking about this particular weapon," Carroll said, raising the rifle higher. "You say you did not hand it to her?"

"I did not hand a weapon to her," Richard replied, "but I did demonstrate for her how to use it in case she would have to defend herself."

"If you will, please," Carroll bristled, "just answer the questions and not volunteer—"

"Just a moment, Your Honor," Mackey said. "This witness has answered the question; that is argumentative, and I object."

"Well, he has answered more than he was asked, I think, is the point," Maier said. He turned to Richard and urged, "Listen to the question and just answer that question."

And so it went. More subdued than at his own trial, Richard gave a slightly different version of the events of November 16, a version clearly skewed in favor of his sister. He took full responsibility, not only for placing the loaded weapons around the house, but for hiding the pets and turning on the lights in the house. Carroll's exasperation mounted as he attempted to lure Richard into repeating a previous assertion that Deborah had picked up and put down the M-1 several times; now the witness recalled seeing his sister hold the weapon only once. The verbal fencing became even more strenuous when Carroll brought up Richard's final conversation with Deborah in the family room, minutes before the shooting.

"My sister just asked me, 'Are you going to shoot Mom?' I think she repeated that a couple of times," Richard said.

"Did she say 'shoot' or 'kill'?" Carroll demanded.

"I'm not too sure."

"Well, let's see if we can refresh your memory," the prosecutor said. Forwood handed him a copy of the transcript of Richard's testimony at his own trial. Carroll read aloud: " '. . . she asked me if I was going to kill Mom, too. . . . I said no. . . . She was upset. She asked me to kill Mom.' "

Mackey provided Richard with another copy of the transcript. After reading quietly for a few moments, he said, "What she said was, if I remember, she already looked upset before—"

"Just a minute," Carroll said. "I asked you—"

"Just a moment," Mackey said, interrupting Carroll's interruption. "The witness has a right to explain."

Maier nodded at Carroll, who tried again. Richard said he remembered Deborah asking him *if* he was going to kill Mom. Carroll interrupted again, seeking clarification of the central point— did Deborah in fact request that he do so—and Mackey interrupted to complain that the prosecutor was being argumentative.

"It's not totally accurate, what she said," Richard said, "because I was asked—"

"I would ask you again," Carroll said. "Did she say—"

"Objection, Your Honor," Mackey insisted. "It's been asked and answered. The witness said it is not totally accurate."

Maier turned to Carroll. "Would you ask your last question again?"

Carroll waved the transcript. "I ask again—is this what your sister said: She asked you to kill your mother, and you answered yes *[sic]*—is that what your sister said?"

"That isn't exactly what she said, but it is close," Richard said.

And that was as close as the jury was going to get to an understanding of the question—was it an inquiry, a request, a command?—Deborah put to her brother moments before he went into the garage.

*   *   *

"Richard, before you shot your father that night, had he made any threats to you?"

Mackey's first question on cross-examination touched off a vehement objection from the prosecution, a conference at the bench, a recess, and a lengthy discussion in chambers. Mackey insisted that the state's examination had raised the issue of Richard's "intentions" that night, and the defense had a right to inquire as to what prompted those intentions. Forwood charged that Mackey merely wanted "to open the infamous door" to a child abuse defense that was improper and irrelevant; he was on the verge of cluttering up the courtroom with the same sort of nonsense that had prevailed at Richard's trial. But Mackey held fast. Before his client could be found guilty of aiding and abetting, he said, the state first had to prove that a crime took place. If their witness—a hostile witness, but their witness just the same—wanted to claim the shooting was self-defense, the jury had a right to hear him.

Judge Maier decided to allow Mackey to proceed, provided that he confine his questions to matters relating directly to Richard's intent to kill. The attorneys returned to the courtroom, and Mackey asked again if Richard's father had threatened him that night.

"He said he didn't know how he was going to do it, but he was going to get rid of me," Richard said.

"And what did you take that to mean?" Mackey asked.

"I thought he was going to kill me."

"Had he ever made threats to you before?"

"I remember one time on a hunting trip in Cheyenne, we were driving back and he just started talking to me. He said, 'Rich, I can handle the problems I face in my work. I have to deal with a lot of assholes, but I can handle it just fine. But when it comes to family, I just lose it. One of these days, I'm going to hit someone so goddamned hard it is going to kill them, and they will deserve it.' And then he stared at me."

"Did you take that as a threat towards yourself?"

"Yes, I did."

"Do you recall an occasion in Arizona where you saw your father shoot at two human beings?"

Richard began to describe the time his father fired in the

direction of the two hunters in the desert. After a few moments Maier asked to see Mackey at the bench.

"It was my understanding," Maier murmured, "that you were going to ask him about his intent to kill his father, not about four years ago in Arizona. . . . he's starting to talk about everything in the world."

Mackey promised to speed things up. He returned to the witness.

"Who placed the guns around the house?" he asked.

"I did," Richard said.

"Did you and your sister enter into any agreement to kill your father?"

"No."

"Richard, who killed your father?"

"I did."

"What did your sister have to do with that?"

"She was only in the house."

"Why did you give her a gun?"

"Because I was afraid that I might get killed."

Once again he described the argument with his mother that night and his subsequent beating by his father. He claimed that Dad had struck Deborah, too, then corrected himself—"I'm not really sure if he did hit her." While he was making preparations to kill Dad, Deborah was "running her fingers through her hair and mumbling to herself." He repeated his assertion that Dad would have killed him if he hadn't shot first. The latter statement was at odds with what he had said at his own trial about his fear that Dad would kill him "mentally," not physically, but it did sound more like an acceptable notion of self-defense.

"Richard, were you charged with killing your father?"

"I was charged with first-degree murder and conspiracy," the witness replied.

"Were you convicted of anything?"

Carroll objected. The last thing he wanted was for this jury to be reminded of the outcome of Richard's trial. But Judge Maier overruled him.

"What crimes were you charged with in the death of your father?" Mackey asked again.

"First-degree murder and conspiracy to commit first-degree murder."

"What crimes were you convicted of?"

"Voluntary manslaughter," Richard said.

Carroll spent the next hour trying to impeach his witness. The district attorney wondered what Dad's threat to "get rid" of his son might mean; if Richard truly feared death or bodily harm that night, or if he simply didn't want to be forced to move out of the house; and why the youth didn't seek help from friends or the authorities again, or run away, maybe find a job and support himself and his sister. Richard replied with increasing impatience and mock politeness, like a jaded native compelled to give directions to an exceptionally thickheaded tourist.

"Why didn't you and your sister both leave?" Carroll asked.

"Sir," Richard sighed, "there was no place permanent I could go."

"You would not consider leaving unless you had some place permanent to go?"

"Sir, I believe that no matter where I went, I would have had to go back to my father."

"You didn't consider this to be an emergency, then, that you better get out of there because your dad might come back and injure you?"

"Sir, I stayed in that house to end the abuse once and for all."

Carroll wouldn't let up. He seemed determined, not only to establish that a crime did take place, but to retry Richard's case all over again—and to vindicate DPASS, the sheriff's office, Major Vegvary, the school nurse, and the rest of the adult world as well. Nothing could have pleased Mackey more; the veteran prosecutor had become so intent on roasting the witness that he appeared to have forgotten why he put him on the stand in the first place. Of the hundreds of questions that made up Carroll's redirect examination, only two addressed Deborah's actions that night. And when those questions were asked, Richard again denied that his sister had anything to do with the shooting.

On his final question, the district attorney managed to wring one entirely expected concession from the witness.

"Don't you think you picked the worst option rather than the best option that was available to you?" Carroll asked.

"Sir, I believe killing my father was wrong," Richard said.

Coming from the state's star witness, it sounded like a very obvious thing to say.

*   *   *

Court resumed on Wednesday morning with the testimony of Gerald Luce, the deputy who had found Deborah in Lions Park the morning after the shooting. The next witness was Michael Brinkman, who again recounted how Richard had told him that Deborah was armed with the M-1 as a "backup"—that she would "follow through" with the "plan" if Richard "froze up" in the garage. Deborah "knew what was to happen that night," Brinkman said.

On cross-examination Mackey quizzed Brinkman about the written statement he had provided the authorities, describing his conversation with Richard. The statement had been prepared, he pointed out, under the helpful supervision of Detective Tim Greene.

"Mr. Greene came back in the room and read the statement that you had written out for him, didn't he?" Mackey asked. "And after that he asked you to include certain other things in that statement that were not there, didn't he?"

"Yes, sir," Brinkman agreed.

"And one of those things was asking you to comment on whether or not Richard and Deborah 'planned' [the shooting], isn't that correct? But you didn't use the word 'planned'—Mr. Greene did, didn't he?"

"I don't—I don't remember the exact word he said," the ROTC captain stammered.

"You told Mr. Brinkerhoff that the word 'planned' was Mr. Greene's, didn't you?"

"Yes, sir."

"And not Richard Jahnke's, was it?"

"No, sir."

Brinkman was followed by Detective Greene himself. Forwood led his chief investigator through a step-by-step account of his actions the morning after the shooting, laying the groundwork for Greene to introduce Deborah's statement. But when Forwood asked Greene to summarize his interview with Deborah, Mackey rose to object.

"That is not the best evidence," he said. "The best evidence is the tape recording they made of a part of that conversation."

Maier hesitated. "Sustained," he said at last.

Forwood asked to approach the bench. Greene's summary would be more "logical," he argued, than the tape recording of the interview, which "wanders back and forth for over an hour and a half.'' Judge Maier retreated; he would allow the witness to paraphrase the transcript of Deborah's statement. If Mackey thought the witness was straying from the text or taking remarks out of context, he could correct matters on cross-examination.

Mackey returned to his seat. He didn't really expect the prosecution to play the tape; he merely wanted to point out that it existed. Actually, it wasn't the ''best evidence'' for either side. He knew, just as well as Forwood did, that the tape was a mess: it was a cheap cassette recorded on a cheap machine, a muffled, scratchy, barely intelligible piece of work. And it was incomplete, too. When Greene had first attempted to listen to it, the detective had accidentally erased several seconds at the beginning, just as he had accidentally shredded his notes of the earlier interview with Deborah. Playing the tape in the courtroom might embarrass Greene, the longwinded Detective Fresquez, and the sheriff's department, but it would have little probative value.

Yet as Mackey saw it, the state's refusal to play the tape helped him a great deal. It left the impression that the prosecution was hiding something. It made the defense out to be the fearless seeker of truth in the case—why, Deborah's statement should not only be discussed, it should be *heard* by everyone—a peculiar position to take, perhaps, given Mackey's losing battle to have the statement suppressed some weeks ago. But the jury didn't know about that. All they knew was that the state had a tape and Forwood didn't want them to hear it. Mackey had bluffed, the state had failed to call, and he was now ready to claim the pot.

At the moment, however, the state was plumbing the statement for the missing pieces to its conspiracy and aiding-and-abetting case. Under Forwood's direction, Greene paraphrased selected passages bearing on Deborah's actions the night of the shooting: her statement that ''her role that night was to be a backup to Richard''; that she had asked for the gun ''that kicks the least''; ''that she and Richard had discussed lighting in the house, placing the family pets in certain areas . . . [and] escape routes''; her ''assessment . . . that what had happened that evening was an 'execution' ''; and finally, ''that her brother didn't verbalize anything specifically'' about what he was going to do, ''but that there was a tacit agreement between the two of them. She agreed with that concept.''

Greene also gave what appeared to be Deborah's version of the infamous ''kill Mom, too'' remark.

"After the weapons had been placed throughout the house, Deborah told me, she asked her brother, 'What about Mom?' And her brother, Richard, told her that he was not going to do anything to Mom, that she was going to be all right. Later on in the interview—after she heard, as she called them, 'shotgun fires,' she observed Richard coming in from the garage area . . . and she at that time asked him, 'What about Mom?' And he indicated to her that the mother was safe."

On cross-examination Mackey approached Greene with a copy of the transcript in his hand. "You started out telling the jury that when Deborah came home that night, there was an 'argument' that took place in the house," Mackey noted.

He glanced down. "The words Deborah actually used to describe that were: 'And he said, well, you—you're such a, you know, shut your mouth, you know, fucking asshole, and you slut, etc., etc. Then, you know, he was just—my mother just goes, oh boo-hoo, boo-hoo, you know, oh these kids, I mean, they're just so terrible to me, and, you know, my father just, yes, yes, I know, they're just a couple of bastards, you know. And we really, you know, got cheated—or something like that . . . so all of a sudden he goes stomp, stomp, stomp, stomp to my brother's room, you know, and bangs on the door, like bang, bang, bang, you know, like the wrath of Hades or something like that.' That's the *argument* Deborah told you about, wasn't it?"

"That's one of them, yes, sir," Greene said.

Mackey pushed on, reading hefty portions of the statement aloud in an effort to "clarify" Greene's testimony. While Greene had cited passages in support of Deborah's role as a "backup" for an "execution" in the making, Mackey presented other passages in which Deborah expressed her belief that Richard was engaged in a "scare tactic." For each statement that suggested that she had somehow conspired by hiding the pets or whatever, Mackey found a corresponding denial. And he took pains to point out that the phrase "tacit agreement" was Greene's, not Deborah's; she had not "agreed with that concept," she'd merely said "uh-huh" when Greene asked her if she had "kind of a tacit agreement" with her brother that "something" had to be done.

On redirect Forwood read aloud other excerpts from the transcript to shore up Greene's original testimony. Mackey then engaged in a rare bout of recross-examination to introduce even more excerpts. By the time Greene stepped down and court adjourned for the noon recess, more than half of the transcript had been read aloud to the jury, with every stomp, bang, and "you know" intact.

Mackey and Brinkerhoff took Deborah to lunch at a nearby restaurant to discuss their next move. Greene was the state's final witness; when they returned to the courtroom, it would be the defense's turn to put on a show. They had witnesses of their own they could call—Maria Jahnke, of course, and Eve Whitcomb— but the crucial decision, still very much up in the air, was whether or not Deborah would take the stand in her own defense.

Mackey knew that his client was deeply frustrated at having to sit silently throughout the court proceedings. At the same time, she was terrified at the prospect of testifying. Last night he and Barrett had tried her out for a couple of hours, throwing the type of questions at her that Tom Carroll might ask. Deborah had responded reasonably well. But an informal mock-trial in a lawyer's office was nothing compared to the pressure of facing a skillful inquisitor in a courtroom packed with reporters. Over lunch Mackey began to tick off the hazards Deborah would face if she decided to testify.

One, Tom Carroll was very good at twisting testimony to suit his own purposes. Deborah had already seen his verbal alchemy at the transfer hearings, when he attempted to characterize Richard Chester Jahnke's alleged fondling of his daughter as "fatherly affection." He would undoubtedly seek to impeach Deborah with carefully selected passages from her statement.

Two, the state had possession of Deborah's diaries, hundreds of pages of very private, angry, and melodramatic writings seized from her room on the night of the shooting. The district attorney had made no attempt to introduce the material as part of his case—he surely realized that Mackey would have objected on grounds of relevancy. But it was possible that Maier would allow Carroll to read certain passages as part of his cross-examination of Deborah. She could find herself in the impossible position of having to defend something she'd written when she was twelve years old, a statement like "I wish my father would drop dead."

Three, the situation was complicated by Carroll's habit of trying his case on rebuttal. The state had subpoenaed more than thirty witnesses and called only eleven; that meant the district attorney had another twenty-odd witnesses waiting in the wings, including other sheriff's deputies, teachers from Central High, and relatives of Richard Chester Jahnke. Some of these witnesses might cast doubt on any claims of child abuse Deborah might make. But if Deborah made no claims, the state couldn't rebut them.

There was one more factor to consider, a concern Mackey didn't voice that day, one he had kept to himself throughout his dealings with Deborah. Ever since he had met her, a familiar phrase had been playing over and over in his mind. It was one of those catch-22 lines from the Vietnam War: *We had to burn the village in order to save it.* Richard Jahnke had held his own against Tom Carroll, but Deborah was a very different sort of person; the memory of her outburst when Richard entered the courtroom was still fresh in Mackey's mind. Putting this emotionally volatile adolescent on the stand, exposing her smoldering anger toward her mother, her nagging sense of guilt over her failure to do more to help her brother, her evident lack of grief over her father's death—tossing this mixed-up package to the jury and expecting them to understand it could prove to be a mistake of Pyrrhic proportions.

Mackey didn't tell Deborah that he was afraid she might break down on the stand. But the other factors he mentioned were enough to give her a sense of what she was up against.

"What do you want to do, babe?" he asked.

"I don't know," she moaned. "I mean, they have my journals—it could be one big character assassination."

Mackey nodded. "Let me tell you what I think we ought to do," he said.

As he outlined his plan, relief began to spread across her face like the sun breaking through a thick bank of thunderheads.

"Yes! Let's do it!" she exclaimed. "Oh, I love it!"

Court resumed at 2:15 P.M., with Jon Forwood's announcement that the state was resting its case. Judge Maier turned to the defense table.

"Mr. Mackey, do you desire to make an opening statement at this time?" Maier asked.

Mackey stood up, moved behind Deborah, and placed his hands on her shoulders, like a teacher showing off his prize pupil. Deborah smiled broadly at the judge.

"Your Honor, at this time the defendant rests," Mackey said.

A murmur of surprise and dismay rippled through the courtroom, like the collective catch in the throat of a crowd in a movie house when the film breaks: *no show today!*

"Very well," Maier said. "Does the state have any rebuttal testimony—ah, obviously, you do not, with none presented. The testimony and evidence in this case are now closed."

The attorneys retreated to Judge Maier's chambers to wrangle over the wording of the instructions the judge would give the jury. As expected, Forwood opposed the inclusion of any instructions regarding the self-defense statute. Mackey argued against Maier's instruction that the jury could find Deborah guilty of the lesser crimes of aiding and abetting second-degree murder or voluntary manslaughter; he felt the judge was giving the jury a "shopping list" to choose from. Judge Maier overruled both objections.

On Thursday morning Jon Forwood delivered the final argument for the state. Juggling key selections from Richard's testimony and Deborah's statement, he contended that Deborah "put the gunman in position to fire the shots."

Richard's testimony, Forwood noted, "contradicts a lot of what was in Deborah's statement. He tries to take all the blame on himself. . . . Well, it is understandable, really. . . . Richard has got nothing to lose. In fact, I would submit he is somewhat caught up in this national frenzy that has been created. He thinks he's a national hero.

"But there is one thing he couldn't get away from on this witness stand—his prior statement, sworn under oath. Did Deborah come out to the garage—and what did she say? 'Are you going to kill Mom?' 'No.' 'Kill Mom, too.' . . . this defendant was as clearly involved in the blood hunt, the death hunt, as her brother. . . . She put Richard in position in the garage, got the dogs out of the way, did everything she could to make sure he fired those shots. . . .

"What meaning are we going to give to 'Thou shalt not kill'? Are we going to throw it in the gutter and let it lie in the filth where they have put another commandment—'Honor thy father and thy mother'?

"Ladies and gentlemen, one word describes this case. Her word." Forwood walked to a blackboard he had brought into the courtroom just for this moment. He seized a piece of bright red chalk and wrote EXECUTION in foot-high letters.

Judge Maier announced a recess. As soon as the jury had left the courtroom, Mackey walked over to the blackboard and erased it.

Mackey addressed the jury for nearly an hour. Perhaps he had been silent too long; with no opening statement under his belt, no witnesses to coax, nothing but his occasionally ferocious cross-examination to test his vocal chords, he seemed overwrought. He spoke quickly, loudly, in an unmistakable tone of sorrow and indignation. It was the most eloquent and passionate piece of advocacy to emerge from either trial.

"It is a lawyer's responsibility to bring you the truth," he said. "The truth was not brought to you by the state of Wyoming. Half-truths have been told you in this case—until forced by cross-examination, sometimes known as the greatest engine for the creation of truth in the world. . . . It was their sworn duty as lawyers to bring you the truth. And they have yet to do it.

"Last May they had an opportunity to prevent all of this. And they did *nothing*. And now they come into court and they say to you blame the children. . . . Richard did wrong. He never should have killed his father. But, you see, to a sixteen-year-old boy, life's not as simple as it is to a lawyer who can walk into this courtroom and play fast and loose with the truth. He had to have resolution, and he went looking for resolution and got none . . . and, you know, it takes *years* to snap the mind of a little boy; to pound him to the point where he can no longer make rational decisions; to pound him into that emotional being that must have been in that house that night; as the mother hugged the father and said, 'Oh, Richard, I love you,' and they went out the door to celebrate their twentieth anniversary, after calling their children bastards and wondering why God visited on them such a horrible thing as to have two children.

"Honor thy father and thy mother, Mr. Forwood said. And that's right. That's right. But, you know, you can't ask children to do that which they are not taught to do. Violence begets violence, just as surely as Maria Jahnke and Richard Chester Jahnke begat these two children.

"We could spend a lot of time talking about what happened to Richard, but we know what the jury did. We are here on account of Deborah. The basics of the law are that she is presumed to be innocent until they present evidence of her guilt beyond a reasonable doubt. . . . You heard how Mr. Greene carried out [his] duty of fairness—by taking a little girl into a room with another big deputy and examining her so that he could ask leading questions, like was it a 'tacit agreement' . . . but they weren't prepared for the answer to one question: 'Would it be fair to say that you and your brother agreed then this had to be done?' And Deborah replied, 'No, we agreed that something had to be done.' God bless them for at least recognizing that *something* had to be done!

"Walk a mile in the moccasins of the people you judge. Go into that house on that night. Feel the intensity of the emotion of the children after the fight with their father. We do not judge the children by the standards of the parents, and thank God in this case we do not. We judge them as they are."

Mackey began to flip through the transcript of Deborah's statement. "They want to quote the Bible," he spat. "Listen to these words: 'I was torn between, I did not want to be like this, and I just said, oh, God, I just wish I wasn't here, you know, and I told him, you know, I'm really scared . . . it just doesn't seem real . . . I just felt kind of indebted to my brother. Because he's been, you know, he's always been very kind to me, very protective of me.'

"Do you know what they want her to do? They want her to honor thy father and mother and throw thy brother to the wolves. That's their theory of how the American family operates. . . . These kids were trapped in the American family gone crazy . . . and out of it came this tragedy. Let's not compound the tragedy."

He wound up back at the defense table, with his hands braced on Deborah's shoulders, his eyes searching out the eyes of the jury.

"I've got to tell you," he said, "as I've stood here and had this opportunity to talk to you—and maybe even yell a little bit, because this is my only chance—I have to tell you, I'm a little frightened that I didn't know the right words and that I don't have a chance to respond. But I know that you will do that for me. . . . I want you to go into that jury room to deliberate. And in all of your deliberations I want you to remember that it means so much to this little girl that the abuse stop here and now, and that the state not take the place of her father."

* * *

Mackey's emotional pleading was met with a shrill response from Tom Carroll. The usually unflappable district attorney seemed at a loss for words; what came out was a string of clichés. The defense's argument was nothing less than "the complete gauntlet of sympathy," he charged. Mackey had omitted the fate of Richard Chester Jahnke, who "will never walk this earth again . . . never experience joy . . . never experience sorrow. He is dead, dead, dead in the cemetery!"

"I say to you that Richard Jahnke has the mark of Cain upon him, and the mark of Cain is upon this defendant," he continued.

"The state's not denying that the father struck the children. I think probably most parents do. I think most parents use moderation. I think probably *all* parents, if they corporally punish their children from time to time, will go in excess of what we call moderation. Nonetheless, you heard from this witness stand that the killer, the murderer, Richard Jahnke, was never badly injured.

" 'Violence begets violence.' If we use that as an excuse, then we could explain all of the [Charles] Mansons and the [Marion] Pruetts; not that I'm comparing this case with them—"

"Your Honor," Mackey protested, "the state is deliberately trying to inflame passion and prejudice by incorporating outside matters."

"It is proper argument," Judge Maier replied.

"Can anybody honestly say that this defendant chose a gun because it kicked the least, but she had no intention of using the gun?" Carroll asked. "And if she didn't know he was going to kill their father, then why would she say, 'Kill Mom, too'?

"That's her state of mind, and she cannot shake loose of that. She is stuck with that. . . . and what a horrible state of mind! . . . I mean, she is not a child. I get a little tired of this 'little girl' business. She's eighteen years old this month. She knows better.

"Sympathize all that you want to, because that's a fine human trait. But do not let sympathy or compassion blind you or control you, in violation of your oath of office as jurors."

Mackey chatted briefly with reporters outside the courtroom about the decision to rest the defense without calling a single witness. "If it works, I'm a genius," he said. "If it doesn't. . . ." He shrugged.

The Barrys spirited Deborah from the courtroom to Eve Whitcomb's house to await the verdict. Deborah was giddy with hopes of acquittal. After this was over, she announced, she was going to move to Boulder, Colorado, or some other progressive college town where she could "really live." She drank several glasses of wine and fell asleep on a bed downstairs. Mackey returned to his office and grabbed a nap on his couch. He was awakened by the noise of a television station's helicopter circling the courthouse.

The jury began its deliberations after lunch. They took a break early in the evening for dinner, reassembled in the jury room, and finally sent word to the judge around half-past nine, after six hours of discussion—roughly the same time frame as that in Richard's case. Actually, the panel had come to its decision several hours earlier. They had delayed announcing it in order to review their reasoning, to reassure each other of its correctness—and, perhaps, for the sake of appearances as well. No one likes a fast jury.

Deborah, the attorneys, and the press were already assembled in the courtroom when the jury filed in, minutes before ten o'clock. Not one of the jurors betrayed any emotion. The foreman handed the verdict forms to the bailiff, who handed them to the court clerk, who read them to the court. Deborah began to tremble; the words hit her like freezing rain.

"... guilty of aiding and abetting voluntary manslaughter ..."

"... not guilty of the crime of conspiracy ..."

Judge Maier thanked the jury and dismissed them. Unlike Judge Liamos, Maier did not revoke the defendant's bond. He released her in the custody of the Barrys pending sentencing. Someone handed Deborah a bouquet of white carnations. She pulled one out and approached Judge Maier as he started to leave the courtroom.

"Thank you for being so kind to me," she murmured, and handed him the flower. The startled Maier nodded, flashed a glacial smile, and vanished into his chambers.

Deborah returned to the defense table, where Mackey, Brinkerhoff, the Barrys, and Eve Whitcomb were waiting for her. She hugged Eve and began to cry.

Mackey stood grimly at her side. Although he would later tell the press that the verdict was a "victory," he was, in fact, perplexed and disappointed. The jury had gone for the least damaging option, short of a full acquittal; but Mackey didn't think that option should have been included in the instructions in the first place. And finding Deborah guilty of the lesser charge wasn't really doing her a favor; in Wyoming, an accessory to a felony is subject to the same penalties as the principal. Like her brother, Deborah was now facing a sentence of up to twenty years in prison.

Maria slipped in front of the bar and waited timidly for Deborah to notice her. Her arms were outstretched; she, too, wanted to hug her daughter. Deborah looked up foggily for a moment, as if studying a stranger. Then she shook her head violently and burrowed deeper into Eve's breast.

Maria turned and wandered slowly, sadly past a flock of reporters who had witnessed her rejection. This time there were no oaths, no curses on her husband's head. She was unsteady on her feet, like a drunk woman or a passenger on a listing deck. Three steps outside the courtroom, she collapsed in a dead faint at the feet of George Hain.

20

The letters arrived a dozen at a time. Then two dozen. Then three. They were stacked in George Hain's office, which had become the unofficial command post for the Committee to Help Richard John Jahnke. Hain and others sifted through them, marking the requests for blank petitions for prompt reply. In less than three weeks the committee logged more than four thousand letters urging leniency for Richard, and one opposed. They also collected ten thousand signatures on locally distributed petitions; no one had time to count the names on the additional petitions coming in from around the country. They bundled up the lot and delivered them to the clerk of the First District Court to await Judge Liamos's inspection.

The defense attorneys were similarly besieged. Louis Epps fielded most of the calls at Jim Barrett's office; Terry Mackey divided the chores between himself and his secretary. More than half of the calls and letters were from victims of child abuse; many felt compelled not only to commiserate but to confess their own dark histories. The memories were painfully fresh, even though in some instances the abuse had occurred half a century ago. Epps soon lost track of the number of callers who confided that they had thought about doing "what Richard did," but they had been too afraid, or they had run away, or the gun had jammed, or some blamed thing. There but for the grace of God go I . . . and I . . . and I. . . .

"I hope Tom Carroll's mail has run like mine," Mackey growled to a visitor. "If it has, he's learned that, with abused children, the thought of killing your parents doesn't start in adolescence. It starts in four- and five-year-olds."

Perhaps the most intriguing plea for mercy was an eight-page letter from a former serviceman, a man who was in a unique position to appreciate Richard's crime and the crime that spawned it.

262

Dear Judge Liamos:

Approximately 10 days ago I picked up my newspaper and began reading the article about a 16-year-old son killing his father. . . . at the name Maria [Jahnke] my eyes sprang open . . . Richard and Maria were my two closest and dearest friends, whom I loved and friendshipped with almost every night 20 years ago while serving in the United States Army. . . .

At that time, Richard Jahnke was dating a young lady named Maria Rodriguez, a lady in every respect and someone I learned to admire and love almost immediately. . . . later Richard and Maria introduced me to a young lady whom I later married, and to us were born two boys. . . . as years went by we lost contact, and as is the case with many military buddies, the separation became permanent. I never heard from Richard and Maria again.

I write this letter today because my heart is deeply saddened over this tragedy. . . . never have I met young Richard Jahnke, neither have I met his sister Deborah—and according to the news reports these two young people shot and killed my friend. . . . My first reaction tells me that I should hate these two, and they should be put away on a permanent basis. I'm sure this is the general thought in the case . . . what the majority of the public will see is that two young people murdered an innocent man. That is only a small side of a big picture. I am one of the unfortunate people who can see the full story. . . .

In reading the newspaper article, one sentence sticks out clearly in my mind. It kept me awake at night and bothered me throughout the day. The statement was made by Maria Jahnke. When someone asked her why she didn't do something about her husband's rage, her reply was, "You don't know what fear does to a person."

Do you know what the word "fear" means to a child? When I was a child my dad beat and whipped his children until their backs, their buttocks, and their legs would bleed. He called this discipline. I called it brutality. He scolded, hollered, and verbally assaulted us. He called this correction. I called it ignorance and mental abuse. . . . Fear and trembling ruled our household like a darkness covers the night. No one dared question my dad's authority. Neither did we question his methods and rules, and this included my mother. . . .

Fear. Do you know what a little boy at five years old tried to do because of fear? This little child filled a pocket with garden lime and began eating it in order to commit suicide, because he was tired of being beaten. He was caught with the lime and emptied his pocket when his older brother explained that he, the five-year-old, would immediately go to hell if he committed suicide. . . .

[Recently] this same boy had the opportunity to be reunited with two of his sisters, and a discussion of childhood came up. . . . [one sister] mentioned that once her father had promised her a whipping . . . in great fear of the harsh beating, this young girl pondered as to how she could poison her father but was afraid that she couldn't pull it off.

That five-year-old boy is me today, that little girl is my grown sister. . . . At age 43 I try to be a good citizen of my community and an asset to my family . . . [but] until one and a half years ago I had fearful dreams and horrifying nightmares about my father chasing me and beating me. My brothers and sisters have all—repeat all—experienced the same dreams.

Funny thing, Your Honor—after Dad died I haven't had the nightmares since. . . .

May God save the court and those innocent children.

[signature]

Confined to a small cell with metal walls painted a sickly green, Richard heard little of the hue and cry raised on his behalf. Maria visited every Sunday, but she had little news to offer. She and her son took turns trying to persuade each other that they were holding up just fine. Barrett and Epps were allowed to visit more frequently, and from them Richard first learned of the disappointing verdict in his sister's trial. By virtue of his dual role as foster parent and school psychologist, Dan Munn was also a frequent visitor. He brought personal messages of encouragement from Troy Schwamb and other committee members.

Richard listened to the messages and nodded politely. A lot of people, it seemed, had high hopes that he was going to get probation. At times he indulged in the fantasy himself. But then he recalled Judge Liamos's words during the plea-bargain discussion—"in all probability he will receive a penitentiary sentence" —and came crashing back to earth. Why should the judge feel any differently, now that he had been convicted of manslaughter?

Seven to fourteen years, Billis had said.

Barrett showed Richard the presentencing report, an extensive document that contained the recommendations of teachers, doctors, and corrections officers. Some of those interviewed believed that Richard could best be rehabilitated at the Wyoming Industrial Institute, the state reform school for boys located outside of Worland. Others favored probation with mandatory psychiatric counseling. No one requested a penitentiary sentence. Barrett told him to hope for the best, expect the worst, and remember that this wasn't the end of the line. In his opinion, they had plenty of grounds for appeal.

Richard asked for books and writing materials to pass the time. The light in his cell was poor, and he soon abandoned the effort. He asked for money to buy food; the gelatinous jail food didn't agree with him. He flushed most of his meals down the toilet and subsisted on stale chocolate-chip granola bars he purchased from the commissary. He was feeling quite light-headed by the time Barrett arrived, around noon on March 18, to hand him his blue suit and escort him into Courtroom B.

After the dimness of his cell, the lights in the courtroom seemed extraordinarily bright. Beyond the spots in his eyes he saw Carroll and Forwood, his mother and sister, Troy Schwamb, the Munns, a few other people from Central, and the familiar crowd of reporters. As Barrett and Epps made the anticipated pleas for probation, Richard tried to focus on Judge Liamos and found that he couldn't. He stood with his head down and listened to Barrett explain that a prison sentence for his client would amount to "the wasting of another life."

Liamos cleared his throat and prefaced the passing of sentence with a few remarks of his own.

"I don't have to tell you that there has been great interest in this case," the ex-Marine said. "I don't know how many letters and cards the Court has received. There are hundreds. The Court has not been able to read all of them, but I have read a lot of them. The vast majority of these communications are from a neighboring state; however, there are some from as far away as both coasts and Canada."

Liamos noted that the Wyoming Code of Judicial Conduct demanded that he not be swayed by such appeals. "I'm sure that we all have compassion for Richard Jahnke," he said. "I would agree wholeheartedly with counsel for the defense that these [presentencing] reports show that Mr. Jahnke would be an excellent probation risk. I disagree with counsel in regard to the picture that has been painted of the state penitentiary, in many respects. It is the Court's experience that many prisoners, especially those of tender years, are treated accordingly."

Liamos fixed his gaze on the defense table. "Mr. Jahnke and counsel, I think it comes down to the proposition that no one should be permitted to act as prosecutor, jury, judge, court of appeal, and executioner without being called to account by society. . . . Richard Jahnke, for the purposes of recognizing and supporting society's law; for its protection; for discouraging other persons from committing acts similar to yours; and to satisfy the need to trust in public justice as opposed to private justice, the Court has decided against probation in your case.

"It is ordered by the Court that you, Richard Jahnke, be remanded to the custody of the Sheriff of Laramie County, Wyoming; that you be delivered within ten days from this date into the custody of the Warden of the Wyoming State Penitentiary; that you then be conveyed by the warden to the penitentiary; and that you be there safely kept, governed, clothed, and subsisted for the period of not less than five years, and not more than fifteen years. . . ."

Maria howled. Deborah wept. Richard didn't even blink. He took it like a man, the strong, silent man his father always wanted him to become.

Within seconds two deputies whisked him back to his cell. Judge Liamos retreated almost as quickly. The moment the door closed behind him, the courtroom erupted in exclamations of anger and shock.

"They're so damned blind," Maria ranted, to no one in particular. "They don't know the pain. They don't know how wicked he was. They don't want to know!"

"What a monstrosity," Deborah sobbed to Troy Schwamb.

"I don't think the man is human!" one woman cried.

Barrett held a press conference at the bottom of the stairs. A seething Troy Schwamb trailed along behind him. Throughout the past few weeks, Schwamb had told reporters he was Richard Jahnke's best friend; he now felt compelled to demonstrate this to the press in the most emphatic way he knew. As the television cameramen trained their minicams on Barrett, Schwamb leaned into view with his middle finger defiantly extended. He was quickly shooed away.

Barrett denounced the sentence as "outrageous" and "unfair." He would appeal to the Wyoming Supreme Court, he said.

"Do you agree with the judge's assessment of the state penitentiary—that prisoners 'of tender years' are 'treated accordingly'?" a reporter asked.

"I don't know what that means," Barrett replied. "I don't know what penitentiary he's been in. I just can't believe this kid has been treated this way."

Troy Schwamb slipped in front of the cameras again and shouted, "He's not sixteen, he's a two-year-old baby in diapers, and they want to send him to prison!"

Barrett spun around and slapped Schwamb on the back of the head. "That's enough," he said. "Go home."

The assembled press watched the display of temper in wonder. Here was the chief defense attorney cuffing a seventeen-year-old kid from the Committee to Help Richard John Jahnke, moments after Richard himself had been sentenced to endure "hard time" —make that homosexual rape and murderous assault by adult convicts—for a minimum of five years without hope of parole. What drama! What irony! What a story!

Six days later—four days before he was due to be transferred to the state penitentiary at Rawlins—Richard was released from the county jail on a $50,000 appeal bond. Judge Liamos had agreed to let him stay with the Munns, Barrett explained, until the high court ruled on the appeal.

"How long have I got, Doc?" Richard asked.

"Oh, maybe six to eight months," Barrett said.

"You're kidding. That long?"

"Maybe even longer."

Richard stuffed his books, letters, and other personal items that had accumulated in his cell over the past month into two plastic garbage bags. Epps and Barrett carried the bags, trailing awkwardly behind their client as he made his way through the thicket of television crews waiting outside. The only reporter to snag an exclusive interview was Kirk Knox, who met up with Richard as he was descending the stairs to the exit.

"How are you, kid?" Knox asked.

Richard shook the reporter's outstretched hand. "I feel pretty good," he said.

The exchange was dutifully reported on the front page of the afternoon *State Tribune,* under the headline JAHNKE YOUTH SAYS IT FEELS GOOD TO BE OUT.

Actually, it felt . . . too strange for words. Richard couldn't stop looking at the sky. He had forgotten how big it was, how utterly, insanely *huge.* The attorneys threw a party for him at Terry Mackey's office; everyone was there, and Deborah, good old spacey Deborah, had made him a pizza—and forgot to cook it. Suddenly all these people were talking to him. He couldn't remember the last time he'd heard so much chatter. He kept looking out the window at the sky. Finally he made his apologies and slipped away. He needed to be alone.

There was a pile of newspaper clippings waiting for him at Barrett's office, a chronicle of the uproar that had followed the news of Liamos's sentence. "We fail to see how 5 to 15 years in the Wyoming State Penitentiary will help Richard Jahnke," read an editorial in the *Casper Star-Tribune.* "Contrary to the assertion made by Judge Liamos, the boy indeed will be thrown to the wolves. He can expect to enter a new period of unimaginable abuse." Kirk Knox's column was titled JAHNKE RESULT NOT SENSIBLE. Even some members of the jury were upset. Hence the screaming headline in the *Globe,* a supermarket tabloid:

JUDGE 'CRUCIFIES' BOY WHO
KILLED A MONSTER

We'd never have convicted
him, say shocked jurors

Other articles pointed out that parricide cases in other states were being handled quite differently. In a recent Florida case, seventeen-year-old George Burns, Jr., shot the abusive George Burns, Sr., in the back six times with a .357 magnum. Young Burns pleaded guilty in adult court to second-degree murder—murder, my friend, not manslaughter—and wound up on probation after a total of four days in jail. According to the Associated Press, no one connected with the case believed that the youth should go to prison, not even the attorneys for the state.

The *Denver Post* unearthed the story of a sixteen-year-old Denver youth who had killed his thirty-eight-year-old abusive father in order to protect his mother and his sister—sound familiar? —from further violence. But the similarities to the Jahnke case ended there. The Denver case was handled in juvenile court, where the youth pleaded guilty to manslaughter and received a suspended two-year sentence. He was now attending school and undergoing therapy.

The moral of the story seemed to be, don't kill your dad in Wyoming. Or, more precisely, don't kill your dad in Laramie County. Barrett's other parricide client—the eighteen-year-old Arapaho Indian who had broken into his abusive father's room and stabbed him to death—had been dealt with in the merciful confines of Wyoming's federal juvenile court. The youth had been sentenced to three years in a juvenile facility.

The flood of phone calls and letters abruptly shifted course. Now the target was Governor Ed Herschler, who had the power to commute Richard's sentence or grant a full pardon. One of the first supplicants was George Hain, who visited Herschler's office two days after the sentencing. Others followed in his wake, despite Barrett's efforts to discourage such visits.

Barrett had worked with Herschler before. In fact, the tall, amiable Democrat—the first three-term governor in the state, "Governor Ed" to the adoring local press—had once pardoned one of Barrett's clients, an elderly bureaucrat convicted of embezzling. Barrett had a strong hunch that Herschler would take an interest in Richard's case, but the governor was a strong-willed man who didn't respond well to people trying to tell him what to do. The defense attorney didn't want any well-intentioned arm twisting to queer the delicate deal he was trying to arrange through intermediaries, which called for Herschler to intervene only after the appeal had run its course.

Barrett explained the situation to Richard one afternoon at the firm, shortly after his release. It was still too early to tell what Herschler might do. Depending on the governor's feelings about the case, it might be better if Richard lost the appeal; then Herschler could come forward with a commutation order. If the Wyoming Supreme Court ruled in Richard's favor, it might mean a new trial, and who knows where that might lead. In any case, it would be wise for Richard to do everything he could in the coming months to "make a good impression" on the press, the courts, the public—and Governor Herschler.

Toward that end, Richard gave his first series of press interviews one snowy afternoon in late March. The requests from local and national media had been piling up ever since the trial. The most patient of the lot now hauled their cameras and microphones into the law library of Trierweiler, Bayless, Barrett, and McCartney, to ask the soft-spoken young parricide how he "felt" about his crime. With Barrett or Epps supervising off camera and a subdued Troy Schwamb watching quietly from the wings, Richard gave his pitch over and over. No, he didn't feel like a hero for killing Dad, what he did was "the wrong solution to a bad problem." Still, he didn't think it was right for the judge "to make an example of me" by sending him to prison, as if granting probation would have meant it was open season on parents for every kid with a key to the family arsenal. And by the way, Deborah didn't have a thing to do with it, she was a basket case that night.

When it was over, Richard felt both exhilarated and tainted. Throughout the trial he had been such a media virgin; now he felt like their whore. They were using him, but he was using them, too. He went over to the Munns' house and watched himself on the evening news. Everyone was impressed. He spoke well; he was a walking, talking advertisement for probation. A little more effort, and he could be the national poster child for some domestic violence prevention group.

The volume of mail addressed to him care of Barrett's office went up. Mixed in with the religious literature, the sympathy cards, and the confessions from other abuse victims were some unexpected propositions. Adoption offers. Offers to write a book or make a movie based on his life story. And something else: unabashed love letters from young women (teenagers? college students? women in their twenties? in some cases it was hard to tell). They had seen him on television or read about him in the paper. They thought he was cute. They wanted to comfort him.

Hell, he thought, I'm larger than life. I even have my own fucking fan club.

Byron and Verla Barry—Art and Petie, as they were known to all their friends—had some inkling of what they were getting into when they agreed to take Deborah Jahnke into their home. Art had thirty years' experience in education, much of it working with troubled adolescents in one capacity or another. Petie had four kids of her own and two stepchildren from Art's previous marriage. And Eve Whitcomb had briefed them on Deborah's compulsive use of the telephone, her incredible nervous energy, her lack of social skills, her efforts to "bend the rules" in order to see Chris Lawrence and other friends, her habit of stashing dirty clothes in her closet for Maria to come pick up and wash— the whole troubling legacy of her isolated existence in the bosom of Richard Chester Jahnke.

In many ways, the Barrys proved equal to the challenge. They removed the phone from Deborah's room so that she would have to use the phone upstairs, in full view of her hosts, in compliance with the terms of her bail. Petie laid down some ground rules about household chores, visiting hours, and the like. Art kept after her to pursue her education through a home studies course. Deborah still engaged in the occasional bit of deviousness—slipping into the kitchen to make a late-night call, or smuggling visitors into her room—but the Barrys were generally aware of her transgressions. By the time her case went to trial, the couple felt they had made significant progress in reclaiming their charge from the darkness in which she had grown up.

The verdict changed all that. Deborah was crushed. She let her studies slide. She resumed her frantic pacing and telephoning. She raided the refrigerator with such locustlike efficiency that Petie took to hiding food from her. Both Mackey and Art tried to tell Deborah it wasn't the end of the world, but the teenager found that a little hard to believe. She told them she'd had a bad feeling about what was going to happen ever since Richard testified about the kill-Mom-too business; *now I know I'm fried,* she thought. Terry's emotional performance in the courtroom had deluded her into thinking she was going to escape; but no, all wrong, the system has a thing about snotty little girls who

bad-mouth their mothers. She was sure to wind up in that new
prison for young murderesses they were building outside Lusk—
time for sweet little Deborah to get the shaft just like her brother—
and people were bitching at her about a few phone calls. I mean,
how ridiculous can you get?

In the last days before her sentencing hearing, Deborah's
agitation reached new heights. She eavesdropped when the probation officer came to interview Petie for the presentencing
report. After the woman left, she demanded that Petie recount the
entire conversation. Mackey handed her the complete report on
the eve of her sentencing. Deborah was aghast to discover what
she considered a highly negative assessment of her by Eve
Whitcomb. She cried most of the night.

The next day—Wednesday, April 27—Deborah walked arm in
arm with Mackey into the courtroom, a look of resignation and
ruin on her face. When Judge Maier asked if she had anything to
say, she deferred to Mackey, who outlined a proposal that had
already been submitted in the presentencing report. The proposal
called for Deborah to be made a ward of the state, with Mackey
appointed legal guardian; she would then be placed on probation
and receive counseling for an indeterminate time at the Excelsior
Youth Center, a custodial institution for emotionally disturbed
teenage girls, located in Aurora, Colorado, a Denver suburb.
While placement in Excelsior would be expensive, up to $30,000
a year, Mackey argued that the move would be more productive
in the long run than sending Deborah to the women's penitentiary
or the state reform school for girls.

Judge Maier asked Carroll if he had any comments. As he had
done in Richard's case, the district attorney declined to make any
recommendations regarding sentencing.

Before passing sentence, Maier read aloud the instructions on self-
defense that Deborah's jury had received. Then he raised his head and
squinted at the reporters in the first two rows of the spectator gallery.

"It apparently is unknown to the public, based upon the
information available to it from media reports, that the jury had
submitted to it the option to find this defendant not guilty if it
found the alleged principal, her brother, was acting in self-
defense," he said. "It is significant to me that the jury rejected
this claim of self-defense. . . . The evidence was sufficient, in my
opinion, to have supported a verdict of aiding and abetting
first-degree murder as charged."

Maier noted that the jury had found Deborah guilty of a lesser offense. He didn't fault them for that. He did, however, take strong exception to the media's coverage of the case.

"The public . . . has been told that this defendant and her brother had no other recourse than to take the action that they did, because it was stated solemnly and repeated continuously by the media that 'society failed them,' society gave them no help in their dilemma. These conclusions were presented to the public as absolute truths by the media, but what does the trial record itself disclose? Let me review for you some of the testimony. . . ."

Maier read aloud eight pages of Carroll's cross-examination of Richard, all of which suggested that Richard could have gone to Major Vegvary, the school nurse, or any number of other adults for protection against his father.

"I mention these matters as one illustration of what I consider incomplete, incorrect, and slanted news given by the media to the public," he said. "I have seen press reports using the words 'incest' and 'rape' with regard to the actions of the deceased father toward this defendant. The only testimony in this regard in this case referred to the deceased 'touching' the defendant—that there was hugging, or putting his hand on her pants, or patting her on the behind . . . and, more importantly, that these things had happened before she was twelve years of age, and never after that."

When he was finished lambasting the press, Maier moved on to the matter at hand. He went over the four major considerations in the judicial determination of sentence: protection of society, rehabilitation of the defendant, deterrence, and punishment. In his view, Deborah posed no further risk to society. Rehabilitation "is not needed," except, perhaps, "in the area of psychological counseling and social counseling, to help her readjust from previous problems of her family and personal life." As for the third factor, "deterrence is a concept difficult to apply because empirical evidence of its success is almost impossible to come by."

However, the judge added, "I believe it necessary to the greater good of society as a whole that defendants found guilty of serious criminal behavior receive swift and certain punishment."

God, here it comes, Deborah thought. *Just get it over with.*

"A wise and learned psychiatrist told me one time that a person who has taken a human life will feel guilt, and that some punishment is necessary for that individual to expiate that feeling of guilt," Maier said. "Deborah Jahnke, would you come forward at this time."

Deborah stood up.

"It is the judgment of this court that you be confined in the Women's Center presently located at or near Evanston in Uinta County, Wyoming, and hereafter to be located at or near Lusk in Niobrara County, Wyoming, for a term of not less than three nor more than eight years. . . ."

An eerie silence reigned in the courtroom, in stark contrast to the gasps of anger and surprise that had greeted Richard's sentence. *Come on, people, say something,* Deborah thought.

"The Court will further provide that if an appeal be in fact filed or your counsel advises me of his intention to do so, that this defendant will be permitted to be released on an appeal bond in the amount of $25,000 cash or surety . . ."

Mackey popped up. "Your Honor, if I might inquire, Miss Jahnke is a child without $25,000. Will the court accept her mother's money?"

"I will accept a property bond," Maier replied.

Mackey exited with his tearful client as she was taken next door to the jail. Reporters headed for the court clerk's office to obtain written copies of Maier's remarks, so that they could print the full text next to their own indignant responses. (Indeed, in blasting the press, the judge had made some questionable claims himself. No reporter present could recall seeing the words "rape" or "incest" in any press reports on the Jahnke case. Dr. Macdonald's testimony at the transfer hearings indicated that Dad put his hands *inside* Deborah's pants, not just on them, as Maier stated. Also, it was difficult to follow Maier's reasoning that the alleged fondling was somehow less offensive because Deborah was less than twelve years old at the time.)

Mackey returned to the courthouse and held the first press conference of his career in the hallway. Visibly distraught, with the television lights catching the dampness in his eyes, he announced, "Now children know there is no relief. The system won't help."

A reporter asked him if he was saying that the system didn't work.

"The system works, and so does my 1957 Ford—not always real good," Mackey replied. "I didn't see much courage in there today."

He fielded a few more questions and then rushed across the street to his office, where Maria Jahnke was waiting for him.

Half an hour later the house on Cowpoke Road had been put up as surety to insure Deborah's release on bond. The women's prison, located on the grounds of the state mental hospital in Evanston, would have to wait a little while. Forever, maybe.

Mackey held a "coming-out" party for his client at his office. When it was over, Deborah left with Art and Petie Barry and their daughter Susan. For several moments they sat in the car without speaking. Deborah giggled.

"God," she said. "I'm sure hard to get rid of."

It was a late spring, the strangest season of their lives. The high priests of society's wrath had spoken; Richard and Deborah had been condemned; the jaws of the penitentiary opened wide for them; and then . . . nothing. An appeal, a reprieve, a stay of punishment. Richard retreated to the Munns' basement to watch television, Deborah got back on the phone at the Barrys and called her friends. Nothing had changed. And yet, it was all different somehow.

A new world beckoned. It was a world of hot studio lights and notoriety, of crusty stares from people at the mall, of encouraging and occasionally seductive letters from people who had read about them in *Newsweek* or *Rolling Stone*. Teenagers they had scarcely known at Central High now invoked their names in a tone of cloying sympathy or harsh resentment. Total strangers offered to buy them presents or take them out to dinner, as some sort of reparation for their years of misery. It was all baffling and magical and not quite real, like a glistening rainbow that could vanish at any moment. For until the five justices of the Wyoming Supreme Court made up their minds, or Governor Herschler made up his, they weren't really free. The prospect of going to prison for three, five, maybe eight or more years—practically a lifetime by any teen's standards—hung over them like a sword of Damocles, suspended by the thread of appeals Barrett and Mackey were weaving.

Like her brother before her, Deborah met with radio, television, and newspaper reporters to honor outstanding interview requests. The interviews were conducted at a brisk pace under the watchful eye of Terry Mackey, who cut off any questions that might have a bearing on the appeal (e.g., "Did you really say, 'Kill, Mom, too'?"). The next day, Richard and Deborah gave their first and only joint interview to ABC's *Good Morning*

America, thereby earning the ire of a producer at NBC, who had been courting the Jahnkes' attorneys for weeks in an effort to snag the controversial siblings for the *Today* show. The *Good Morning America* segment was taped in a studio provided by Cheyenne's KYCU-TV, a CBS affiliate; the *CBS Morning News* responded by running an interview Deborah had given to KYCU the day before.

Years earlier, Deborah had confided to her diary, "My biggest ambition in life is to some day become an actress. That's all I dream about. I'd like very much to change my name—perhaps to something unique like—Brooke Amberley. . . . I want Love and Fame so badly!" She now had fame, of a sort, but it wasn't quite what she had expected. The press treated her the same way the prosecution did—as an accessory, a bit player. The focus was elsewhere, on her brother, the real star of the show. She tried to tell the reporters a thing or two about all the other kids she knew who had problems at home. Honest, we're not as weird as you think, she said, maybe somebody ought to investigate why the schools or social services aren't doing more about it; I mean, it's really too bad my father had to die for all you people to wake up and look at what's going on. But few comments of that nature found their way into print or on the air.

The interviews soon became an object of bitter humor for both Richard and Deborah. They even developed a routine for their own amusement. Troy or some other friend would shove an imaginary microphone into Richard's face and ask inane questions. Richard would give equally inane replies. Then the "interviewer" would turn to Deborah.

"I agree with my brother," she would say. "Whatever he says goes for me, too. I'm just an extension of Richard."

Her life in the public eye ended abruptly, shortly after it began. With the appeal pending, Mackey proceeded with his plan to have Deborah placed in the Excelsior Youth Center in Aurora. Her stay would be paid for by the state of Wyoming, which assumed custody of the eighteen-year-old through a court order issued in May. Mackey was promptly appointed her legal guardian.

Deborah balked. Barrett and the Munns and Dr. Barry were working on getting Richard back into the Cheyenne school system next fall. She didn't see why she had to be packed off to some creepy home for girls with emotional problems, one hundred miles from her friends and whatever was left of her family, when her little brother was going to be allowed to go to high school and maybe even graduate like a normal teenager. It wasn't fair. It wasn't fair at all.

Mackey insisted that the "structured environment" at Excelsior would do her some good. She'd get some badly needed counseling and an opportunity to get her high school diploma, maybe even go to college on a day pass. A voluntary move to an institution like Excelsior was good public relations, too; whatever time she spent there could conceivably be regarded as time served on her sentence by the Wyoming Supreme Court or Governor Herschler. Besides, he couldn't ask the Barrys to house her indefinitely, and there was nowhere else in Cheyenne she could go.

"Trust me," he said.

Deborah gave in reluctantly. A ward of the state of Wyoming, she left Cheyenne in late May to seek treatment and "rehabilitation" in Colorado. She was no longer available to the press, but the legal issues raised by her case had sparked a debate that continued to rage in the Denver papers months after the trials had ended.

She found some comfort in an opinion piece that appeared in the *Denver Post* shortly after her arrival. The article challenged the judges' reasoning that the teenagers should be imprisoned to "discourage others," as Judge Liamos put it, "from committing acts similar to yours." "To make an example of Richard and Deborah Jahnke is to suggest that society fears a sudden outbreak of parricide more than it fears the common practice of child abuse," the writer argued. "It is to aggravate the tragic consequences of a crime while ignoring its causes."

By the time that article was published, events in Cheyenne had led many citizens to ponder the mysteries of cause and effect. One particularly disturbing echo of the Jahnke case had people asking themselves whether the sentences imposed on Richard and Deborah had any deterrent value at all. On May 11, the day after the pair appeared on *Good Morning America* together, an eighteen-year-old student at Cheyenne's East High School surrendered to a police SWAT team after a two-hour confrontation at his house. According to newspaper reports, the incident began after the youth threatened "to do what Jahnke did to his father."

21

What Tom Carroll had termed the "glare of publicity" surrounding the Jahnke case reached its apotheosis in August of 1983, when a CBS news crew arrived in Cheyenne to research a story on the parricide for an upcoming episode of *60 Minutes*. Producer Allan Maraynes, reporter Ed Bradley, and a film crew from the top-rated weekly program spent two days interviewing principals in the case and shooting footage of the house at 8736 Cowpoke Road. District Attorney Carroll declined to be interviewed; it was his policy, he said, not to discuss any of his cases publicly.

By the time the *60 Minutes* team appeared on the scene, both Richard and Deborah had been through a veritable gauntlet of press interviews. Both were reluctant to face the cameras one more time, particularly for a "television news magazine" with a reputation for high-pressure investigative journalism. Richard had already declined an invitation to appear on Phil Donahue's television talk show, telling Barrett, "No way—that guy's *rude!*" It took some friendly persuasion from Barrett and Mackey to convince their clients that this was an opportunity to plead their cause to a staggeringly large audience, and perhaps give the Wyoming Supreme Court and Governor Herschler some food for thought. But if the teenagers' precarious legal position was an argument for appearing on the program, it was also a reason for caution. As one of the conditions for granting an interview, Mackey stipulated that Bradley would not be allowed to question Deborah about her role in the events of November 16.

The situation was further complicated by the growing rift between Maria Jahnke and the law firm of Trierweiler, Bayless, Barrett, and McCartney. Maria had never forgiven Jim Barrett for not consulting her before putting Richard on the stand. Barrett insisted he needed a free hand to represent Richard's best interests. Following his release from jail on an appeal bond, Richard had become openly hostile to his mother, a development she

278

blamed on the increasing influence of Richard's new circle of "friends," including his lawyers. Maria had more or less accepted that her relationship with Deborah would always have its share of heartache; but now she felt that both her children had been taken from her.

Money was another sore point. Barrett had initially told Maria that the criminal defense for her children would cost around $25,000. When Terry Mackey was retained to represent Deborah, the figure was raised to $50,000. After the trials were concluded, Barrett informed Maria that the attorneys had "run over budget." The legal bills totaled more than $94,000. Much of the overrun had to do with expenses, not attorney's fees. Given the tremendous cost of hiring private investigators, locating witnesses, and staging two trials, it is possible that Barrett's early estimates had been simply too optimistic, but Maria was furious. Her children were facing prison sentences, and the trials had devoured a substantial chunk of the money her husband had left her.

Shortly before the *60 Minutes* crew arrived, Maria Jahnke and Jim Barrett settled their differences—legally, at least—in writing. Maria agreed to pay Richard's outstanding legal bills, including the cost of preparing a transcript of his trial to be submitted to the Wyoming Supreme Court in the course of his appeal. In return, Barrett agreed not to hold her liable for any further expenses; he would be working on the appeal gratis from now on. Maria also broke off her relationship with Barrett's partner, Dick Trierweiler, who was handling the negotiations with various television producers vying for the rights to the Jahnkes' life story. She retained another Cheyenne lawyer, Peter McNiff, to represent her interests in any forthcoming film or book deal.

McNiff urged Maria not to grant *60 Minutes* an interview. She had little to gain, he said, and everything to lose. Given the electronic media's habit of turning complex issues into showdowns between white-hats and black-hats, she was likely to emerge as the villain of the piece. But other advisers reminded Maria of another truism of television journalism: the people who didn't talk to *60 Minutes* came off looking like they were hiding something. Better to take your chances in a sit-down interview than to be filmed running to your car in some shopping-mall parking lot.

Maria agreed. Eager to make a good impression, she purchased a new set of furniture for the living room; the pieces were delivered only hours before the *60 Minutes* crew visited her. Ed Bradley sat in a chair that, according to the bright orange price tag that still hung from one arm, was a RED TAG SPECIAL.

Bradley's interviews with Richard and Deborah were conducted back to back at the Excelsior Youth Center. Barrett and Mackey were present off camera throughout the proceedings. At one point, Mackey interrupted the taping to instruct Deborah not to answer a question that verged on forbidden territory—her "intentions" on the night of the shooting—but for the most part, the sessions went smoothly. As Bradley saw it, this was not a situation that called for aggressive interrogation techniques. His job was to get the teenagers talking, speaking from the gut, and then to sit back and listen. That didn't prove difficult.

Bradley found Richard Jahnke particularly fascinating. Far from being camera-shy, the youth was an expressive, articulate, highly emotional subject, clearly "psyched" for the task at hand. Bradley decided to let him roam. At times thirty or forty seconds went by without either one saying a word, a terribly long silence by film interview standards, but Bradley's patience was rewarded. Richard's hatred of his father, his sense of helplessness and disgust, the tremendous anger coursing through his system—it all bubbled to the surface once more, just as it had in the courtroom. But now there was more reflection, more control, and more acid in his voice. His eyes burned with intense outrage and frustration as he talked about the prison sentences awaiting him and his sister.

Listening to Richard, Bradley knew he had a winner. This was high emotion. This was effective television. This was going to be one heck of a powerful story, even by the blockbuster standards of *60 Minutes*.

That summer the Jahnke family concluded negotiations for the creation of a television "docudrama" based on their life story. The TV movie would be produced by Taper Media Enterprises, a subsidiary of the Mark Taper Forum theater company in Los Angeles. The agreement called for the Jahnkes' "exclusive" cooperation in researching and preparing a script for the movie, giving the family a ready excuse to refuse further requests for media interviews.

Although at least three other production companies had

attempted to obtain the rights to the story, Taper Media had managed to woo the family and their attorneys with the right blend of persistence and tact. Producer Elizabeth Daley, one of the directors of Taper Media, had come to Cheyenne only days after Richard's sentence was announced; Maria had first met her in Dick Trierweiler's office, as she was arranging her son's release from jail on an appeal bond. Throughout the subsequent negotiations, Daley had stressed the Mark Taper Forum's reputation for quality. She suggested that the television script could provide the basis for a stage play as well.

Taper paid $5000 in option money for the rights to the Jahnkes' story, with the promise of a much more substantial payment, in the neighborhood of $40,000, to be paid when the movie went into production. It was hardly an astronomical sum, particularly by television standards, but many people in Cheyenne were under the impression that it was much more. Indeed, rumors were spreading that *People* and *60 Minutes* had paid the Jahnkes for their interviews; what was the world coming to, they wanted to know, when kids can deep-six their dear old daddy and then get rich telling people about it?

The rumors were, of course, totally unfounded. The Jahnkes were far from wealthy. More than a third of Richard Chester Jahnke's life insurance money had already been spent on his funeral and his children's legal fees. Much of what was left had been used to pay off the mortgage on the house on Cowpoke Road.

Maria had decided to buy the house outright, against the advice of George Hain and practically everyone else she knew. Hain and the others had urged her to sell the house and move away from Cheyenne. How can you live there, they said, with all those painful memories? Don't you want a fresh start, Maria? But what did they know? The house was all she had, and Maria was starting to like Cheyenne. Nobody said bad things to her when she went out in public, not to her face, anyway. Some people even *smiled* at her. And Richie and Deborah weren't the only ones to get letters; Maria did, too. She threw away the hateful ones and kept the nice ones. Quite a few of the writers were local people. But the memories, the notoriety, wouldn't it be better—no, she liked the house. She liked the neighborhood. Nobody was going to make her move. She was going to fix the damaged garage door and stay right here in Cowboy Country, thank you.

As if to prove her independence from her erstwhile advisers, she made several more purchases. She treated herself to some new clothes, a VCR, a home satellite dish, a trip to Hawaii, and a membership in a health spa, where she quickly shed thirty pounds. Some of her friends told her she was acting like a kid let loose in a candy store; she'd better be careful or there would be nothing left. She told her friends to mind their own business. Richard had left the money to her, not the children; she was entitled to spend a little on herself, for the first time in her life. Besides, the kids were getting plenty. Hadn't she footed the bill for two trials? Didn't she buy them plenty of presents for Christmas and their birthdays? Wasn't the lion's share of the money from the movie deal going into trust funds to pay for their college education, once the legal system was through with them? What more did they want?

Maria couldn't understand it. The more she tried to do for her children, the more they seemed to avoid her. Two bumper stickers plastered on the back of her station wagon told the rest of Cheyenne how she felt—I ♥ RICHIE, I ♥ DEBBIE, they said—but her children rarely visited her. Deborah was a hundred miles away at Excelsior; the emotional distance between mother and daughter was even greater. Richard was still in Cheyenne, staying with the Munns, but for the past few months he had barely spoken to his mother.

He had his own circle of admirers now. People couldn't do enough for him; what did he need a mother for? He tooled around town with his buddy Troy Schwamb, in a sporty Mazda RX-7 borrowed from a young widow who had been one of the most ardent supporters of the Committee to Help Richard John Jahnke. Young girls flirted with him at the mall, but he wasn't into dating ninth-graders anymore; his taste had matured. He went out with girls his own age or even older and spent freely on them, running through the pocket money he'd earned doing some filing at Barrett's firm or grilling patties at Burger King, a summer job provided by George Hain. He came to Maria only when he needed more money, and then they quarreled.

One dusty July afternoon, shortly before Cheyenne's annual Frontier Days celebration, he showed up at the house with an armful of purchases—new shirts, an expensive new jacket. He demanded to be reimbursed for what it had cost him to buy them. Maria gave him the money but then complained about his spending habits. He responded by complaining about hers; he might go to prison in the fall, he pointed out—what was her excuse? He accused her of not caring what happened to him. The cruelest charge of all, though, was merely an echo of what other people were saying about the Jahnke case—that "the wrong people" were on trial.

"It's your fault that Dad died," Richard said.

"How can you say that?" Maria moaned.

"It's true. You know it's true."

Maria knew nothing of the kind. After her son left, she cried and prayed for strength. She was alone now, a poor widow estranged from her own children. She chalked it up to bad luck, ignorant judges, and the malignant interference of strangers.

On Sundays she drove to Olivet Cemetery to visit her husband's grave. The grave stood adjacent to the road, in a patch of sunlight atop a gentle ridge at the northeast end of the cemetery. Maria had purchased a double plot with the intention of being buried beside him. She had since changed her mind; the other nameplate on the tombstone would remain forever blank. It was just as well; she knew Richard wouldn't want to be too close to anybody. Still, she made sure the grave always had plenty of fresh flowers. She visited often, spending quiet hours alone with her thoughts. If Richard could hear her, she told herself, he'd understand. He wouldn't condemn her for what had happened.

He'd know it wasn't her fault.

When classes resumed at East High School in the fall, seventeen-year-old Richard Jahnke answered the first bell with the rest of the senior class. His return to the Cheyenne public school system had been arranged by superintendent of schools Art Barry and Jack Iverson, East's sympathetic principal. The outcome of Richard's appeal was still uncertain, but Barry and Iverson believed that the youth deserved an opportunity to "try to put his life back together" in as normal a setting as possible, for however long it lasted.

Richard had hoped to return to Central High, with Troy Schwamb and the rest of his new friends. Barrett had dissuaded him; the shooting was still a sensitive topic at Central, particularly in the ROTC department. Instead, he was allowed to make up his junior year with special tutoring over the summer. His arrival at East was greeted with some curiosity on the part of his classmates, but interest in the convicted killer in their midst quickly gave way to more pressing concerns: college applications, the latest Van Halen or Talking Heads album, the coming weekend's social calendar. The novelty of Cheyenne's most sensational crime was wearing off; in many eyes, Richard Jahnke was just another transfer student from East's crosstown rival.

Richard did his best to encourage that impression. He became a photographer for the school paper. He joined the local chapter of Distributive Education Clubs of America (DECA) and went to a convention in Boise, Idaho, with the rest of the group. Troy had given him some tips about how to carry himself with the ladies, and he had no trouble getting dates. Yet he couldn't escape the sense that he was leading a double life. What good was a quick trip to Boise when a five-year trip to prison was only a phone call away? Did the girls who went out with him really like him, or did they just want to be seen with the Boy Who Killed His Father? Who was he, really?

He wasn't sure. Dan Munn told him he was trying to grow up too fast; he should try to cool out, relax, be a teenager for a change. But he couldn't go back. That world didn't exist anymore. He had destroyed it one night in the garage.

One day he ran into Greg Porter at the Frontier Mall. Greg hugged him like a long-lost brother and invited him to his house. He showed him the coveted saber of the battalion commander, the emblem of leadership both youths had vied for so earnestly in ROTC. Richard offered his congratulations, but it all seemed so unimportant now. Their rivalry was a couple of lifetimes ago.

In October Barrett told him he had some good news. After weeks of confidential discussions through intermediaries, Governor Herschler had committed himself. If Richard lost his appeal, Herschler would step in and commute his sentence. Herschler didn't believe that probation would be "appropiate," but Richard wouldn't be going to prison, either. The worst he had to fear was a few months or years at the boys' school at Worland—four years tops, since the juvenile facility couldn't hold him past the age of twenty-one. It was vital, Barrett added, that Richard not breathe a word of this to anyone.

Richard could hardly contain himself. No hard time for killer Jahnke! Yet the euphoria faded quickly. Serving time in a boys' school . . . well, it was still time—four years was a bitch of a long time, if you thought about it—and what if the Wyoming Supreme Court ordered a new trial, what if something terrible happened to Governor Ed, God bless him, before the court made up its collective mind? He didn't want to sound like an ungrateful little snot, but freedom still seemed far, far away.

The imponderables of his situation weighed heavily on him. He tried to talk about them with the local psychiatrist he was seeing once a week. What oppressed him wasn't just the uncertain future, or the impossibility of being just another kid at East High. He was still smothering in the unresolved past. He had talked so often and so publicly about the terrible things that had happened to him, from the earliest beatings to the moment he pulled the trigger, that the whole story had become a bit unreal to him, like the plot of a lame soap opera. In trying to make sense of it, he first had to hack his way through a dense thicket of rationalization, everything from the standard clinical and legal excuses for what he did to the pop-psychology theories offered by friends. Some of his friends had told him that his father had a death wish, that Mom had been setting him up to kill Dad ever since he was a little boy, that he had been acting as the "unconscious agent" of one or both parents when he went into the garage.

"What do *you* think, Richard?" the psychiatrist asked.

"I don't know," he said.

The psychiatrist and the Munns urged him to try to talk things out with his mother. Until he came to grips with the anger he felt toward her, the soap opera was just going to get worse. He packed an overnight bag and went back to the house with the intention of spending the weekend with her. The first day, though, they quarreled again, about money, the attorneys, and who was to blame for everything rotten in the world. Your fault. Your fault.

"You just came here to torment me, didn't you?" Maria cried.

Richard realized she was right. You blew it again, sonny. You carved Mom out of your life just like Dad, only this time you did it with words. Nice work.

He grabbed his bag and stomped out of the house; his own father couldn't have done it better. Maria called after him, pleading, come back, you're all I have left. He made it to the end of the driveway, then turned around and ran back. He found his mother crying in her room.

"You're not going to hurt yourself, are you?" he asked.

He hugged her and burst into tears.

They talked for hours. Maria tried to explain how it was for her: how she had loved her husband, loved them all, but she had been so afraid, so terribly afraid. And now that she was alone in the house, she couldn't sleep. She was nervous all the time. She'd go to the supermarket and buy food for the whole family. As she was putting it away she'd think, wait a minute, I don't have a family anymore. She'd rush to have the laundry done and dinner ready at five o'clock, everything had to be just right, and then she'd remember that her husband was dead, he wasn't coming home after all. But she still heard him sometimes. She heard him whistle—remember how he whistled, Richie, when he came home from work? And she heard his footsteps in the driveway, as if he was coming back to get her. It sounds crazy, yes—but still. The sounds, the tension, they wouldn't go away. She was afraid to go out alone at night. She was so afraid, so terribly afraid.

Richard stayed with her for the rest of the weekend. He felt as if he was seeing his mother for the first time.

Two weeks after Richard's visit, Maria Jahnke checked into Memorial Hospital, complaining of nervous exhaustion. A few days later she checked out and started seeing a psychologist at the Southeast Wyoming Mental Health Center. She also began to spend more time out of the house, first as a volunteer at the local Veterans Administration hospital, then as a residential counselor at Meadowlark House, a home for unwed mothers.

The job at Meadowlark required her to sleep there three nights a week. It was a good job, she told friends, very fulfilling—"like being a regular mother," she said.

On November 16, 1983, the first anniversary of the death of Richard Chester Jahnke, Terry Mackey presented Deborah's appeal to the five justices of the Wyoming Supreme Court. He began his argument by quoting G. K. Chesterton: "Children are innocent and love justice, while most adults are wicked and beg mercy."

"Deborah Ann Jahnke, a child, does not seek mercy before this court, and she sought none before her jury," Mackey said.

"She seeks justice. Mercy may be easier to identify than justice, but it is justice and not mercy which is the business of this court."

Jim Barrett had appeared before the justices several weeks earlier, in the second week of September, to appeal three crucial rulings in Richard's case. Judge Liamos had erred, Barrett contended, by excluding from the *voir dire* examination any questions on the jury's attitudes about child abuse and justifiable homicide; by refusing to permit Dr. John Macdonald's expert testimony; and by handing down an "excessive" prison sentence.

Mackey was challenging the sentence imposed on his client, too. But the bulk of Mackey's appeal was devoted to three other issues: Judge Maier's decision to admit testimony concerning Deborah's statement to the detectives; the Wyoming statute that allowed District Attorney Carroll to charge juveniles as adults solely at his own discretion—a statute that Mackey charged was "unconstitutional on its face"; and finally, Maier's instructions to the jury that they could find Deborah guilty of the lesser offense of aiding and abetting voluntary manslaughter.

Unlike the tortuously slow appeals process in other states, it is customary for the Wyoming Supreme Court to rule on appeals in thirty to sixty days after they have been filed. The Jahnke appeals were an exception. At the time Mackey pleaded Deborah's case before the high court, the anticipated "deadline" for a decision in Richard's case had already passed. Now Deborah began a vigil of her own.

She had been living at the Excelsior Youth Center for the past six months, long enough to manifest an impeccable outward conformity to its rules while cultivating a deep-seated abhorrence of the place. Every day the voice on the intercom awakened her at 6:45; she was expected to have her room ready for inspection by 7:30. Breakfast was followed by a brief group counseling session, then morning classes, lunch, afternoon classes, dinner with the half-dozen girls who shared her cottage, study hall, more group counseling and "peer talks," miscellaneous chores, lights out at 10:15, bathroom locked at 10:20. And then it all started over again.

She wrote long, lonely letters to Mackey complaining about the facility's barrackslike atmosphere, the sheer tedium of her daily routine, the lack of privacy, and her desperate need to talk to someone close to her own age and interests. She didn't see how she was supposed to learn to be normal when her companions were runaways, drug abusers, hookers, and some rather scary, violent types, all younger than herself. Mackey told her to bite the bullet. The reports he was receiving from her counselors indicated that Deborah was doing her homework, progressing in her therapy, and learning to accept responsibility. She might not admit it, but the counselors believed Deborah Jahnke secretly craved the sort of "structured existence" Excelsior offered.

Deborah collected her high school diploma and returned to Cheyenne for a brief visit a few days before Christmas. To practically everyone she met, she posed a blunt question: "Do you think I've changed?" With few exceptions, they agreed that she had. Even Eve Whitcomb found her to be more reserved, more in control of herself—not relaxed exactly, Whitcomb had never seen Deborah relaxed; but she had gained a certain maturity. Nonetheless, Mackey insisted that she return to Excelsior until the appeal was resolved.

"I don't see why I have to be treated like a four-year-old," Deborah protested. "I hate it there."

"Trust me," Mackey said.

"You always say that."

The new year arrived without any word from the Wyoming Supreme Court regarding the Jahnkes' appeals. Aside from the family and its small circle of supporters, it is doubtful that many people in Cheyenne took note of the high court's delay. The case had ceased to be the focus of public attention months ago. Cheyenne had other things on its mind: President Reagan's plan to place MX missiles in nearby Minuteman silos, the political wrangling of the state legislature, the perennial debate over how to attract new businesses to the area. Yet the man in the street soon found the Jahnke case staring him in the face again, whether he liked it or not.

On January 22, 1984, the Los Angeles Raiders gained their third National Football League championship by defeating the Washington Redskins 38–9 in Super Bowl XVIII. CBS followed up its live coverage of the game with a "Super Bowl Sunday special edition" of *60 Minutes*. The lineup for the program, certain to be the highest-rated episode of *60 Minutes* for the entire season, had been carefully selected by executive producer Don Hewitt. The lead piece was Ed Bradley's seventeen-minute report on the Jahnkes, "Dirty Little Secret." (The title was surely more ironic than *60 Minutes* had intended; it echoed a line in "Dirty Laundry," the song about sensationalistic TV journalism that was playing on the radio when Richard shot his father.)

Several million Super Bowl viewers—Washington Redskins fans, probably—switched off their sets before the familiar stopwatch began to tick. But the carryover audience was large enough to guarantee that "Dirty Little Secret" would be one of the most popular *60 Minutes* segments of all time. An estimated 46 million Americans (27,400,000 households) watched as Sandy Hain described the "bloodcurdling screams" she'd heard coming from the Jahnke house, and Bradley prodded a sheepish Frank DeLois into admitting, once more, that he "forgot" to leave his card with Richard when he investigated the child abuse report six months before the shooting. Skillful editing served to dramatize the conflicts within the house on Cowpoke Road as only television can. One highly effective cut moved from Deborah insisting that her mother knew that her father fondled her ("On more than one occasion, she has seen it") to Maria stumbling over the word "molestation" as she denied the charge.

As Bradley had expected, the report's most powerful moments came in a series of tight close-ups of Richard Jahnke, who recalled his father's "evil voice" and merciless treatment of him with the uncanny talent for mimicry he had first displayed at his trial. Angry, bitter, and occasionally sarcastic, Richard concluded by blasting the judges who had sentenced him and his sister.

"Doesn't fourteen years of a person's life count?" he asked. "Here I am facing five-to-fifteen years, and my sister—three-to-seven [sic] years in prison—for what? Because she was going through a nervous breakdown? What did they want her to do—stop me? The only way she could have stopped me was to kill me."

He bowed his head. "Seems like both of our lives are wrecked."

The switchboard at CBS headquarters in New York City lit up with calls that night. Over the next few days the mail room logged more than a thousand letters in response to "Dirty Little Secret." What was surprising about the mail was not its volume but its overwhelming one-sidedness. Most of the writers praised the report; 154 of them offered assistance to the Jahnkes, from free legal advice and counseling to adoption; only ten objected to the program.

Reaction to the broadcast in Cheyenne was more restrained. If any local viewers had been expecting 60 Minutes to shed fresh light on the Jahnke case, they were disappointed. Much of what "Dirty Little Secret" had to say was old news. Contacted by a local reporter for his opinion, Terry Mackey volunteered that he was satisfied with the program's accuracy, and let it go at that. Tom Carroll had no comment.

Michael Brinkman, now a freshman at the University of Wyoming, watched Richard's performance with a mixture of amusement and disbelief. This wasn't the Richard Jahnke he used to know, the tight-lipped, gung-ho cadet who didn't want to talk about his problems. This was one Angry Young Man, gnashing his teeth and playing the crowds.

To a large degree, Deborah was insulated from further public scrutiny by virtue of her confinement at Excelsior; the 60 Minutes treatment had little effect on her situation. But Richard had to go to school the next day and face a classroom full of people who had seen him on TV. Dan and Corrine Munn warned him that he would probably have to fend off a great deal of renewed interest in the case.

"No problem," Richard said. "I can handle it."

Yet the Munns saw an obvious change in his behavior over the next few weeks. His grades were starting to slide. He was spending more time at the Frontier Mall, waiting for someone—the young girls, maybe—to notice him. He was partying more frequently and staying out later, operating on the general theory that he had better learn whatever he could—about strip poker, Jack Daniels, what the stars looked like from the back seat of a car at three o'clock in the morning, and a dozen other matters—before the Man came to take him away. In short, he was showing the symptoms of senioritis, a disease of the grade-point average, brought on by the distractions, pressures, and anxieties of the senior year, compounded by an extreme case of notoriety and an attack of jailhouse blues. Dan Munn told him, gee, Richard, I know we encouraged you to act like a teenager for a change, but don't you think you're overdoing it?

"No problem," Richard said. "Everything's fine."

At East they were saying: if you want to get laid, go out with Jahnke. That wasn't true, of course; raw sex didn't appeal to him all that much. But in between the good, stable, level-headed relationships he said he wanted, he did manage to have a few alien encounters. At the height of his playboy period, a former Miss Wyoming called him up and asked him out on a date. The Munns tried to talk him out of it: Richard, this has got to be some weird publicity stunt, she's several years older than you are. But how many guys get a crack at a genuine Miss Wyoming? She arrived one Sunday morning wearing an ingenious corduroy jumpsuit with a zipper down the middle. She took him to services at her church, then out for pizza. When she laughed, her breasts bobbed up and down. She laughed a lot. Richard liked her. He invited her into his room when they returned. She sat on his bed and talked about her personal relationship with the Lord. End of discussion. End of date.

It didn't take many alien encounters to convince him that some people found him appealing for reasons that had nothing to do with him. They weren't interested in Richard Jahnke. They weren't even all that interested in the Boy Who Killed His Father. It didn't matter who he was or what he'd done; he could be Charles Manson or Johnny Carson, for all they cared. He was a celebrity, a face beamed into people's living rooms. That made him important. That made *you* important, if you happened to know him.

Pretty sick stuff; yet there were times when he enjoyed the attention, God knows. And when his psychiatrist tried to draw him out on the subject, to get all those mixed-up feelings about his very public life out on the table, he retreated behind the hard shell of his boyish smile.

No problem, doc. No problem.

As the months dragged on with no news from the high court, the smile became as brittle as a leftover Christmas cookie. Richard took to leaving the room whenever someone started to ask him about the appeal. Despite his reconciliation with his mother last fall, he found it difficult to control his temper around her. One evening Maria asked him to bring in the garbage cans from the edge of the darkened driveway.

"What are you afraid of, Mom?" Richard snapped. "There's only one murderer in Cheyenne, and that's me!"

In March he had a falling out with his sister. Perhaps the break was inevitable, given the long-simmering resentment each harbored for the other. Circumstance had hurled them into a series of fairy-tale-like roles: Hansel and Gretel, Rapunzel and the prince, Little Red Riding Hood and the woodsman. But underneath it all, they really weren't that close. Publicly, Deborah praised her brother for his courage, his sensitivity, his intelligence, his good looks; privately, she envied his popularity and his freedom. Richard grew weary of her praise, her envy, and her obvious dependence on him; he could handle the hero worship from others, but not from his own sister. One night, following a raucous party in celebration of Deborah's nineteenth birthday, they set about shattering each other's illusions about the relationship and wound up not speaking to each other.

Deborah returned to Excelsior in the grip of a profound depression. Her counselors told her she was resisting therapy. She began to adorn her letters to friends with drawings of tombstones and daggers dripping blood. Richard turned his attention to the upcoming senior prom. No problem, folks. No problem. No problem. Noproblemnoproblemnoproblem.

In May Richard gave an exclusive interview to his school paper, the East High *Thunderbolt*. "Thank you so much for making this year my best so far," he told his classmates. "This school has provided me with the most normal atmosphere possible, which has helped me to deal with the strain of my situation." Two weeks later he attended graduation ceremonies with the rest of the senior class. As he walked on stage to collect his diploma, the audience roared its approval. A television cameraman stationed in the balcony zoomed in for a close-up.

On the first of June Jim Barrett filed a petition with the Wyoming Supreme Court requesting permission to place Richard Jahnke in Bethesda Hospital, a Denver psychiatric hospital specializing in the treatment of adolescents, "for purposes of further and more intensive psychological therapy." Richard's psychiatrist had been urging such a move for months, but it had been delayed in order to allow Richard to graduate with his friends.

Five days later, with Barrett's petition still pending, the high court released its 98-page decision in Richard's appeal. The justices upheld the conviction by a vote of 3–2. Writing for the majority, Justice Richard Thomas described the basis of Richard's defense as "the concept that one who is a victim of family abuse is justified in killing the abuser." That notion, Thomas reasoned, is "antithetical to the mores of modern civilized society. . . . To permit capital punishment to be imposed upon the subjective conclusion of the individual that prior acts and conduct of the deceased justified the killing would amount to a leap into the abyss of anarchy.''

In a brief, concurring opinion, Justice Charles Stuart Brown, a devout Mormon, added a few rhetorical flourishes of his own. "Appellant is handsome, personable, intelligent, and ready of tongue. He is an all-American boy, except that he has a predilection toward patricide," Brown wrote. "This is a textbook case of first-degree murder."

Brown offered a novel interpretation of Richard's behavior in the garage: he blew his ROTC whistle "to freeze his victim." The testimony painting Richard Chester Jahnke as "cruel, sadistic, and abusive" struck him as "greatly exaggerated." And, like Tom Carroll and Judge Maier before him, Justice Brown bemoaned the publicity the case had received.

"We make folk heroes out of our criminals," Brown wrote. "The more bizarre or unusual the murder, the greater the proliferation of songs, poems, and books. The public's thirst for this sort of literature will not be stilled. If a person wants to become famous and even wealthy, he just needs to commit a grotesque crime."

The dissenting opinions offered by Justice Robert Rose and Justice Joseph Cardine took issue with Liamos's restrictions on expert witness testimony and *voir dire,* respectively. Justice Rose's lengthy rebuttal (59 pages) offered Barrett no small measure of consolation:

The theory of Richard Jahnke's defense was misunderstood by the prosecuting attorney, the trial court, and now, I submit, this court. This was indeed a proper case of self-defense, and the offer of proof was made on the recognized grounds that battered children behave differently than other children. . . . Richard Jahnke did not offer Dr. Macdonald's testimony to establish *insanity* or any form of diminished capacity; his defense was *sanity,* i.e., the reasonableness of the behavior of a brutalized human being . . . the defendant *intended* to use deadly force against his father because he believed he was in imminent danger. Whether that belief was the reasonable belief of a battered, 16-year-old, sane human being was the issue—not his intent.

Eight days later, on June 14, 1984, Governor Ed Herschler

called a long-awaited press conference. "I don't believe that I can ignore the compelling circumstances of the Jahnke case," he said. In the governor's opinion, the sentence imposed by Judge Liamos and affirmed by the Wyoming Supreme Court was "too harsh."

Herschler's commutation order would send Richard Jahnke to Denver's Bethesda Hospital for a period of two to four months for "evaluation"—in other words, he would receive the inpatient psychiatric treatment his attorney had requested. Jahnke would pay for the cost of his hospital stay "to the greatest extent of his ability." Then he would be placed in the custody of the superintendent of the Wyoming Industrial Institute, to serve the remainder of his sentence among the eighty-one juvenile offenders incarcerated there.

The total sentence amounted to three years and thirteen days. On June 27, 1987, the day he turned twenty-one, Richard John Jahnke would be a free man.

22

It is a sunny morning in early October of 1984. Cheyenne is in the warm, dry grip of Indian summer. A slight breeze tugs at the stalks of prairie grass outside. The wind never stops blowing in Cowboy Country; at times, though, it recedes to a soothing murmur, like the undulations of a distant sea. Maria Jahnke has a pot of coffee brewing in the kitchen. She greets her visitor at the door, leads him to a couch in the family room, serves him coffee. She sits on another couch across from him, her hands clasped in her lap.

"I have a hard time talking, because I'm basically a shy person, but I'll try my best," she says. "Would you like to see a few pictures?"

The photo albums are stacked neatly in a corner of a hall closet. That seems to be where they belong. An Aristotelian sense of order prevails in the house on Cowpoke Road; every object has its place, its fixed position in the universe. It must reside there and nowhere else. So it is with the photo albums. One could no sooner envision them thrust untidily under a coffee table than one could imagine paperbacks strewn across Deborah's room, socks on Richard's desk, a loaded .38 on top of Richard Chester Jahnke's gun cabinet. Maria has sold the guns, put away the books and clothes, stacked the photo albums and scrapbooks in the closet. Her housekeeping is impeccable. Every room is as neat as a showroom at a furniture store, as if no one had ever lived there.

Maria hasn't looked at the photo albums for months. She retrieves them from the closet, spreads them open on the couch, and slowly turns the pages. The past returns, or rather, one version of the past. For Maria's pictures are no different from the millions of snapshots taken by parents everywhere. They are a family chronicle of birthday parties, first communions, trips to the zoo; portraits of smiling children, vacationing relatives, and pets blinded by flashbulbs; great and banal moments in the history of the tribe, frozen in time, to be handed down from generation to generation. The Book of Kodak. The Book of Polaroid.

Maria narrates. See here, that's Richie in his sailor suit, he was so adorable. That's Deborah dressed up for a pageant at school—she was always a very classy lady, so feminine. That's Richie and his dad in the pool in Arizona—he probably drowned him that day. He used to do it to Deborah, too, but Richie was the one who got drowned the most. Sometimes I thought he was gonna kill that poor kid. . . .

There is something troubling about the ordinariness of the Jahnke family albums. You expect less wholesomeness, fewer smiles. You expect the faces of young Richie and Deborah to shine with pain; they do not. You expect a picture of eighteen-year-old Private Jahnke posing beside a tank to be a revelation of character, but the image is mute, unyielding. You expect some hint of impending tragedy; but even a picture of father and son taken in Arizona before a hunting trip—a shot of Richard Chester Jahnke and his son clad in camouflage outfits, offering their rifles for inspection—seems less ominous than it should.

Occasionally a picture leaps out at you, as if you've seen it before—and, of course, you have. Several of Maria's snapshots were made available to the press at the time of the trials. They have since appeared again and again in newspapers and magazines and on television. Through repetition these images have assumed a sinister import. The most widely circulated of the lot is a 1979 photo of a balding, cigar-chewing Richard Chester Jahnke flanked by twelve-year-old Richard and thirteen-year-old Deborah, with an empty stretch of Arizona desert as a backdrop. It is impossible to look at this awkwardly huddled trio without being annoyed at the impenetrableness of Dad's sunglasses, the proprietary manner in which he drapes his arms over his son and daughter, the aloofness. But this reaction surely owes something to the public life the photo has attained.

What you see in Maria's pictures depends largely on what you are looking for. A few weeks before Richard's trial, Jim Billis sat down with the photo albums and went through them with a magnifying glass. The private investigator counted twelve pictures, taken when Richard and Deborah were small children, in which one or the other appears to have been freshly beaten. ''All kids have bruises on their knees, but I found bruises on the knees, under the eyes, on the sides of the head, on the forehead—all undetectable to the naked eye," Billis would later recall. Enlargements were not produced at the trial, he explained, because "it was too much, or not enough," to stand up in court.

Maria has shown the albums to several people since the day her husband died, but it is more difficult for her each time. The photos stir up too many conflicting memories, too many contrary emotions. She studies her wedding pictures for several moments in silence. When she speaks, her small voice is heavy with sadness.

"When I see his picture, I remember how wonderful he used to be, and what our life turned into," she says. "You know, I had a fairy-tale marriage, and it ended, and it was horrible. Whatever happened? What makes people change?"

She turns the page. A trim, smiling Richard Chester Jal e, clad only in bathing trunk, stands on the beach with the ocean behind him. He is looking directly at the camera.

"That was in Puerto Rico, before we were married," she says. "We didn't have much money. We had to be careful, but there was always some party with my friends or something. We went to the beach a lot. We always found places to go for a little money. He used to get paid once a month, and he'd give me the money to help me save for the wedding. Even before the engagement, he used to do that. He'd say, 'Here, you take it. With you holding it, I won't blow it all at the same time.'

"That was one of the things that I—it gave me a good feeling, how he trusted me. He was always very truthful, and he left everything to me. And that was one of the problems I was having—this man trusted me so much. In fact, a couple of months before he died, he told me, 'There's only one person in the world I trust, and it's you.' That gave me a good feeling, so I had a hard time testifying. When all this happened, I had to come out and tell the truth, and I felt like I was betraying him. I had to tell the truth because I love my children. And my word means a lot to me, you know. At the same time, it killed me. He was dead, but that really doesn't matter. He trusted me completely."

A few pages later, she is confronted with an unusually somber portrait of Richard and Deborah, aged five and six. They are dressed in heavy coats and stocking caps, ready to brave the snowbound Chicago streets.

"Look at their eyes. I always fed them and took care of them so well, and they always had circles under their eyes. I said, boy, my kids never look healthy. You know, I was always trying to protect the kids. That was my goal. Sometimes I think I protected them too much.''

"Protected them from what? The outside world?" the visitor asks.

Maria nods. "From him and the world, too. I thought protecting them would be the right way to show my love for them. But it wasn't, of course. So I did a lot of wrong, too. But at the time that was the only way I knew how to be a good mother. That's the first instinct of a mother, protect her children. Even an animal—what do they do, they protect their little babies. I said, I'm going to be the best mother in the whole wide world. Because my mother was so bad to me, see. So that was my goal, to be a good mother and a good wife.''

Her eyes drift back to the photograph. "Richard was always a very kind little kid," she says. "I will always remember him that way. And Deborah, she was a real nice girl, but then she started to change. She was always an individual, and I had a harder time getting through to her, but I loved them both the same. They say, oh, you love one more than the other—I don't. I love them both the same. But I see the differences in them, too. I could always reach Richard more. Deborah slips through my fingers.''

She closes the album and puts it aside. "It has been hard for me, but things are getting better," she says. "That doesn't mean—see, there are things that will stay with me. Even with all the therapy I get, they will stay with me all my life. To this day, no one can slam a door without me feeling like my heart's gonna come out of my mouth. If I'm in the bathroom and somebody bangs on the door—forget it. That drives me crazy. Because that's what *he* used to do. But I feel I finally have buried him. Especially after making peace with Richard.

"It used to be, I couldn't get to sleep in this house. I finally got to sleep when Richard was sent to Bethesda, and we started seeing each other more often. We finished therapy together a couple of weeks ago, and I think we have accomplished a lot. We're closer now than we ever have been before. There have been a lot of misunderstandings. Too many people tearing us apart instead of bringing us together. But I must say, in the end we have become closer than ever.''

"What about Deborah?" the visitor asks.

"I was picking Deborah up at Excelsior on Mondays during the summer and taking her to see Richard. Then school started, and I don't see her so much. She calls me every Thursday. I think what Deborah needs is the freedom to do the things she wants to do. The last couple of weeks since she's started school she's been so happy. Her education is very important to her, and when she's going to school and her mind is occupied, I see a sort of serenity in her. She's so anxious to make something of herself, to prove herself."

"So what are your plans now? Are you going to stay here?"

"I love it here. I have friends here now, and that's very important. My children come first, but my friends come second. And I love the job at Meadowlark, working with those girls. They tell me, 'We need you,' and I say, 'Boy, I need you more than you need me.'

"I want to get married again, but I want to work, too. I don't want to be anybody's possession. It's important to have your own interests, and it's important to have friends, too. Friendship is so important to a marriage. Richard and I, we had this passionate love for each other in the beginning, but we were never friends. Never.

"I do want to get married again, but I'm determined that I will not fall into the same pattern again. I will not allow it. I will not. I will not allow another human being to do what two did to me already. . . . Do you want more coffee?"

Three months later, Maria is on the phone, announcing her engagement. Her fiancé is John Druce, a thirty-two-year-old part-owner of a local auto repair business.

"The wedding is scheduled for September," she says. "I want to be sure—I'm sure of him, but I want to be sure of myself. You'd like him. He's the opposite of Richard. He's more like Gary Cooper—very quiet, laid-back. We've been friends for over a year. Last summer we started to date, and it was just dating for a while. And then he came out and told me, you know, that he cared for me. We weren't expecting it, it just happened. But we were friends first, and that's very important to me. It wasn't like, oh, we're madly in love; the love has just grown.

"You have to make time for my wedding."

* * *

"You know, for the first seven years of my life, my mother was an excellent parent. She was a little too strict with Richard and me, but at least she tried. I guess she thought she was protecting us.

"But my father—that's another story. I *always* really hated my father. I don't remember ever loving him. And he hated me, too. Maybe not always. I remember, like, with the sexual stuff, when I was eleven, he started treating me like a girlfriend. And I think one of the reasons he hated me so much was because I rejected him. Sexually, I mean.

"I can sincerely say that I still hate my father. In a sense, it really hasn't registered with me that he's dead. I dream about him a lot. In my dreams, you know, I'm walking around somewhere, and I see him, and I say, 'Dad, aren't you supposed to be dead?' And he just laughs at me.

"I dream a lot about my father."

Deborah Jahnke is having lunch at Kato's on the Square, a fashionable garden-level restaurant in downtown Denver's Larimer Square. A year has passed since Terry Mackey filed her appeal with the Wyoming Supreme Court—a year in limbo, Deborah calls it. She still lives at Excelsior, her room, board, and counseling paid for by the state of Wyoming. Every weekday morning she boards a bus that takes her downtown to Metropolitan State College, where she is taking classes in literature, philosophy, dance, art history, and French. The state of Colorado pays for her tuition. She is expected to be back in her cottage at Excelsior by half-past six in the evening.

The arrangement is an improvement over her previous twenty-four-hour confinement at the youth center, but she admits to being restless. She has no social life and only limited contact with her classmates. Indeed, these weekly lunches with a friend constitute her only regular opportunity for conversation outside of a clinical setting. Her voice is strong, expansive. There is no trace of an accent, English or otherwise. With her horn-rimmed glasses, casual clothes, and occasionally emphatic gestures, she looks and sounds exactly like what she is—a somewhat bookish college student, trying to make a point.

"When I think about it, I guess I can understand my father a little bit," she says. "I mean, why he was the way he was. When I was little, he used to tell me how lucky I was. When he was a child, he said, he didn't get enough to eat, he didn't have enough clothes, he had to go to work at a young age—it sounded like he was treated badly by his parents. And I don't think he had very many friends. While the other guys were having fun, he was working after school. Then, of course, he turns eighteen, joins the army, gets married, has kids—he didn't have time to develop or have fun. And he blamed us for that.''

"You were in the way," her friend says.

"That's right. And my mother—well, her whole way of life— you respect your elders no matter what, you respect your husband and do what he says no matter what. That was really indoctrinated in her. It's taken me a long time to forgive her. But I don't have to worry about that stuff anymore. I'm almost twenty years old. I don't have to live with my mother; I don't give a damn about what happened between us when I was twelve. Life goes on.''

"What about your brother?"

"Growing up with Richard was like growing up with a third parent. There was a point, when we were going through the trials together, when we became really good friends. And then I went off to Excelsior—and now, I don't know, now—I really don't like myself when I'm around Richard.''

"What do you mean?"

"I just seem to act younger than I really am—like, help me, Richard, give me some advice. You know, a lot of people identified with Richard and admired him. I spoiled him, too. I thought Richard was perfect. I saw him as Apollo and myself as Dionysus. And for a long time, I was really jealous. Don't get me wrong—I didn't want people to think I was a hero. I didn't do anything; I was just there, in the house, that night. But damn, I just wish that people would have been able to appreciate me for other reasons. . . .

"At times, though, it seemed like Richard was the only one who could understand the way I was feeling. Before the trials started I told him, 'I don't know if you've read any of the depositions, but I hope we aren't tried together, because I'll just pull you down. Everybody thinks I'm crazy, and some things are going to be brought up that are going to embarrass you.' And he said, 'That's all right. I love you anyway.' I was always really different and eccentric, ever since I was very young—and people misinterpret that as being crazy. But Richard understood about that kind of thing.''

"You mean about your behavior—"

"Yeah. I mean, there are all these stories about me. I don't know what you've heard. Maybe you think I'm pretty weird, too. But I wasn't crazy. Like the time I told one of my teachers I was an orphan—that was a class I hated. I always got in trouble for talking, and one day the teacher told me she was going to call my parents. I told her she couldn't do that, and she asked why not, and I had to think of something fast, so I told her my parents were dead. I was just trying to come up with anything I could, so she wouldn't call my father.

"And then, those last few months—well, Richard says I was having a nervous breakdown. I don't know. All these weird things were happening. It really started in the spring, when my father started patrolling around the house with a gun. He'd done that before, but then it seemed like he was out there practically every night. I'd go to bed, turn off the light, and I would see my father's silhouette outside my window. I couldn't sleep. And when my father came home, he would whistle this really obnoxious whistle, and I would get really nervous and start shaking. It was so loud and piercing; at times I'd get so nervous, I'd have to run to the bathroom and throw up. I was just a nervous wreck. My memory was going. Toward the end I couldn't even remember what class I was going to. And you know, I was afraid to tell people. I mean, what are they going to do? They'll just tell my father or have me shut away.

"That summer it got to the point where I was having these hallucinations. All these imaginary friends I used to have—you know, Anna and Reinhart and so on—I'd wake up, and I'd see one of them standing over me, saying, 'Deborah, Deborah, wake up.' It wasn't a dream; I was fully awake. But I couldn't feel anything. So finally, I just cut myself—it wasn't a paper clip, it was a razor blade, one of my father's. I just slashed myself across the wrist three times, and I thought, God, this really hurts.

"But I didn't want to kill myself. I just wanted to feel something. It's so hard to explain, but that's how it was. I wasn't suicidal. But I'll tell you who was."

"Who?"

"If you look under the furniture in my room, in the corner there's some discoloration—a stain on the rug. What happened was, one day I heard all this commotion in the hall. My father was threatening to shoot himself. And I thought, oh my God, he's going to take us all with him. I really thought he would. I was just standing there, waiting for the shots, and I lost control of my bladder.''

"Richard and your mother remember that incident, too," her companion says. "Richard says it happened just a few months before he died. He thought the threat had something to do with the fact that your father had been reported for child abuse, and he felt his career was ruined."

"Could be. I thought it happened earlier than that."

There are other conversations over the next few weeks, in restaurants in Denver and Cheyenne. One day her companion shows Deborah a copy of the notes taken by Dr. John Macdonald on the evening of February 16, 1983, the third day of Richard's trial, the night Richard broke down and told his attorneys the details of the shooting for the first time. In many respects, Macdonald's hastily jotted record of Richard's "confession" follows the testimony Richard gave in court very closely. Of course, the "Macdonald version" is greatly condensed. Indeed, its terseness is one of its virtues, provided one is sufficiently informed about the case to fill in the missing pieces. Here is Richard's description of his vigil in the garage:

> I had speed loaders
> Marine [knife]
> 12 gauge
> whistle
> I felt I was a soldier
> he wasn't my father he was the enemy

Yet Richard revealed certain key details to his attorneys that night that he did not repeat on the stand. For example, according to the Macdonald version, Richard had originally planned to use the Sako .30-06 rifle to kill his father, "but I was shaking too bad—I was afraid I'd miss and shoot Mom." So he settled on the riot gun. And the Macdonald version contains a variant account of the conversation between Richard and his sister only minutes before the shooting:

> I told Debra to stay away

Debra are you going to kill mom too
       Kill mom too

I said No
        She wouldn't be that way
Debra said it was a phantasy

There is no reason to doubt that, at the time he testified at his
own trial, Richard sincerely believed his sister had asked him to
kill their mother. He had refused, telling Deborah that Mom
"wouldn't be that way" if Dad wasn't around. But when he
appeared at Deborah's trial, Richard hedged. The interruptions
by both the prosecution and the defense prevented him from
"correcting" his previous testimony, but it is clear that he was
trying to suggest that he might have misunderstood her; perhaps
she was merely repeating her question, "Are you going to kill
Mom, too?"—rather than urging him to do so.

Deborah reads over the passage in Macdonald's notes again
and again. "So what do you think it means?" she asks.

"Suppose you tell me," her companion says.

"I don't know. I know Richard wouldn't make stuff up. I'm
not saying those things weren't said." Her face reddens. "I'm
really confused about that, because at one point Richard told me I
never said 'Kill Mom too.' "

"But could you have said it?"

"I don't know. I remember being really pissed at her that night
after my father came home and started beating Richard. Because
I have big ears, you know, and I specifically did not hear—
Richard did not say to my mother that she was a martyr and she
was not a good parent and all those other things. She lied to my
father about what Richard said. And she was in the room when
my father was beating the shit out of Richard. And she's just,
like, 'Oh, he said this and he said this,' and of course that's
going to enrage my father even more. So Richard got a hell of a
beating again. I remember being incredibly pissed. Like, how
could she do that, what a damn hypocrite she is. I really felt like,
for the most part, she was on my dad's side.

"And there was a certain amount of fear. I felt like, well,
she's going to lie to the authorities, she's going to call me a liar
and call Richard a liar. All that was going through my mind, too.
You know, I might have said it. I don't know for sure. I do admit
I was feeling a bit vindictive."

"What about this line: 'Debra said it was a phantasy'?"

"I went back and forth. You know, on one hand I was scared, and I'd tell myself, this is serious, something terrible is going to happen. But on the other hand—like I told the police, at first I thought it was just going to be a scare tactic or a threat. Richard didn't say how or where he was going to do it, and for a while it seemed like he was just playing this role.

"And I thought, okay, nothing else has worked. Maybe this will work."

The town of Worland lies in the middle of the Bighorn Basin of northern Wyoming, three hundred and fifty miles from Cheyenne and one hundred miles from the nearest interstate highway. To the traveler bound for Yellowstone or the big-sky country of Montana, Worland is just another homely "point of interest" in the heart of the real West, a pocket of amenities flanked by the Bighorn Mountains on the east, the Wind River Indian Reservation on the south, and the Continental Divide on the west. But to the ten thousand inhabitants of Washakie County, the town is much more. The sugar refinery on the southeast side of town processes the beets harvested on rolling farmland for miles around; the local bowling alley and video arcade do a raging business every weekend. Worland is the county seat, its center of agriculture, commerce, entertainment—and justice.

Five miles south of town, on the other side of the winding Bighorn River, stands a weathered, three-story structure of pale yellow brick, surrounded by cottages and storage sheds. The main building is a hollow rectangle, with barred windows looking out upon an enclosed courtyard. It resembles a hospital, a fort, a cloistered monastery; in a sense, it is all of these. Built in 1915, the Wyoming Industrial Institute was conceived as a state reformatory for young men and juveniles. It has since become a facility for juveniles only; in 1984 it was renamed the Wyoming Boys School. At present, there are approximately ninety residents, aged twelve to twenty, although the school has received boys as young as ten years old. The majority have been convicted of felonies in juvenile court. The typical sentence is six months.

For the past quarter of a century, the school has been the kingdom of a wry, avuncular man named Buck Kuchel, a former deputy warden of the state penitentiary at Rawlins. When Kuchel first came to Worland, he found a makeshift school with no

certified teachers and a vocational program that stressed agriculture and manual labor. Corporal punishment was the chief means
of social control. Nearly half of his charges were repeat offenders, with many more graduating to the penitentiary. The new
superintendent set about acquiring the funds for a "decent"
educational program, vocational training in a variety of modern
trades, and "respectable" living quarters to replace the decrepit
dormitory. Twenty-four years later, the Wyoming Boys School is
staffed with a small, dedicated crew of certified teachers and
caseworkers; other major improvements, such as respectable housing, await the whims of the state legislature.

While the school remains a dreary, old-fashioned reformatory
in appearance, Kuchel has achieved other, subtler changes in the
spirit of the place. In recent years, the school has adopted an
honor system. The "inmates" are no longer locked in their
rooms at night. Many are allowed to go home on the bus for
major holidays. Although he is planning to retire in the spring of
1986, Kuchel still takes a keen personal interest in his boys—just
like Spencer Tracy's Father Flanagan in the 1938 movie *Boys
Town*.

"We don't have as many problem people here anymore because we don't treat them as badly," the superintendent declares.
"The kids haven't changed, we've changed."

Kuchel boasts that there have been few escape attempts under
the new system. The rate of recidivism has also declined. That
doesn't mean the Wyoming Boys School will ever suffer from a
lack of clientele; some of the superintendent's present charges are
the sons of boys he hosted twenty years ago. And, like Tracy's
Father Flanagan, Kuchel is far from the stereotype of the bleeding heart. A quote from Mark Twain adorns his office door:
"Few sinners are saved after the first twenty minutes of a sermon."

Richard Jahnke arrived in Kuchel's kingdom on October 15,
1984, after four months of residential psychiatric treatment at
Bethesda Hospital in Denver. His stay at Bethesda had been
expensive (the medical and hospital bills reportedly totaled close
to $48,000, with the Jahnkes' private health insurance paying
more than half of the amount, the state of Wyoming paying the
rest) but free, for the most part, of media coverage. The move
from the hospital's prim, secluded, twenty-acre campus to the
narrower confines of the reformatory triggered a resurgence of

press interest in Denver, Casper, and Cheyenne, but Kuchel swiftly denied reporters' requests to interview Richard.

"Enough is enough," he said.

Initially, the superintendent had some questions of his own about Richard Jahnke. At the very least, he wondered if his institution's most celebrated guest might be idolized by some of the younger boys. Yet Kuchel was soon satisfied that Richard Jahnke was not going to be one of his "problem people." In fact, he was sufficiently pleased with Richard's attitude and performance to bestow upon him Buck Kuchel's finest accolade. Richard Jahnke, he told the curious, is "a fine boy." He would be allowed to receive regular visitors and holiday leaves just like the rest of the fine boys.

So it comes to pass that, two months after his arrival, Richard Jahnke shakes hands with a lone visitor in a small office overlooking the barren courtyard. The two have met before. They will meet again—several times—before the visitor's work is done. This is not another newspaper interview, not another therapy session, but an opportunity of sorts, an invitation to wrestle with the lingering past, the elusive future. It is a chance to "tell his story" one last time, and, perhaps, a chance to tell the whole story, with its burden of family secrets, for the first time.

Richard's grip is firm. His hair is longer, his voice calmer than when the visitor last saw him, twenty months ago. His capacity for self-criticism, always keen, has increased. The boyish smile, the epicene good looks remain unchanged. Except for the lines under his eyes, and, of course, the blue jeans and flannel shirt, he might have stepped out of a Pre-Raphaelite painting of ethereal, mysterious youth. He settles into a chair and tugs at his watchband.

"I was really surprised by this place, after two years of fear about where I was going to end up," he says. "I was expecting a lot of rednecks being tough on me, beating me up or something. There have been problems with some of the kids testing me, a few tacky jokes, but I've been doing pretty good with the others. Look around. Sure, it's a place for incarceration. But it isn't a bad place.

"Monday's usually a slow day. On Mondays I read in my room, work on my accounting. I'm not sure yet if I'm going into business. I might try psychology. You know, after watching all these shrinks in action, I got interested in it. Anyway, on Tuesdays and Fridays I work in the commissary. On Wednesdays I see a psychologist in town. And I have school five days a week in the afternoon. A few refresher courses. Weekends—well, there's a lot of free time here, so I volunteered to be a score-keeper for the basketball games. That way you get out more often.

"It's been a real change for me. Time to cool out. You know, right after the trial, everybody was worried about me going around acting like a hero. It was confusing at first, but after a while, I fell for it. I started living in this fantasy, that I could do anything, that everything was going to be given to me on a silver platter. That I was better than other people, I guess. Because I had this support group of people that—hell, they treated me like a saint. I had this one woman telling me all this shit about how I was the one diamond on the beach and all the rest was dirt. And you know, the Munns kept trying to discourage that stuff, but I wouldn't listen to them. People said they were going to take care of me and send me to college. People wanted to adopt me. Girls were after me. I was going to be a warrior for peace and stop all child abusers. Help all the children I could. It was pretty unrealistic.

"Then, for some reason, toward the end of my senior year, I started wanting to die. I started having fantasies about burglars coming in and killing me. I think I was just tired of it, tired of being Richard Jahnke, the guy who shot his father. It was really weighing on me, because in so many ways I was so close to having a good life and being normal, but then so far away. . . .

"By the time I got to Bethesda, I was lost. I mean, they'd ask me questions in group [therapy], and I didn't know how to answer them. I'd answer them like I was still doing PR for the trial. One day my doctor took me outside and started asking me all these questions about whether I thought killing Dad was wrong. At first I said no—because the rest of my family's better off. But then I said well, yeah, it was really terrible, and I fell into pat answers again, just like a press interview. And he said, 'Richard, most of what you just told me is pure bullshit. I don't think you know what you really feel anymore.' That hit home really bad. I didn't talk to him for two or three days. But he was right. I'd been avoiding facing up to a lot of things, and I just decided that I didn't want to do that anymore. . . ."

"So what do you believe now?" his visitor asks. "Was it wrong to kill him?"

"Now that I'm out of that situation, I can say, of course it was wrong. The guilt—it's been pretty constant. I mean, I did end his life, and that was wrong. But see, I'm also starting to understand how the whole situation was set up for me. In that environment, Dad had to be the way he was, and I became the way I was. I can accept that. But I can't say if I'd do anything differently now, because I'm not in that situation anymore. It's hard for me to believe I'm talking about the same person when I talk about what I'm like now. . . .

"One thing I came to realize that was very tragic for me. I did not know my father. I only saw his cruel side. He very rarely talked to me, you know. Only once in a while, I saw this half-buried side of him, these small glances of what else he could be. It's been the same with Mom—I've just been getting to know her over this last year, through therapy together and stuff. I never really knew who she was before. And now I know she's there for me.

"Anyway, I want to know who my father was, but that means sorting through a lot of strange experiences. At the trial, I had to paint a certain picture of him. And it wasn't quite right. You know, for me, Dad's mental abuse did much more harm than the physical abuse, but people don't understand that. So what was I going to do? I had to make Dad look like Satan II."

"Are you saying your father wasn't that violent?"

"No, I'm not. But certain things—like when he said he'd get rid of me—I said it for the trial, but I never really believed Dad would kill me. Deborah might have believed that, but I didn't. I just thought he would always make life rougher, and that really got to me. That's what I meant about Dad killing me mentally. I didn't think I'd ever be anything. I mean, I started to find an identity for myself in ROTC, but then that all fell apart. And I felt like I was going to be nothing my whole life, and I couldn't stand that. That pressure that Dad had on us, it just kept building. And I had to do something, or I'd end up killing myself.

"Ever since I was young, I had these fantasies about Dad beating up Mom, and me coming to the rescue and beating him up or killing him. That started in Arizona, but it really blossomed in Cheyenne, because that's when Deborah and I started to talk. That's the only thing I could talk to her about, you know—killing Dad, getting rid of Dad. That's the only way she ever let me into her life. So I talked about that. It was never we, it was always me killing him.''

"Were you serious?''

"It was kind of hypothetical, kind of wishful. Kind of like we're fantasizing about it, but in reality we probably won't do it. I got the sense I was entertaining her when I was talking about the ways I was going to kill him. And then, you know, it just got worse and worse. I remember having all these arguments with Mom, where she'd say, 'He'll get his. God will punish him.' And I'd say, 'He'll get his, but *I'm* going to do it.' And that made her very angry. . . .

"Toward the end I started keeping weapons in my room. I had some guns that Dad gave me, but he took them away from me. And one time he found a weapon that I made for him from a weight bar. It was a ball and chain hooked to a bar. He found it under my bed and took it away. I lied and said it was for my Halloween costume. Bullshit. He knew what it was for. It was for him.''

He pauses, sips water from a coffee mug.

"There's one thing Mom will never admit to herself, but I swear it's true. One night—this would have been around late September of 1982—Dad threatened to make me quit ROTC. Now that might sound like something simple, but ROTC was my only life. I stayed up all night thinking about it. I hadn't slept much in weeks, and now I was thinking, you know, what am I going to do? Thinking about him calling me down all the time, calling me a faggot. Finally, around three o'clock in the morning, I went into Mom's room and got the shotgun from under her bed. And as I was taking it out of the room, heading for his room, I hit the barrel on the doorway. Mom woke up. I told her I was going to kill him. I started walking down the hallway, and she stopped me. 'Give me the gun.' That's all she said.

"The next day I was sitting in the family room watching TV, and Dad walked by carrying the shotgun. I looked at him, and the way he looked at me—I don't know if he knew. He just gave me this strange look. I think Mom told him something about the shotgun—something like, take that gun out of here, it's making me nervous. But that look—I don't know if she told him. He put the gun in his room.

"When I talk to Mom in therapy about that night, she can't remember. Even now, in therapy, she doesn't recall it ever happening. I guess I can understand how she'd want to block that off.''

"Was that the same shotgun you took into the garage two months later?"

"Yeah. One more thing. A couple of weeks later, something happened that was really hard for me, that almost broke my sanity. In fact, it probably did. After building up so much hate for him and making the decision that I had to do it, had to get rid of him, something happened. I was involved in a fight at school or something; anyway, I got a black eye. He came into my room. Normally, he would have just started pounding and yelling. But no, he just hugged me and told me, I love you. And that really ripped through my skull.

"I hugged him, too, and I told him I loved him. And I meant it. But then I thought to myself, it's too late. It's too late. That was in October.

"And then, that night in the garage, it was the same feeling all over again. It's too late. I just remembered all that had happened, everything he did. That's one thing about Mom, it's like she forgot what happened yesterday. But I couldn't. I saw Mom and Deborah being destroyed. A lot of it was my feelings about me, too—what he did to me. Thinking that he would always do that as long as he lived. I had all this fear and pain and anger and hate in me, and it was too late to stop it.

"And then there he was. I mean, one minute I'm sitting there listening to the radio, and the next I hear him coming up the driveway. It had been a fantasy for so long, and here comes the reality. Then I started to chicken out. When he was getting out of the car, I thought, No, no, I'm not going to do this, I can't do this. But I looked around, and I had all the guns out, everything was already prepared. I was committed. I was committed.

"All my senses were very acute. I could hear Mom talking to him, so I knew she was on the other side of the driveway. And I was fighting with myself, saying no, I can't, and finally I just— that was when I blew my sergeant major's whistle.

"I didn't feel the recoil or anything. The gun jammed, but I was able to pull it through and keep shooting, because of the adrenaline I had. It was like I was shooting an automatic or something. I couldn't stop it. I was fighting to stop, but I couldn't. It was too late.''

*   *   *

The next day Richard shows his visitor around the grounds. At dawn a treacherous fog hugged the road, and the windshields of cars were glazed with ice. But then the sun broke through and burned off the fog, and now, shortly after noon, the temperature is a balmy thirty-six degrees Fahrenheit, the sky almost spotlessly blue. It is warm enough for Richard to walk around the small campus without a coat. There is not a great deal to see: the classrooms, the gymnasium, the cafeteria, the commissary. In the commissary Richard has his own desk, tucked among shelves of clothes, soap, stationery, and gleaming rows of canned goods. Twice a week he delivers supplies to the school's various departments in a small pickup truck.

Richard walks slowly, circling the main dormitory and the outlying buildings. His breath is visible in the crisp December air.

"This feeling I have of wanting to know Dad—it's really important to me," he says. "Kind of a hunger. Last year, when I was alone, I'd go visit Dad's grave. I'd just sit there and talk. I guess that sounds kind of strange. But I wanted him to know— even though I knew he probably couldn't hear me—I wanted to tell him that, now that I'm out of that situation, I understand that he wasn't the devil. He was a good person at one point, but he changed. I get the feeling he never did what he wanted to with his life. He had this marriage he didn't want, these kids he didn't want. He was trapped. And I'd talk about that, and tell him, you know, I wish all of this didn't happen, but it did. And I'd think about how I wished I knew more about him. . . .

"You know, for about a year after the shooting, I had nightmares about him. I had one just about every week at first. Then they tapered off to once a month. In most of them, he's not dead, he's alive; but his breathing is very haggard. He's wounded. He's really hurt bad. He has problems moving. And his face is always in the shadows, so I can't see it. But I know it's him, and right away I have to start fighting him off. He's coming after me, he's really angry with me, and all I can do is put him to rest. Then, in some of the later dreams, it isn't just that I have to stop him. I want to. I want to.

"The dreams stopped when I went to Bethesda. You know why? Through therapy I finally figured out why his face was always in shadow—because he was me. Parts of me that were like him, things he'd passed on to me, that I was trying to kill off. Because, see, I have a lot of Dad's habits and personality.

And directly after the shooting, I tried to deny all that. I tried to get it all out of my system at once. That's why I was so soft-spoken; I was trying to make my personality as unlike his as I could. Every time I saw something of him in me—you know, expressions that were his, or if I laughed the way he did, certain mannerisms—I couldn't stand myself.

"I had to learn that I can't change myself like that. I'm stuck with me. There are things about me that remind me of Dad, and what I did, and I'm just going to have to learn from that and live with it."

They stop beside the sign that marks the entrance to the reformatory. No high wall separates Buck Kuchel's kingdom from the rest of Washakie County; there is not even a fence, barbed-wire or otherwise, to mark the edge of the property. Twenty paces in front of them, trucks roll by on the naked highway. Richard could keep walking, if he chose—any of Kuchel's fine boys could, if they were feeling foolish enough.

But the road leads nowhere of interest, and Richard hopes for another way out. He fully expects that he will not have to serve all of the remaining thirty months of his sentence. If he stays out of trouble, it is likely that he will get time off for good behavior. He is prepared to wait, he says. Time passes slowly for him, and his fondest dream is the dream of convicted felons everywhere—a full pardon.

"I talked to the caseworker a little about it," he says. "If I don't leave here by way of a pardon—let's say it's just normal parole or something—then I'm going to try to get my rights back anyway. As it stands now, I can't vote. I can't leave the country, because I can't get a visa. I can't own firearms, which I don't want. But there are a lot of jobs that I can't have. And that's the main reason I'd like to get the conviction erased. At some point in my life, I'd like to fill out a job application and—you know, where they ask you, have you ever committed a felony, what is it—I'd rather not have to say, I shot my father.

"I know it may take a while. But a few years down the road, maybe I'll be able to pick up a pardon from some governor. In the meantime, I don't feel the need to make a lot of plans. I just want to give myself some freedom. I want to go to college. I want to improve myself. But mainly, I just want to be with people who don't see me as Richard Jahnke.

"I know I'm going to hold off from marriage for a while.

There are a lot of problems with relationships I still have to work out. I'm going to try to learn from Dad's mistakes, too. I've met a lot of people who have the freedom that I fantasize about. Yet they lock themselves in their own cell, their own hell. That's what Dad did. Maybe he could have got a divorce, maybe he could have done something else, I don't know exactly. But I don't want to make the same mistakes. When I get out, I want it to be a time for me.

"I'm just starting to look into the opportunities I might have. Who knows, I might end up being a guru in South America, sitting on a hill, telling people things to confuse them. Whatever happens, I'm just going to be me. And it's okay if I want to wear a flannel shirt with a T-shirt underneath"—he tugs at his shirt, exposing the white undershirt—"the way Dad used to. It's okay. It's part of me. After all, I am his son."

He kicks a pebble with his toe. It skips toward the road, comes to rest on the embankment. Richard looks out across the road, past the barren fields, to the distant mountains, as if seeking the elusive parent, the imagined home, the true point of beginning.

EPILOGUE

HAVERHILL, Mass.—A 16-year-old accused of slaying his father with a shotgun had been beaten for years and after being hit with a hammer "just couldn't take it any more," says the boy's brother.

—The Associated Press, 12/22/83

POMONA, Calif.—A teenager who killed his father after years of abuse was sentenced Friday to serve five years' probation as a refugee worker in Hong Kong by a judge who received 700 letters of advice on the case from across the nation.

—The Associated Press, 2/25/84

TAMPA, Fla.—A teenager who witnesses said emerged from his house crying "I shot my dad" has been charged with first-degree murder in the shotgun slaying of his father, who the youth said had beat him regularly. The suspect, 15, told friends at Van Buren Junior High School early last week that "one of these days I'm going to kill my dad," said one classmate.

—The Associated Press, 1/13/85

On December 12, 1984, the Wyoming Supreme Court upheld the conviction of Deborah Jahnke for aiding and abetting voluntary manslaughter. As in Richard's case, the high court split 3–2 over the decision, with Chief Justice John Rooney, Justice Richard Thomas, and Justice Charles Stuart Brown affirming the conviction, and Justice Joseph Cardine and Justice Robert Rose dissenting. Writing for the majority, Justice Thomas found that Judge Maier was "justified" in refusing to suppress Deborah's statement to the detectives, in instructing the jury that Deborah could be found guilty of the lesser included offense of aiding and abetting manslaughter, and in the sentence he meted out. As for

Mackey's contention that the district attorney's discretionary power to try juveniles as adults was unconstitutional, Thomas replied, "There is no constitutional right to be tried as a juvenile."

Chief Justice Rooney's concurring opinion speculated that if Richard and Deborah had pleaded "not guilty by reason of mental illness or deficiency, temporary or otherwise, the jury may well have acquitted them. Appellant and her brother did not do so, but opted to rely on self-defense. A court cannot properly find self-defense when the homicide is committed from ambush."

Once again, Justice Stuart Brown offered the most scathing opinion of the lot. "The Jahnke cases are reminiscent of the apocryphal accused who murdered his parents and then appealed to the court for mercy because he was an orphan," Brown wrote. "The news media latched on to these cases and carried a preposterous story with missionary zeal to the public. . . . [they] purified and sanctified Richard and Deborah Jahnke, who emerged heroes, worthy of praise. We have witnessed a remarkable feat of image building. The Richard Jahnke and Deborah Jahnke perceived by the public are an invention of the news media, and bear little resemblance to the persons who executed and aided in executing their father. The news media should bear a heavy burden for what they have done.

"Juries and courts in this state will not buy into any story of self-defense as justifiable homicide when it is so patently unbelievable. . . . Deborah Jahnke was no less culpable than Richard. She did not pull the trigger, but she participated in the planning and was a backup if Richard failed in the execution. In one sense, Deborah Jahnke was more culpable than Richard; she wanted to kill the mother also."

Justice Cardine, joined in his dissent by Justice Rose, marveled at the harsh words of his colleagues. "It is surprising how often good, honest men, acting in utmost good faith, can look at the same facts and circumstances so differently," Cardine wrote. Deborah was "a scared little girl, fragmented, out of touch with reality," subject to "incommunicado custodial interrogation" without the aid of counsel or any other adult. Cardine believed that her statement should have been suppressed, and that Judge Maier had compounded the error by allowing Tim Greene to paraphrase and interpret what Deborah had told him. Greene's unusual testimony had resulted in "overwhelming prejudice" against the defendant; if the statement was going to be presented at all, Cardine argued, then the jury should have been allowed to read the entire transcript.

The high court's ruling touched off a predictable response from the Wyoming media. Judge Maier's criticism of the trial coverage had struck many reporters as inappropriate, at best, but Justice Brown's suggestion that the press had "invented" the Jahnkes elevated judicial imperiousness to a new level. "The impression of the slain IRS agent as an abusive father was not something dreamed up outside the courts and the criminal justice system but one that originated within it," noted a huffy editorial in the *Wyoming State Tribune*. "So far no one has come forward to present an image that is other than that, or to adequately refute his children's and wife's stories." A cartoon in the *Casper Star-Tribune* depicted Chief Justice Rooney scolding a bedraggled Deborah Jahnke while Justice Brown berates another waif named "Press."

While the press was fuming, Terry Mackey put in a call to the governor's office. Six days later, with Christmas only a week away, Governor Herschler intervened again. Saying that he had "a little difficulty" accepting the idea that Deborah Jahnke should be sent to prison for three to eight years while her brother served three years at a juvenile facility, Herschler commuted her sentence to one year of probation, to be preceded by a month of "intensive psychiatric evaluation" at the Excelsior Youth Center.

Thirty days later, a freshman from Colorado named Deborah Ann Jahnke enrolled at the University of Wyoming at Laramie.

WASHINGTON, D.C.—Law enforcement officers treat acts of violence within a family less seriously than other violent crimes, contributing greatly to the widespread abuse of spouses, children, and the elderly, a Justice Department task force reported Wednesday.

After a year of study, the Attorney General's Task Force on Family Violence pointed to apathy and misguided practices by police, prosecutors, and judges as major causes of rising family violence across the nation . . .

—*Los Angeles Times*, 9/20/84

In early 1983, before the trial of Richard Jahnke began, the Wyoming state legislature voted to change the statutory definition of childhood. Under the revisions to the state's Child Protective Services Act of 1977, the word "child" may now be applied to any person under the age of twenty; previously, one ceased to be regarded as a child in Wyoming at the age of sixteen. Supporters of the change say that it gives child abuse investigators the go-ahead to intervene more aggressively in cases of abused adolescents aged sixteen to nineteen.

In 1984 the legislature modified its concurrent jurisdiction laws, restricting but not curtailing the discretionary power vested in county and district attorneys. Juveniles seventeen years old or older who are charged with certain serious offenses—first- or second-degree murder, first-degree arson, aggravated robbery, first- or second-degree sexual assault, and so on—may still be prosecuted as adults. But juveniles who are sixteen or younger must first be charged in juvenile court, regardless of the offense. In other words, if the Jahnke case were to repeat itself today, Tom Carroll could prosecute seventeen-year-old Deborah Jahnke in adult court, as before; but Carroll would have to request a transfer hearing before he could try sixteen-year-old Richard in adult court.

That same year, an increase in state funding and internal reallocation of personnel allowed Laramie County DPASS to double the number of full-time caseworkers in its child protection intake unit, from two to four. The move was accompanied by greater emphasis on departmental supervision of the front-line caseworkers to ensure proper follow-up of abuse and neglect reports.

Local and state officials have consistently denied that such measures were adopted in reaction to the Jahnke case. In any event, the typical monthly caseload of child abuse investigators at Laramie County DPASS remains well above the standard of twenty-five cases per worker recommended by the National Association of Social Workers; the county's staff has doubled, but the number of reported cases of abuse and neglect has increased by a staggering 349 percent over two years. In 1982, the agency investigated 131 such cases, including Richard's report in May of that year. In 1983, the number of reports went up to 294; in 1984, the total was 578.

Common sense suggests that the increase should be attributed not to a massive surge of child abuse in Laramie County, but to more conscientious reporting of an existing problem, spurred on by child abuse workshops in the schools, public-service announcements on radio and television, and other "consciousness-raising" efforts that were part of the intense local reaction to the trials of Richard and Deborah Jahnke.

> RAWLINS, Wyo.—Prison overcrowding forced Gov. Ed Herschler to commute the prison sentences of 46 Wyoming Penitentiary inmates in June—the largest mass release of prisoners in the institution's history.
>
> —United Press International, 7/13/84

If a curious taxpayer takes the time to add up the number of police man-hours, the trial expenses, the bills for counseling and psychiatric treatment at out-of-state facilities, and the expense of preparing official responses to both appeals, he will discover that the prosecution of Richard and Deborah Jahnke cost Laramie County and the state of Wyoming in excess of a quarter of a million dollars. This figure excludes the cost of Richard's room and board at the Wyoming Boys School, the money Maria Jahnke spent on the trials, and whatever price one wishes to assign to the embarrassment and negative publicity suffered by the state of Wyoming and the city of Cheyenne.

The taxpayer might calculate that $250,000 is a fair piece of change, even in these inflationary times. It could serve as a down payment for any one of several community services: a child abuse education program in the schools, a team of DPASS caseworkers specializing in the volatile field of adolescent abuse, more battered women's shelters, or a wider range of placement alternatives for adolescents than the choice offered to Richard Jahnke—seventy-two hours in the county jail or a group home—when he reported his father for child abuse. The taxpayer might conclude that if public officials had allocated $250,000 to one of these areas before Richard shot his father, they might have saved the county and the state a much greater expense (and considerable embarrassment) down the line. The investment might also have saved the life of Richard Chester Jahnke.

Another taxpayer, equally tight-fisted, might point out that the above is a simple exercise in hindsight. But many people involved in the Jahnke case have a penchant for hindsight. Jim Barrett has speculated that if District Attorney Tom Carroll had accepted a plea-bargain offer that would have placed the Jahnkes in juvenile court, Richard and Deborah would probably have received the same sentences that they ultimately served—a light sentence in a juvenile facility for Richard, Deborah on probation— but without all the expense and publicity of two adult trials.

Tom Carroll refuses to speculate on such matters. Tom Carroll does not indulge in hindsight.

9:00 > Movie: *Right to Kill?* *** IRS agent Richard Jahnke Sr. (Frederic Forrest) submits his wife (Karmin Murcelo), daughter (Justine Bateman) and son, Richard Jr. (Christopher Collet), to daily mental and physical abuse. A social worker suggests they work it out themselves. Richard Jr. goes first with a shotgun. (Premiere) (1985) (NR) (CC)

—USA Today, 5/22/85

The promised "docudrama" based on the Jahnke parricide aired on ABC at the tail end of the 1984–85 season, a season loaded with disturbing tales of child abuse and teenage pregnancy, alcoholism, and suicide. According to *TV Guide*, the two top-rated made-for-television movies of the season were both docudramas of family violence, ripped from yesterday's headlines: *The Burning Bed*, starring Farrah Fawcett as a battered wife who incinerates her abuser, and the miniseries *Fatal Vision*, the story of a Green Beret convicted of murdering his wife and children. The ABC executives who agreed to take on the Jahnke project were evidently counting on the truth of Justice Stuart Brown's lament that "the public's thirst" for bizarre true crime stories "will not be stilled." They weren't disappointed. *Right to Kill?* aired in the middle of the highly competitive May "sweeps week" and placed a respectable fifth in the week's ratings.

The two-hour, three-million-dollar movie was the first network film to be produced by Taper Media Enterprises, in association with Telepictures Productions. It was directed by John Erman (director of the controversial TV movie *The Atlanta Child Murders*) and featured a deft script by Joyce Eliason, who interviewed Maria, Deborah, and Richard Jahnke in Cheyenne in February of 1984. (An opening note announces that "this dramatization . . . is based on court records, personal interviews, and investigative reports.") Maria and Deborah subsequently visited the set—*Right to Kill?* was shot "on location" in Dallas, Texas—to confer with the actors portraying them.

Right to Kill? received highly favorable reviews from television critics across the country, who praised its solid performances and better-than-average production qualities. The movie has a tasteful, understated sense of drama not found in most commercial television efforts. *Right to Kill?* may not hedge as much as the question mark in its title—as one reviewer put it, "in its heart, this film is completely on the side of the boy murderer" —but it does manage to present Richard's difficulty in seeking protection from his father with an unusual degree of credibility.

Yet, for all its virtues, *Right to Kill?* is also an example of commercial television's timidity, its simplifications, its inability, even in these taboo-breaking times, to confront the sheer messiness of a "true" story. As in the vast majority of docudramas, the emphasis is on drama, not documentary. Numerous details were altered to suit the convenience of the filmmakers—and, presumably, to appease the network censors. Several of the film's most dramatic scenes are complete fabrications. In the film, young Richard quits the Central High Rangers because his ROTC instructor told others about the abuse report; in reality, the two events are six months apart and have little connection to each other. The night of the shooting, Justine Bateman's Deborah breaks down while helping Richard empty the garbage, then begs her brother, tearfully and at length, not to shoot their father; the real Deborah did neither. The last half-hour consists of a series of contrived speeches between the Jahnkes and Jim Barrett, with lines cobbled from trial testimony. The trials and the subsequent uproar about the case receive scant mention in a quick scrawl at the end.

Many of the film's dramatic shortcuts are perhaps unavoidable, but others seriously undermine the ostensible point of the story. *Right to Kill?* minimizes the mental, verbal, and physical abuse the Jahnkes suffered. There is little reference to the years of humiliation the children endured before the move to Cheyenne. One could hardly expect an explicit portrayal of the alleged fondling of Deborah Jahnke, but the subject is mentioned only once, in a frantic conversation between mother and daughter. It is indicative of television's peculiar moral standards that the shooting is depicted as even more brutal than it actually was—the first shot hurls Richard Chester Jahnke onto the windshield of his car, in full view of a horrified Maria—while the viewer is deprived of even a taste of the sort of vicious, obscene language that was daily fare in the Jahnke household. Consequently, the average viewer may regard Richard's rush to the gun cabinet and ultimately to the garage as provocative behavior, insufficiently provoked.

At the same time, the script would seem to support Justice Brown's charge that the media was inclined to "purify and sanctify" Richard and Deborah Jahnke. The teenagers are seen as more naive and far more attached to each other than they really were. There is no indication of the growing tension between them and their mother, and no mention of "Kill Mom, too." The character of Maria is sanitized, too. Faced with conflicting testimony, the filmmakers decided to avoid any suggestion that Maria might have contributed to the final battle between father and son. In the movie version, Dad comes home during the argument between Richard and Mom in the kitchen, not afterward, and Mom whisks Dad away to dinner rather than telling him that she and her son "had words" or that Richard called her a "martyr" and a "terrible mother."

Such omissions belie the psychological complexities of the story. In many ways, *Right to Kill?* is a docudrama of exceptionally high quality. It may even be regarded as a public service. But it is also an example of the limitations of the medium. Television demands a clean kill.

Publicly, the Jahnkes expressed satisfaction with the movie that had been made about them. Justine Bateman's shrill, hysterical performance made the real Deborah Jahnke wince, but she consented to interviews on behalf of the project anyway. When she and Maria appeared on the talk show *Hour Magazine* to promote the film, host Gary Collins asked Deborah if her mother had ever abused her. Deborah denied it.

By the time the Jahnke case was reincarnated as a made-for-television movie, many of the players in the real drama were leading quite different lives. Others had returned to business as usual.

In 1984 Frank DeLois resigned his job as a family/community services specialist with Laramie County DPASS and moved to another state. Stan Torvik, director of Wyoming Health and Social Services, also resigned that year to head a corporation that planned to build a private psychiatric facility for adolescents in Cheyenne. At his final press conference, Torvik warned of "large numbers of potentially suicidal youth" in the state.

After thirteen years as a judge in the Sixth Judicial District, Paul Liamos lost a retention vote in the fall of 1984 and is no longer on the bench. According to news reports, his defeat had less to do with the stiff sentence he gave Richard Jahnke than with his perceived "leniency" in other cases and attorneys' dissatisfaction with his habit of scheduling late-night court sessions.

Jim Barrett and Louis Epps left the law firm of Trierweiler, Bayless, Barrett, and McCartney to open their own practice in Cheyenne. Terry Mackey still practices law from his downtown office, and Tom Carroll is still the chief prosecutor of Laramie County, with Jon Forwood at his side.

Eve Whitcomb and Dan Munn are still working in the Cheyenne school system. Donald Morris now teaches a course in "contemporary problems" at High School III, the city's "alternative" high school. The Jahnke case is a topic of frequent discussion in the course's child abuse unit.

Robert Vegvary left the ROTC program at Central High after three years to pursue an advanced degree in psychology.

When last seen, Greg Porter, Michael Brinkman, Eric Needham, Eric Lee, and Troy Schwamb were all enrolled at the University of Wyoming at Laramie. Chris Lawrence was working in Utah.

On September 9, 1985, acting on the strong recommendations of Buck Kuchel, doctors in Denver and Worland, and others, Governor Ed Herschler ordered Richard Jahnke's release from the Wyoming Boys School on parole. The executive order called for Richard to live and work in Cheyenne for an indeterminate period, not to exceed twenty months.

Five days later, on Saturday, September 14, Maria Rodriguez Jahnke married John Druce. The Catholic ceremony was held at Saint Mary's Cathedral in Cheyenne. The bride wore an ivory lace dress and was attended by her daughter, Deborah, twenty, and her son, Richard, nineteen.

After the wedding, Deborah Jahnke changed her name and moved to another state.

Richard Jahnke returned to his mother's house in Cheyenne.

AUTHOR'S NOTE

Some of the material presented in this book is based on court transcripts, police and medical records, private investigators' reports, newspaper articles, and other documents pertaining to the murder trials of Richard and Deborah Jahnke. However, such impersonal sources yielded only a small part of the very personal story I have sought to tell, and I have relied to a much greater extent on my own interviews with the Jahnkes and those who knew them. I have tried to re-create key conversations and events—and, in some instances, thoughts and attitudes as well—as faithfully as the memories of the participants will allow. Certain conversations and court testimony have been greatly condensed, but I have made no attempt to fictionalize the Jahnkes' story; every scene that is not derived from my own observation has its basis in official records or eyewitness accounts. To the extent that I have succeeded in conveying actual experiences in the words of the people who lived them, *The Poison Tree* may be considered a "true" story.

Many people contributed to this project by providing letters, notes, diaries, and precious insights and personal recollections. My greatest debt is to Deborah, Maria, and Richard Jahnke, who spent many hours with me recounting their experiences in vivid and often painful detail. Their candor and patience is a tribute to their desire to have "the whole story" told at last. Their one editorial request of me was that the book be as accurate as possible.

Jim Barrett, Terry Mackey, and Louis Epps were generous with their time and with their formidable knowledge of the case. Equally valuable was the assistance of Dr. John M. Macdonald of the University of Colorado Health Sciences Center; Buck Kuchel, Les Poszgi, and the hospitable staff of the Wyoming Boys School; Mel Dickerson of the Excelsior Youth Center in Aurora, Colorado; Dr. Richard Krugman of the Henry Kempe National Center for the Prevention and Treatment of Child Abuse

325

and Neglect; and Elizabeth Daley of Taper Media Enterprises, who supplied me with copies of Taper's interviews with the Jahnkes and other documents at an early stage of my research.

Citing the existing policy of the Laramie County district attorney's office, Tom Carroll and Jon Forwood declined to comment on the Jahnke case. Both men, however, were kind enough to provide needed information on other subjects, including themselves.

I am also grateful to the following individuals for their cooperation: Art, Petie, and Susan Barry; Jim Billis; Janet Booth; Ed Bradley; Michael Brinkman; Roger and Jacqueline Carrel; Richard Foster; George and Sandy Hain; Walter Headley; Cindy Holste; Kirk Knox; Chris Lawrence; Eric Lee; James Martin; John Marvel; Ralph McConahy; Donald Morris; Dr. Raymond Muhr; Dan and Corrine Munn; Eric Needham; Michael Norwitz; Gayle Plato; Greg Porter; Mark Rech; Troy Schwamb; Stan Torvik; Robert Vegvary; Edwina Waldrip; Carolyn Wheeler; Eve, Gaines, Jason, and Matthew Whitcomb; Dorothy and Stella Zielinski; and Donna Zimny. Several other people assisted in various ways but asked to remain anonymous, so my debt to them must remain anonymous as well.

This project could not have been undertaken at all without the helping hand of Susan Murcko, senior editor of *Rolling Stone*, who dispatched me to Wyoming to cover the Jahnke trials for that magazine; the persistence of my agent, Gwen Edelman; and the encouragement of my editor at Putnam, Chris Schillig. My special thanks to them, and to Roxanna, for her steadfast belief that the story could be told.